BEST AMERICAN
ESSAYS

BENJAMIN FRANKLIN.

Né à Boston, dans la nouvelle Angleterre le 17 Janvier 1706

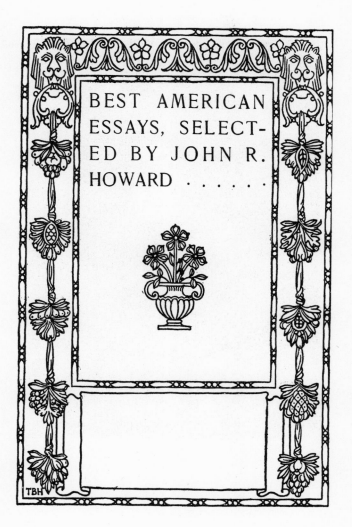

BEST AMERICAN
ESSAYS, SELECT-
ED BY JOHN R.
HOWARD . . . . . .

BEST AMERICAN ESSAYS

SELECTED BY

JOHN RAYMOND HOWARD

Essay Index Reprint Series

BOOKS FOR LIBRARIES PRESS

FREEPORT, NEW YORK

First Published 1910
Reprinted 1969

STANDARD BOOK NUMBER:
8369-1140-7

LIBRARY OF CONGRESS CATALOG CARD NUMBER:
73-86761

PRINTED IN THE UNITED STATES OF AMERICA

PREFACE

AMONG reflective writers the Essay has been a favorite literary mode, commending itself also to readers. Briefer, less formal, and less complete than the treatise, it is indeed rather an incentive to thought upon a theme than exhaustive treatment. Without definite orderliness, it allows great freedom, and its desultory reflections may be observant or learned, grave or gay, graceful or earnest, at the mood of the writer.

It comes in many guises, — in literary discussion or criticism, as in the articles herein by Poe and Longfellow; in demonstration of theories or advocacy of principles, as in Hamilton's "Federalist" papers; in allegorical fancies, conveying social or ethical ideas, as in many of the sketches of Irving, or Hawthorne, or Curtis; in contemplative passages during the flow of narrative fiction, as Fielding's introductions to the divisions in "Tom Jones," or Mrs. Stowe's chapter herein from "The Minister's Wooing"; in presentation of suggestive thoughts on science, or art, or any partial elements of a great subject; even in familiar letters, real or imitative, as Bacon describes Seneca's Epistles to Lucretius, which, he says, "are but essays, that is, dispersed meditations"; and in other ingenious methods of gaining the attention and interest of readers.

Bacon is credited with inventing the name, as well as unique in mastery of the thing, in his famous "Essays." While both the French and the Germans have notable examples of the Essay, it is in English literature that the fashion most abounds. American writers at first naturally followed English models; yet the sensible Franklin, the cogent Hamilton, the serious-minded Channing, began American thinking very early; Emerson — *the* American essayist, *par excellence* — struck an entirely original note, and his influence, with the fresh variations of American life and interest, has had great effect upon succeeding writers.

The Essay has never been more generally and acceptably cultivated than in recent years among American authors, but the necessary limitations of such a collection as the present compel a restriction to writers not now living, — and, indeed, to a comparatively few of those. The separate notices prefacing our varied selections give reasons for their inclusion.

Poe, in his essay on "The Philosophy of Composition" (pp. 87–106), says, with special reference to poems: "If any literary work is too long to be read at one sitting, we must be content to dispense with the immensely important effect derivable from unity of impression; for if two sittings be required,

the affairs of the world interfere, and everything
like totality is at once destroyed." This limit of
space and consequent need of compact expression
draw from Hamilton W. Mabie — himself a successful essayist of our day — this discriminating remark:[1] "One must be a master of the art to pack
a thought within the confines of a sonnet and yet
evoke its complete suggestiveness; and one must
command the higher resources of thought and of
speech to put a philosophy into an essay."

These elements, it is believed, will be found well
exemplified in the Essays here presented. It would
be easy to double the number of authors worthy
of representation. Indeed, such a selection as this
involves the careful reading of many more writers,
not only, but of various productions of each —
"many called, few chosen." The essential aim is to
arrive at a choice that shall be representative of the
best in quality and variety, while restricted to such
a number as may come within the limits of the
"handy volume."

Lowell, recommending wise choice in books, says:
"I should be half inclined to say that any reading
was better than none, allaying the crudeness of the
statement by the Yankee proverb which tells us that,
'though all deacons are good, there's odds in deacons.'" Surely, in this gathered company there are
of the best.

[1] "The Essay and Some Essayists."

CONTENTS

BENJAMIN FRANKLIN

1706–1790

AMONG the many brilliant names illumining the revolutionary and constructive periods of the young American nation, men great in intellectual and moral stature, common sense incarnated in BENJAMIN FRANKLIN has made his name, his deeds, and his sayings the most familiarly known in the civilized world.

His lowly origin, and his patient, steady rise from the Boston tallow-chandler's apprentice to the Philadelphia printer, writer, editor, clerk of the legislature, British Colonial Postmaster-general, Commissioner for the Colonies in England, Ambassador to France, President of Pennsylvania, and member of the Constitutional Convention of 1787, are known of all. His many inventions, his scientific experiments and conclusions, his admirable citizenship, his diplomacy abroad, were all based upon the broadest good sense; while his industrious pen set forth his ideas with a logic so forcefully simple, enlivened by humor and a ready wit, that it bore the sanity of his mind throughout America and Western Europe. His discovery of the electrical nature of lightning and his influence in freeing America, led Turgot, the great French minister of finance, to write under his portrait: —

Eripuit cælo fulmen, sceptrumque tyrannis.[1]

Perhaps the most characteristic product of Franklin's pen was "Poor Richard's Almanac" — a kind of literature common in his day of few books — which he published annually from 1733 to 1758, with a yearly sale of 10,000 copies. His preface to the issue for 1758, which has been reprinted hundreds — perhaps thousands — of times as "The Way to Wealth," is here reproduced, as well as one of his letters to a friend in Paris, containing his witty essay known as "The Whistle." FRANKLIN's Autobiography is a wonderful narrative, its simple lucidity making it one of the classics of the language.

[1] He snatched the thunderbolt from heaven, and the scepter from tyrants.

THE WAY TO WEALTH

THE PREFACE TO

POOR RICHARD'S ALMANAC

FOR 1858

IN his Autobiography, Franklin writes of the Almanac as follows: —

"I endeavored to make it both entertaining and useful; and it accordingly came to be in such demand, that I reaped considerable profit from it, vending annually near ten thousand. And observing that it was generally read, scarce any neighborhood in the province being without it, I considered it as a proper vehicle for conveying instruction among the common people, who bought scarcely any other books; I therefore filled all the little spaces that occurred between the remarkable days in the calendar with proverbial sentences, chiefly such as inculcated industry and frugality as the means of procuring wealth, and thereby securing virtue; it being more difficult for a man in want to act always honestly, as, to use here one of those proverbs, '*It is hard for an empty sack to stand upright.*'

"These proverbs, which contain the wisdom of many ages and nations, I assembled and formed into

3

a connected discourse, prefixed to the almanac of 1757,[1] as the harangue of a wise old man to the people attending an auction. The bringing all these scattered counsels thus into a focus enabled them to make greater impression. The piece, being universally approved, was copied in all the newspapers of the [American] continent; reprinted in Britain on a broadside, to be stuck up in houses; two translations were made of it in French, and great numbers bought by the clergy and gentry, to distribute *gratis* among their poor parishioners and tenants. In Pennsylvania, as it discouraged useless expense in foreign superfluities, some thought it had its share of influence in producing that growing plenty of money which was observable for several years after its publication."

COURTEOUS READER,

I have heard that nothing gives an author so great pleasure, as to find his works respectfully quoted by other learned authors. This pleasure I have seldom enjoyed. For though I have been, if I may say it without vanity, an *eminent author* of *Almanacs* annually, now for a full quarter of a century, my brother-authors in the same way, for what reason I know not, have ever been very sparing in their applauses; and

[1] He wrote the "harangue" in 1757, preparing it for the Almanac of 1758.

no other author has taken the least notice of me, so that did not my writings produce me some solid *pudding*, the great deficiency of *praise* would have quite discouraged me.

I concluded at length, that the people were the best judges of my merit; for they buy my works; and besides, in my rambles, where I am not personally known, I have frequently heard one or other of my adages repeated, with, *as Poor Richard says*, at the end on't; this gave me some satisfaction, as it showed, not only that my instructions were regarded, but discovered likewise some respect for my authority; and I own, that to encourage the practice of remembering and repeating those sentences, I have sometimes *quoted myself* with great gravity.

Judge, then, how much I must have been gratified by an incident I am going to relate to you. I stopped my horse lately where a great number of people were collected at a vendue of merchant goods. The hour of sale not being come, they were conversing on the badness of the times, and one of the company called to a plain, clean old man with white locks, "Pray, Father Abraham, what think you of the times? Won't these heavy taxes quite ruin the country? How shall we be ever able to pay them? What would you advise us to?" Father Abraham stood up and replied, "If you'd have my advice, I'll give it you in short, for *A word to the wise is enough*, and *Many words won't fill a bushel*, as Poor Richard says."

They joined in desiring him to speak his mind, and gathering round him, and he proceeded as follows: —

Friends, says he, and neighbors, the taxes are indeed very heavy, and if those laid on by the government were the only ones we had to pay, we might more easily discharge them: but we have many others, and much more grievous to some of us. We are taxed twice as much by our *Idleness*, three times as much by our *Pride*, and four times as much by our *Folly*, and from these taxes the commissioners cannot ease or deliver us by allowing an abatement. However, let us hearken to good advice, and something may be done for us; *God helps them that help themselves*, as Poor Richard says in his *Almanac* of 1733.

It would be thought a hard government that should tax its people one-tenth part of their *Time*, to be employed in its service, but *Idleness* taxes many of us much more, if we reckon all that is spent in absolute *Sloth*, or doing of nothing, with that which is spent in idle employments or amusements, that amount to nothing.   Sloth, by bringing on diseases, absolutely shortens life. *Sloth, like rust, consumes faster than labor wears, while the used key is always bright*, as Poor Richard says.   But *Dost thou love life? then do not squander Time, for that's the stuff life is made of*, as Poor Richard says.

How much more than is necessary do we spend in sleep? forgetting, that *The sleeping fox catches no poultry*, and that *There will be sleeping enough in the grave*, as Poor Richard says. If time be of all things the most precious, *Wasting of time must be*, as Poor Richard says, *the greatest prodigality;* since, as he elsewhere tells us, *Lost time is never found again;* and what we call *Time enough, always proves little enough.* Let us then up and be doing, and doing to the purpose; so, by diligence, shall we do more with less perplexity. *Sloth makes all things difficult, but industry all things easy*, as Poor Richard says; and *He that riseth late must trot all day, and shall scarce overtake his business at night;* while *Laziness travels so slowly that Poverty soon overtakes him*, as we read in Poor Richard, who adds, *Drive thy business, let not that drive thee*, and *Early to bed and early to rise makes a man healthy, wealthy, and wise.*

So what signifies *wishing* and *hoping* for better times? We may make these times better, if we bestir ourselves. *Industry need not wish*, as Poor Richard says, and *He that lives on hope will die fasting. There are no gains without pains; then help, hands, for I have no lands;* or, if I have, they are smartly taxed. And, as Poor Richard likewise observes, *He that hath a trade hath an estate*, and *He that hath a calling hath an office of profit and honor;* but then the trade must be worked at, and the calling well followed, or neither the estate nor the office will enable us to pay our taxes. If we are industrious we shall never starve; for, as Poor Richard says, *At the working-*

man's house hunger looks in, but dares not enter. Nor will the bailiff or the constable enter, for *Industry pays debts while despair increaseth them.*

What though you have found no treasure, nor has any rich relation left you a legacy, *Diligence is the mother of good luck*, as Poor Richard says, *and God gives all things to industry.* Then *Plough deep while sluggards sleep, and you shall have corn to sell and to keep*, says Poor Dick. Work while it is called to-day, for you know not how much you may be hindered to-morrow, which makes Poor Richard say, *One to-day is worth two to-morrows;* and farther, *Have you somewhat to do to-morrow? Do it to-day.* If you were a servant, would you not be ashamed that a good master should catch you idle? Are you then your own master, *Be ashamed to catch yourself idle*, as Poor Dick says. When there is so much to be done for yourself, your family, your country, and your gracious king, be up by peep of day. *Let not the sun look down and say, Inglorious here he lies.* Handle your tools without mittens; remember that *The cat in gloves catches no mice!* as Poor Richard says. 'Tis true there is much to be done, and perhaps you are weak-handed; but stick to it steadily, and you will see great effects, for *Constant dropping wears away stones;* and *By diligence and patience the mouse ate in two the cable;* and *Little strokes fell great oaks*, as Poor Richard says in his *Almanac*, the year I cannot just now remember.

Methinks I hear some of you say, "Must a man afford himself no leisure?" I will tell thee, my friend, what Poor Richard says, *Employ thy time well, if thou meanest to gain leisure;* and, *Since thou art not sure of a minute, throw not away an hour.* Leisure is time for doing something useful; this leisure the diligent man will obtain, but the lazy man never; so that, as Poor Richard says, *A life of leisure and a life of laziness are two things.* Do you imagine that sloth will afford you more comfort than labor? No, for as Poor Richard says, *Trouble springs from idleness, and grievous toil from needless ease. Many without labor would live by their wits only, but they break for want of stock;* whereas industry gives comfort, and plenty, and respect. *Fly pleasures, and they'll follow you. The diligent spinner has a large shift;* and *Now I have a sheep and a cow, everybody bids me good-morrow,* all which is well said by Poor Richard.

But with our industry we must likewise be steady, settled, and careful, and oversee our own affairs *with our own eyes,* and not trust too much to others: for, as Poor Richard says: —

> *I never saw an oft-removed tree*
> *Nor yet an oft-removed family*
> *That throve so well as those that settled be.*

And again, *Three removes is as bad as a fire;* and again, *Keep thy shop, and thy shop will keep thee;*

and again, *If you would have your business done, go; if not, send.* And again, *He that by the plough would thrive, himself must either hold or drive.*

And again, *The eye of a master will do more work than both his hands;* and again, *Want of care does us more damage than want of knowledge;* and again, *Not to oversee workmen is to leave them your purse open.* Trusting too much to others' care is the ruin of many; for, as the Almanac says, *In the affairs of this world men are saved, not by faith, but by the want of it;* but a man's own care is profitable; for saith Poor Dick, *Learning is to the studious, and Riches to the careful;* as well as, *Power to the bold, and Heaven to the virtuous.* And farther, *If you would have a faithful servant, and one that you like, serve yourself.* And again, he adviseth to circumspection and care, even in the smallest matters; because sometimes *A little neglect may breed great mischief,* adding, *For want of a nail the shoe was lost; for want of a shoe the horse was lost; and for want of a horse the rider was lost,* being overtaken and slain by the enemy, all for want of a little care about a horseshoe nail.

So much for *Industry,* my friends, and attention to one's own business; but to these we must add *Frugality,* if we would make our industry more certainly successful. *A man may,* if he knows not how to save as he gets, *keep his nose all his life to the grindstone, and die not worth a groat at last. A fat kitchen makes a lean will,* as Poor Richard says; and —

Many estates are spent in the getting,
Since women for tea forsook spinning and knitting,
And men for punch forsook hewing and splitting.

If you would be wealthy, says he in another Almanac,
think of saving as well as of getting. *The Indies have
not made Spain rich; because her outgoes are greater
than her incomes.* Away, then, with your expensive
follies, and you will not have so much cause to complain of hard times, heavy taxes, and chargeable
families; for as Poor Dick says : —

Women and wine, game and deceit,
Make the wealth small and the wants great.

And farther, *What maintains one vice would bring up
two children.* You may think, perhaps, that a *little*
tea, or a *little* punch now and then, diet a *little* more
costly, clothes a *little* finer, and a *little* more enter-
tainment now and then, can be no great matter; but
remember what Poor Richard says, *Many a little
makes a mickle;* and farther, *Beware of little expenses;
a small leak will sink a great ship;* and again, *Who
dainties love, shall beggars prove;* and moreover, *Fools
make feasts, and wise men eat them.*

Here are you all got together at this vendue of
fineries and knick-knacks. You call them *goods;*
but, if you do not take care, they will prove evils
to some of you. You expect they will be sold cheap,
and perhaps they may for less than they cost: but,
if you have no occasion for them, they must be *dear*

to you. Remember what Poor Richard says: *Buy
what thou hast no need of, and ere long thou shalt sell
thy necessaries.* And again, *At a great pennyworth
pause a while.* He means, that perhaps the cheap-
ness is apparent only, and not real; or the bargain,
by straitening thee in thy business, may do thee more
harm than good. For in another place he says,
Many have been ruined by buying good pennyworths.
Again, Poor Richard says, *'Tis foolish to lay out
money in a purchase of repentance;* and yet this folly
is practised every day at vendues for want of minding
the *Almanac. Wise men,* as Poor Richard says, *learn
by others' harms; fools, scarcely by their own;* but
Felix quem faciunt aliena pericula cautum.[1] Many a
one, for the sake of finery on the back, has gone with
a hungry belly, and half-starved their families.
Silks and satins, scarlets and velvets, as Poor Richard
says, *put out the kitchen fire.* These are not the
necessaries of life; they can scarcely be called the
conveniences; and yet, only because they look pretty,
how many *want* to *have* them! The *artificial* wants
of mankind thus become more numerous than the
natural; and, as Poor Dick says, *For one poor person
there are a hundred indigent.* By these, and other
extravagances, the genteel are reduced to poverty,
and forced to borrow of those whom they formerly
despised, but who through industry and frugality
have maintained their standing; in which case it

[1] Happy he, whom others' perils make cautious.

appears plainly, that *A ploughman on his legs is higher than a gentleman on his knees*, as Poor Richard says. Perhaps they have had a small estate left them, which they knew not the getting of, — they think, *'Tis day, and will never be night;* that *A little to be spent out of so much is not worth minding;* (*A child and a fool*, as Poor Richard says, *imagine twenty shillings and twenty years can never be spent,*) but *Always taking out of the meal-tub, and never putting in, soon comes to the bottom;* then, as Poor Dick says, *When the well's dry, they know the worth of water.* But this they might have known before, if they had taken his advice. *If you would know the value of money, go and try to borrow some;* for *He that goes a borrowing, goes a sorrowing*, and indeed so does he that lends to such people, when he goes *to get it in again.*

Poor Dick further advises, and says : —

> *Fond pride of dress is, sure, a very curse;*
> *Ere fancy you consult, consult your purse.*

And again, *Pride is as loud a beggar as Want, and a great deal more saucy.* When you have bought one fine thing, you must buy ten more, that your appearance may be all of a piece; but Poor Dick says, *'Tis easier to suppress the first desire, than to satisfy all that follow it.* And 'tis as truly folly for the poor to ape the rich, as for the frog to swell in order to equal the ox.

> *Vessels large may venture more,*
> *But little boats should keep near shore.*

'Tis, however, a folly soon punished; for, *Pride that dines on vanity sups on contempt*, as Poor Richard says. And in another place, *Pride breakfasted with Plenty, dined with Poverty, and supped with Infamy.* And after all, of what use is this pride of appearance, for which so much is risked, so much is suffered! It cannot promote health or ease pain; it makes no increase of merit in the person; it creates envy; it hastens misfortune.

> *What is a butterfly? At best*
> *He's but a caterpillar drest,*
> *The gaudy fop's his picture just,*

as Poor Richard says.

But what madness must it be to *run in debt* for these superfluities! We are offered, by the terms of this vendue, six months' credit; and that, perhaps, has induced some of us to attend it, because we cannot spare the ready money, and hope now to be fine without it. But, ah! think what you do when you run in debt; *You give to another power over your liberty.* If you cannot pay at the time, you will be ashamed to see your creditor; you will be in fear when you speak to him; you will make poor, pitiful, sneaking excuses, and by degrees come to lose your veracity, and sink into base downright lying; for, as Poor Richard says, *The second vice is lying, the first is running in debt;* and again, to the same purpose, *Lying rides upon debt's back;* whereas a free-born Englishman ought not to be ashamed or afraid to see or speak to any man living. But poverty often deprives a man of all spirit and virtue; *'Tis hard for an empty bag to stand upright!* as Poor Richard truly says. What would you think of that prince, or that government, who should issue an edict forbidding you to dress like a gentleman or gentlewoman, on pain of imprisonment or servitude? Would you not say, that you are free, have a right to dress as you please, and that such an edict would be a breach of your privileges, and such a government tyrannical? And yet you are about to put yourself under such tyranny, when you run in debt for such dress! Your creditor has authority, at his pleasure, to deprive you of your liberty, by confining you in jail for life, or to sell you for a servant, if you should not be able to pay him.[1] When you have got your bargain, you may, perhaps, think little of payment; but *Creditors* (Poor Richard tells us) *have better memories than debtors;* and in another place says, *Creditors are a superstitious sect, great observers of set days and times.* The day comes round before you are aware, and the demand is made before you are prepared to satisfy it; or if you bear your debt in mind, the term which at first seemed so long, will,

[1] Imprisonment for debt was common then, and in England for long afterward.

as it lessens, appear extremely short. *Time* will seem to have added wings to his heels as well as his shoulders. *Those have a short Lent*, saith Poor Richard, *who owe money to be paid at Easter.* Then since, as he says, *The borrower is a slave to the lender, and the debtor to the creditor*, disdain the chain, preserve your freedom, and maintain your independency. Be *industrious* and *free ;* be *frugal* and *free.* At present, perhaps, you may think yourself in thriving circumstances, and that you can bear a little extravagance without injury; but,

> *For age and want, save while you may,*
> *No morning sun lasts a whole day,*

as Poor Richard says.   Gain may be temporary and uncertain; but ever, while you live, expense is constant and certain; and *'Tis easier to build two chimneys than to keep one in fuel*, as Poor Richard says; so, *Rather go to bed supperless than rise in debt.*

> *Get what you can, and what you get hold ;*
> *'Tis the stone that will turn all your lead into gold,*

as Poor Richard says.   And when you have got the Philosopher's stone, sure you will no longer complain of bad times, or the difficulty of paying taxes.

This doctrine, my friends, is reason and wisdom; but, after all, do not depend too much upon your own industry and frugality and prudence, though excellent things: for they may all be blasted without the blessing of Heaven; and therefore, ask that blessing humbly, and be not uncharitable to those that at present seem to want it, but comfort and help them. Remember Job suffered, and was afterwards prosperous.

And now, to conclude, *Experience keeps a dear school, but fools will learn in no other, and scarce in that;* for it is true, *We may give advice, but we cannot give conduct,* as Poor Richard says. However, remember this, *They that won't be counseled, can't be helped,* as Poor Richard says: and farther, that, *If you will not hear reason, she'll surely rap your knuckles.*

———

Thus the old gentleman ended his harangue. The people heard it, and approved the doctrine, and immediately practised the contrary, just as if it had been a common sermon; for the vendue opened, and they began to buy extravagantly, notwithstanding all his cautions, and their own fear of taxes. I found the good man had thoroughly studied my *Almanacs,* and digested all I had dropped on those topics during the course of five-and-twenty years. The frequent mention he made of me must have tired any one else; but my vanity was wonderfully delighted with it, though I was conscious that not a tenth part of the wisdom was my own which he ascribed to me, but rather the gleanings that I had made of the sense of all ages and nations. However, I resolved to be the better for the echo of it; and, though I had at first determined to buy stuff for a new coat, I went away resolved to wear my old one a little longer. Reader, if thou wilt do the same, thy profit will be as great as mine.

> *I am as ever,*
> > *Thine to serve thee,*
> > > RICHARD SAUNDERS.

July 7, 1757.

THE WHISTLE [1]

NOVEMBER 10, 1779.

I RECEIVED my dear friend's two letters, one for Wednesday, one for Saturday. This is again Wednesday. I do not deserve one for to-day, because I have not answered the former. But, indolent as I am, and averse to writing, the fear of having no more of your pleasing epistles if I do not contribute to the correspondence, obliges me to take up my pen; and as Mr. B. has kindly sent me word that he sets out to-morrow to see you, instead of spending this Wednesday evening, as I have done its namesakes, in your delightful company, I sit down to spend it in thinking of you, in writing to you, and in thinking over and over again your letters.

I am charmed with your description of Paradise,

---

[1] A letter to Madame Brillon.

and with your plan of living there; and I approve much of your conclusion, that in the meantime we should draw all the good we can from this world. In my opinion, we might all draw more good from it than we do, and suffer less evils, if we would take care not to give too much for *whistles*. For to me it seems that most of the unhappy people we meet with are become so by neglect of that caution.

You ask what I mean? You love stories, and will excuse my telling one of myself.

When I was a child of seven years old, my friends on a holiday filled my pocket with coppers. I went directly to a shop where they sold toys for children: and, being charmed with the sound of a *whistle* that I met by the way in the hands of another boy, I voluntarily offered and gave all my money for one. I then came home, and went whistling all over the house, much pleased with my *whistle*, but disturbing all the family. My brothers and sisters and cousins, understanding the bargain I had made, told me I had given four times as much for it as it was worth; put me in mind what good things I might have bought with the rest of the money, and laughed at me so much for my folly, that I cried with vexation; and the reflection gave me more chagrin than the *whistle* gave me pleasure.

This, however, was afterwards of use to me, the impression continuing on my mind, so that often, when I was tempted to buy some unnecessary thing, I said to myself, *Don't give too much for the whistle:* and I saved my money.

As I grew up, came into the world, and observed the actions of men, I thought I met with many, very many, who *gave too much for the whistle.*

When I saw one too ambitious to court favor, sacrificing his time in attendance on levees, his repose, his liberty, his virtue, and perhaps his friends, to attain it, I have said to myself, *This man gives too much for his whistle.*

When I saw another fond of popularity, constantly employing himself in political bustles, neglecting his own affairs and ruining them by that neglect, *He pays, indeed,* said I, *too much for his whistle.*

If I knew a miser, who gave up any kind of a comfortable living, all the pleasure of doing good to others, all the esteem of his fellow-citizens, and the joys of benevolent friendship, for the sake of accumulating wealth, *Poor man,* said I, *you pay too much for your whistle.*

When I met with a man of pleasure, sacrificing every laudable improvement of the mind, or of his fortune, to mere corporal sensations, and ruining his health in their pursuit, *Mistaken man,* said I, *you are providing pain for yourself instead of pleasure; you give too much for your whistle.*

If I see one fond of appearance, or fine clothes, fine houses, fine furniture, fine equipages, all above his fortune, for which he contracts debts, and ends his career in a prison, *Alas!* say I, *he has paid dear, very dear, for his whistle.*

When I see a beautiful, sweet-tempered girl married to an ill-natured brute of a husband, *What a pity,* say I, *that she should pay so much for a whistle!*

In short, I conceive that great part of the miseries of mankind are brought upon them by the false estimates they have made of the value of things, and by their *giving too much for their whistles.*

Yet I ought to have charity for these unhappy people, when I consider, that with all this wisdom of which I am boasting, there are certain things in the world so tempting, for example, the apples of King John, which happily are not to be bought; for if they were put up to sale by auction, I might very easily be led to ruin myself in the purchase, and find that I had once more given too much for the *whistle.*

Adieu, my dear friend, and believe me ever yours, very sincerely and with unalterable affection,

B. FRANKLIN.

ALEXANDER HAMILTON

1757–1804

BORN on the West Indian island of Nevis, of Scottish-French ancestry, this remarkable youth at the age of fifteen entered King's College (now Columbia) in New York. Poetry, philosophy, history, commerce, finance, were his studies outside regular courses. He was an ardent American patriot; published, when only seventeen, striking essays on the rights of the colonists; leaped into notice as a speaker arousing the people to arms, and at the age of nineteen (1776) joined the Revolutionary forces as a captain of artillery.

At twenty-one he was on WASHINGTON'S staff as confidential aid serving through the war, and attaining the rank of major-general. His diplomatic skill was of great value to his chief, and his bravery and military genius were notable.

After the war HAMILTON became a leading member of the New York bar, served in the State legislature, in Congress, and was an influential member of the Constitutional Convention of 1787. Whether as writer, orator, or counselor, he shone a star of the first magnitude. His greatest fame has a twofold radiance. With MADISON and JAY, he was joint author of the renowned essays in favor of the new Constitution, known as "The Federalist," which probably more than anything else influenced its adoption, HAMILTON writing the largest proportion of the separate papers. From those unquestionably HAMILTON'S two are here presented.

After WASHINGTON became President, HAMILTON was the first Secretary of the Treasury, and here won his other greatest fame, as the finance minister who brought order out of chaos with his masterly plans. WEBSTER said of him: "He smote the rock of the national resources, and abundant streams of revenue gushed forth. He touched the dead corpse of the Public Credit, and it sprung upon its feet."

HAMILTON'S disagreements with BURR resulted in a foolish duel, in which this great genius passed away at the early age of forty-eight and at the height of his splendid career.

24

DEFECTS OF THE ORIGINAL CONFEDERATION

From "The Federalist." No. XXII

To the People of the State of New York:

In addition to the defects already enumerated in the existing federal system, there are others of not less importance, which concur in rendering it altogether unfit for the administration of the affairs of the Union.

The want of a power to regulate commerce is by all parties allowed to be of the number. The utility of such a power has been anticipated under the first head of our inquiries; and for this reason, as well as from the universal conviction entertained upon the subject, little need be added in this place. It is indeed evident, on the most superficial view, that there is no object, either as it respects the interests of trade or finance, that more strongly demands a federal superintendence. The want of it has already operated as a bar to the formation of beneficial treaties with foreign powers, and has given occasions of dissatisfaction between the States. No nation acquainted with the nature of our political association would be unwise enough to enter into stipulations with the United States, by which they conceded privileges of any importance to them, while they were apprised that the engagements on the part of the Union might at any moment be violated by its members, and while they found from experience that they might enjoy every advantage they desired in our markets, without granting us any return but such as their momentary convenience might suggest. It is not, therefore, to be wondered at that Mr. Jenkinson, in ushering into the House of Commons a bill for regulating the temporary intercourse between the two countries, should preface its introduction by a declaration that similar provisions in former bills had been found to answer every purpose to the commerce of Great Britain, and that it would be prudent to persist in the plan until it should appear whether the American government was likely or not to acquire greater consistency.[1]

Several States have endeavored, by separate prohibitions, restrictions, and exclusions, to influence the conduct of that kingdom in this particular, but the want of concert, arising from the want of a general authority and from clashing and dissimilar views in the State, has hitherto frustrated every experiment of the kind, and will continue to do so as long as the same obstacles to a uniformity of measures continue to exist.

[1] This, as nearly as I can recollect, was the sense of his speech on introducing the last bill. — PUBLIUS.

The interfering and unneighborly regulations of some States, contrary to the true spirit of the Union, have, in different instances, given just cause of um·brage and complaint to others, and it is to be feared that examples of this nature, if not restrained by a national control, would be multiplied and extended till they became not less serious sources of animosity and discord than injurious impediments to the intercourse between the different parts of the Confederacy. "The commerce of the German empire [1] is in continual trammels from the multiplicity of the duties which the several princes and states exact upon the merchandises passing through their territories, by means of which the fine streams and navigable rivers with which Germany is so happily watered are rendered almost useless." Though the genius of the people of this country might never permit this description to be strictly applicable to us, yet we may reasonably expect, from the gradual conflicts of State regulations, that the citizens of each would at length come to be considered and treated by the others in no better light than that of foreigners and aliens.

The power of raising armies, by the most obvious construction of the articles of the Confederation, is merely a power of making requisitions upon the States for quotas of men. This practice, in the course of the late war, was found replete with obstructions to

[1] Encyclopædia, article "Empire." — PUBLIUS.

a vigorous and to an economical system of defense. It gave birth to a competition between the States which created a kind of auction for men. In order to furnish the quotas required of them, they outbid each other till bounties grew to an enormous and insupportable size. The hope of a still further increase afforded an inducement to those who were disposed to serve to procrastinate their enlistment, and disinclined them from engaging for any considerable periods. Hence, slow and scanty levies of men, in the most critical emergencies of our affairs; short enlistments at an unparalleled expense; continual fluctuations in the troops, ruinous to their discipline and subjecting the public safety frequently to the perilous crisis of a disbanded army. Hence, also, those oppressive expedients for raising men which were upon several occasions practiced, and which nothing but the enthusiasm of liberty would have induced the people to endure.

This method of raising troops is not more unfriendly to economy and vigor than it is to an equal distribution of the burden. The States near the seat of war, influenced by motives of self-preservation, made efforts to furnish their quotas, which even exceeded their abilities; while those at a distance from danger were, for the most part, as remiss as the others were diligent in their exertions. The immediate pressure of this inequality was not in this case, as in that of the contributions of money, alleviated by the hope of a final liquidation. The States which did not pay their proportions of money might at least be charged with their deficiencies; but no account could be formed of the deficiencies in the supplies of men. We shall not, however, see much reason to regret the want of this hope, when we consider how little prospect there is, that the most delinquent States will ever be able to make compensation for their pecuniary failures. The system of quotas and requisitions, whether it be applied to men or money, is, in every view, a system of imbecility in the Union, and of inequality and injustice among the members.

The right of equal suffrage among the States is another exceptionable part of the Confederation. Every idea of proportion and every rule of fair representation conspire to condemn a principle, which gives to Rhode Island an equal weight in the scale of power with Massachusetts, or Connecticut, or New York; and to Delaware an equal voice in the national deliberations with Pennsylvania, or Virginia, or North Carolina. Its operation contradicts the fundamental maxim of republican government, which requires that the sense of the majority should prevail. Sophistry may reply, that sovereigns are equal, and that a majority of the votes of the States will be a majority of confederated America. But this kind of logical legerdemain will never counteract the plain suggestions of justice and common sense. It may happen that this majority of States

is a small minority of the people of America; [1] and
two-thirds of the people of America could not long
be persuaded, upon the credit of artificial distinctions and syllogistic subtleties, to submit their
interests to the management and disposal of one-
third. The larger States would after a while revolt
from the idea of receiving the law from the smaller.
To acquiesce in such a privation of their due importance in the political scale, would be not merely to
be insensible to the love of power, but even to sacrifice the desire of equality. It is neither rational to
expect the first, nor just to require the last. The
smaller States, considering how peculiarly their
safety and welfare depend on union, ought readily
to renounce a pretension which, if not relinquished,
would prove fatal to its duration.

It may be objected to this, that not seven but
nine States, or two-thirds of the whole number, must
consent to the most important resolutions; and it
may be thence inferred, that nine States would
always comprehend a majority of the Union. But
this does not obviate the impropriety of an equal
vote between States of the most unequal dimensions
and populousness; nor is the inference accurate in
point of fact; for we can enumerate nine States which

[1] New Hampshire, Rhode Island, New Jersey, Delaware,
Georgia, South Carolina, and Maryland are a majority of
the whole number of the States, but they do not contain one-
third of the people. — PUBLIUS.

contain less than a majority of the people; [1] and it is constitutionally possible that these nine may give the vote. Besides, there are matters of considerable moment determinable by a bare majority; and there are others concerning which doubts have been entertained, which, if interpreted in favor of the sufficiency of a vote of seven States, would extend its operation to interests of the first magnitude. In addition to this, it is to be observed that there is a probability of an increase in the number of States, and no provision for a proportional augmentation of the ratio of votes.

But this is not all; what at first sight may seem a remedy, is, in reality, a poison. To give a minority a negative upon the majority (which is always the case where more than a majority is requisite to a decision), is, in its tendency, to subject the sense of the greater number to that of the lesser. Congress, from the non-attendance of a few States, have been frequently in the situation of a Polish diet, where a single VOTE has been sufficient to put a stop to all their movements. A sixtieth part of the Union, which is about the proportion of Delaware and Rhode Island, has several times been able to oppose an entire bar to its operations. This is one of those refinements which, in practice, has an effect the reverse of what is expected from it in theory. The neces-

[1] Add New York and Connecticut to the foregoing seven, and they will be less than a majority. — PUBLIUS.

sity of unanimity in public bodies, or of something
approaching towards it, has been founded upon a
supposition that it would contribute to security. But
its real operation is to embarrass the administration, to destroy the energy of the government, and
to substitute the pleasure, caprice, or artifices of an
insignificant, turbulent, or corrupt junto, to the regular deliberations and decisions of a respectable majority. In those emergencies of a nation, in which
the goodness or badness, the weakness or strength of
its government, is of the greatest importance, there
is commonly a necessity for action. The public
business must, in some way or other, go forward.
If a pertinacious minority can control the opinion
of a majority, respecting the best mode of conduct-
ing it, the majority, in order that something may be
done, must conform to the views of the minority;
and thus the sense of the smaller number will overrule
that of the greater, and give a tone to the national
proceedings. Hence, tedious delays; continual negotiation and intrigue; contemptible compromises of
the public good. And yet, in such a system, it is
even happy when such compromises can take place:
for upon some occasions things will not admit of
accommodation; and then the measures of government must be injuriously suspended, or fatally
defeated. It is often, by the impracticability of obtaining the concurrence of the necessary number of
votes, kept in a state of inaction. Its situation must

always savor of weakness, sometimes border upon anarchy.

It is not difficult to discover, that a principle of this kind gives greater scope to foreign corruption, as well as to domestic faction, than that which permits the sense of the majority to decide; though the contrary of this has been presumed. The mistake has proceeded from not attending with due care to the mischiefs that may be occasioned by obstructing the progress of government at certain critical seasons. When the concurrence of a large number is required by the Constitution to the doing of any national act, we are apt to rest satisfied that all is safe, because nothing improper will be likely *to be done;* but we forget how much good may be prevented, and how much ill may be produced, by the power of hindering the doing what may be necessary, and of keeping affairs in the same unfavorable posture in which they may happen to stand at particular periods.

Suppose, for instance, we were engaged in a war, in conjunction with one foreign nation, against another. Suppose the necessity of our situation demanded peace, and the interest or ambition of our ally led him to seek the prosecution of the war, with views that might justify us in making separate terms. In such a state of things, this ally of ours would evidently find it much easier, by his bribes and intrigues, to tie up the hands of government from making peace, where two-thirds of all the votes

were requisite to that object, than where a simple
majority would suffice. In the first case, he would
have to corrupt a smaller number; in the last, a
greater number. Upon the same principle, it would
be much easier for a foreign power with which we
were at war to perplex our councils and embarrass
our exertions. And, in a commercial view, we may
be subjected to similar inconveniences. A nation,
with which we might have a treaty of commerce,
could with much greater facility prevent our forming
a connection with her competitor in trade, though
such a connection should be ever so beneficial to
ourselves.

Evils of this description ought not to be regarded
as imaginary. One of the weak sides of republics,
among their numerous advantages, is that they afford
too easy an inlet to foreign corruption. An hered-
itary monarch, though often disposed to sacrifice
his subjects to his ambition, has so great a personal
interest in the government and in the external glory
of the nation, that it is not easy for a foreign power
to give him an equivalent for what he would sacrifice
by treachery to the state. The world has accordingly been witness to few examples of this species
of royal prostitution, though there have been abundant specimens of every other kind.

In republics, persons elevated from the mass of the
community, by the suffrages of their fellow-citizens,
to stations of great preëminence and power, may find

compensations for betraying their trust, which, to any but minds animated and guided by superior virtue, may appear to exceed the proportion of interest they have in the common stock, and to overbalance the obligations of duty. Hence it is that history furnishes us with so many mortifying examples of the prevalency of foreign corruption in republican governments. How much this contributed to the ruin of the ancient commonwealths has been already delineated. It is well known that the deputies of the United Provinces have, in various instances, been purchased by the emissaries of the neighboring kingdoms. The Earl of Chesterfield (if my memory serves me right), in a letter to his court, intimates that his success in an important negotiation must depend on his obtaining a major's commission for one of those deputies. And in Sweden the parties were alternately bought by France and England in so barefaced and notorious a manner that it excited universal disgust in the nation, and was a principal cause that the most limited monarch in Europe, in a single day, without tumult, violence, or opposition, became one of the most absolute and uncontrolled.

A circumstance which crowns the defects of the Confederation remains yet to be mentioned, — the want of a judiciary power. Laws are a dead letter without courts to expound and define their true meaning and operation. The treaties of the United States, to have any force at all, must be considered as part of the law of the land. Their true import, as far as respects individuals, must, like all other laws, be ascertained by judicial determinations. To produce uniformity in these determinations, they ought to be submitted, in the last resort, to one SUPREME TRIBUNAL. And this tribunal ought to be instituted under the same authority which forms the treaties themselves. These ingredients are both indispensable. If there is in each State a court of final jurisdiction, there may be as many different final determinations on the same point as there are courts. There are endless diversities in the opinions of men. We often see not only different courts but the judges of the same court differing from each other. To avoid the confusion which would unavoidably result from the contradictory decisions of a number of independent judicatories, all nations have found it necessary to establish one court paramount to the rest, possessing a general superintendence, and authorized to settle and declare in the last resort a uniform rule of civil justice.

This is the more necessary where the frame of the government is so compounded that the laws of the whole are in danger of being contravened by the laws of the parts. In this case, if the particular tribunals are invested with a right of ultimate jurisdiction, besides the contradictions to be expected from difference of opinion, there will be much to fear from the bias of local views and prejudices, and from the interference of local regulations. As often as such an interference was to happen, there would be reason to apprehend that the provisions of the particular laws might be preferred to those of the general laws; for nothing is more natural to men in office than to look with peculiar deference towards that authority to which they owe their official existence. The treaties of the United States, under the present Constitution, are liable to the infractions of thirteen different legislatures, and as many different courts of final jurisdiction, acting under the authority of those legislatures. The faith, the reputation, the peace of the whole Union, are thus continually at the mercy of the prejudices, the passions, and the interests of every member of which it is composed. Is it possible that foreign nations can either respect or confide in such a government? Is it possible that the people of America will longer consent to trust their honor, their happiness, their safety, on so precarious a foundation?

In this review of the Confederation, I have confined myself to the exhibition of its most material defects; passing over those imperfections in its details by which even a great part of the power intended to be conferred upon it has been in a great measure rendered abortive. It must be by this time evident to all men of reflection, who can divest themselves of the prepossessions of preconceived opinions, that it is a system so radically vicious and unsound, as to admit not of amendment but by an entire change in its leading features and characters.

The organization of Congress is itself utterly improper for the exercise of those powers which are necessary to be deposited in the Union. A single assembly may be a proper receptacle of those slender, or rather fettered, authorities, which have been heretofore delegated to the federal head; but it would be inconsistent with all the principles of good government, to intrust it with those additional powers which, even the moderate and more rational adversaries of the proposed Constitution admit, ought to reside in the United States. If that plan should not be adopted, and if the necessity of the Union should be able to withstand the ambitious aims of those men who may indulge magnificent schemes of personal aggrandizement from its dissolution, the probability would be, that we should run into the project of conferring supplementary powers upon Congress, as they are now constituted; and either the machine, from the intrinsic feebleness of its structure, will molder into pieces, in spite of our ill-judged efforts to prop it; or, by successive augmentations of its force and energy, as necessity might prompt, we shall finally accumulate, in a single body, all the most important prerogatives of sovereignty, and thus entail upon our posterity one of the most execrable forms of government that human infatuation ever contrived. Thus we should create in reality that very tyranny which the adversaries of the new Constitution either are, or affect to be, solicitous to avert.

It has not a little contributed to the infirmities of the existing federal system, that it never had a ratification by the PEOPLE. Resting on no better foundation than the consent of the several legislatures, it has been exposed to frequent and intricate questions concerning the validity of its powers, and has, in some instances, given birth to the enormous doctrine of a right of legislative repeal. Owing its ratification to the law of a State, it has been contended that the same authority might repeal the law by which it was ratified. However gross a heresy it may be to maintain that *a party* to a *compact* has a right to revoke that *compact*, the doctrine itself has had respectable advocates. The possibility of a question of this nature proves the necessity of laying the foundations of our national government deeper than in the mere sanction of delegated authority. The fabric of American empire ought to rest on the solid basis of THE CONSENT OF THE PEOPLE. The streams of national power ought to flow immediately from that pure, original fountain of all legitimate authority.

PUBLIUS.

OBJECTS AND POWERS OF A FEDERAL UNION

From "The Federalist." No. XXIII

To the People of the State of New York:

The necessity of a Constitution, at least equally energetic with the one proposed, to the preservation of the Union, is the point at the examination of which we are now arrived.

This inquiry will naturally divide itself into three branches — the objects to be provided for by the federal government, the quantity of power necessary to the accomplishment of those objects, the persons upon whom that power ought to operate. Its distribution and organization will more properly claim our attention under the succeeding head.

The principal purposes to be answered by union are these — the common defense of the members; the preservation of the public peace, as well against internal convulsions as external attacks; the regulation of commerce with other nations and between the States; the superintendence of our intercourse, political and commercial, with foreign countries.

The authorities essential to the common defense are these: to raise armies; to build and equip fleets; to prescribe rules for the government of both; to direct their operations; to provide for their support.

These powers ought to exist without limitation, *because it is impossible to foresee or define the extent and variety of national exigencies, or the correspondent extent and variety of the means which may be necessary to satisfy them.* The circumstances that endanger the safety of nations are infinite, and for this reason no constitutional shackles can wisely be imposed on the power to which the care of it is committed. This power ought to be coextensive with all the possible combinations of such circumstances; and ought to be under the direction of the same councils which are appointed to preside over the common defense.

This one of those truths which, to a correct and unprejudiced mind, carries its own evidence along with it; and may be obscured, but cannot be made plainer by argument or reasoning. It rests upon axioms as simple as they are universal; the *means* ought to be proportioned to the *end;* the persons, from whose agency the attainment of any *end* is expected, ought to possess the *means* by which it is to be attained.

Whether there ought to be a federal government intrusted with the care of the common defense, is a question in the first instance open for discussion; but the moment it is decided in the affirmative, it will follow, that that government ought to be clothed with all the powers requisite to complete execution of its trust. And unless it can be shown that the circumstances which may affect the public safety are reducible within certain determinate limits, unless the contrary of this position can be fairly and rationally disputed, it must be admitted, as a necessary consequence, that there can be no limitation of that authority which is to provide for the defense and protection of the community, in any matter essential to its efficacy — that is, in any matter essential to the *formation*, *direction*, or *support* of the NATIONAL FORCES.

Defective as the present Confederation has been proved to be, this principle appears to have been fully recognized by the framers of it; though they have not made proper or adequate provision for its exercise. Congress have an unlimited discretion to make requisitions of men and money; to govern the army and navy; to direct their operations. As their requisitions are made constitutionally binding upon the States, who are in fact under the most solemn obligations to furnish the supplies required of them, the intention evidently was, that the United States should command whatever resources were by them judged requisite to the "common defense and general welfare." It was presumed that a sense of their true interests, and a regard to the dictates of good faith, would be found sufficient pledges for the punctual performance of the duty of the members to the federal head.

The experiment has, however, demonstrated that

this expectation was ill-founded and illusory; and the observations, made under the last head, will, I imagine, have sufficed to convince the impartial and discerning, that there is an absolute necessity for an entire change in the first principles of the system; that if we are in earnest about giving the Union energy and duration, we must abandon the vain project of legislating upon the States in their collective capacities; we must extend the laws of the federal government to the individual citizens of America; we must discard the fallacious scheme of quotas and requisitions, as equally impracticable and unjust. The result from all this is that the Union ought to be invested with full power to levy troops; to build and equip fleets; and to raise the revenues which will be required for the formation and support of an army and navy, in the customary and ordinary modes practiced in other governments.

If the circumstances of our country are such as to demand a compound instead of a simple, a confederate instead of a sole, government, the essential point which will remain to be adjusted will be to discriminate the OBJECTS, as far as it can be done, which shall appertain to the different provinces or departments of power; allowing to each the most ample authority for fulfilling the objects committed to its charge. Shall the Union be constituted the guardian of the common safety? Are fleets and armies and revenues necessary to this purpose? The government of the Union must be empowered to pass all laws, and to make all regulations which have relation to them. The same must be the case in respect to commerce, and to every other matter to which its jurisdiction is permitted to extend. Is the administration of justice between the citizens of the same State the proper department of the local governments? These must possess all the authorities which are connected with this object, and with every other that may be allotted to their particular cognizance and direction. Not to confer in each case a degree of power commensurate to the end, would be to violate the most obvious rules of prudence and propriety, and improvidently to trust the great interests of the nation to hands which are disabled from managing them with vigor and success.

Who so likely to make suitable provisions for the public defense, as that body to which the guardianship of the public safety is confided; which, as the center of information, will best understand the extent and urgency of the dangers that threaten; as the representative of the WHOLE, will feel itself most deeply interested in the preservation of every part; which, from the responsibility implied in the duty assigned to it, will be most sensibly impressed with the necessity of proper exertions; and which, by the extension of its authority throughout the States, can alone establish uniformity and concert in the plans and measures by which the common safety is to be secured? Is there not a manifest inconsistency in devolving upon the federal government the care of the general defense, and leaving in the State governments the *effective* powers by which it is to be provided for? Is not a want of coöperation the infallible consequence of such a system? And will not weakness, disorder, an undue distribution of the burdens and calamities of war, an unnecessary and intolerable increase of expense, be its natural and inevitable concomitants? Have we not had unequivocal experience of its effects in the course of the revolution which we have just accomplished?

Every view we may take of the subject, as candid inquirers after truth, will serve to convince us, that it is both unwise and dangerous to deny the federal government an unconfined authority, as to all those objects which are intrusted to its management. It will indeed deserve the most vigilant and careful attention of the people, to see that it be modeled in such a manner as to admit of its being safely vested with the requisite powers. If any plan which has been, or may be, offered to our consideration, should not, upon a dispassionate inspection, be found to answer this description, it ought to be rejected. A government, the constitution of which renders it unfit to be trusted with all the powers which a free people *ought to delegate to any government,* would be an unsafe and improper depositary of the NATIONAL INTERESTS. Wherever THESE can with propriety be confided, the coincident powers may safely accompany them. This is the true result of all just reasoning upon the subject. . . . For the absurdity must continually stare us in the face of confiding to a government the direction of the most essential national interests, without daring to trust to it the authorities which are indispensable to their proper and efficient management. Let us not attempt to reconcile contradictions, but firmly embrace a rational alternative.

I trust, however, that the impracticability of one general system cannot be shown. I am greatly mistaken, if anything of weight has yet been advanced of this tendency; and I flatter myself, that the observations which have been made in the course of these papers have served to place the reverse of that position in as clear a light as any matter still in the womb of time and experience can be susceptible of. This, at all events, must be evident, that the very difficulty itself, drawn from the extent of the country, is the strongest argument in favor of an energetic government; for any other can certainly never preserve the Union of so large an empire. If we embrace the tenets of those who oppose the adoption of the proposed Constitution, as the standard of our political creed, we cannot fail to verify the gloomy doctrines which predict the impracticability of a national system pervading the entire limits of the present Confederacy.

PUBLIUS.

WILLIAM ELLERY CHANNING

1780–1842

OF New England birth and training, a grandson of WILLIAM ELLERY, one of the signers of the Declaration of Independence, a graduate of Harvard, and for many years a distinguished Unitarian pastor in Boston, Dr. CHANNING was one of the earliest of the essentially literary men of America. Calm, serene, philosophical, poetic, of loftiest spirituality and just discrimination in many realms of thought, he was distinctly an essayist, although in the pulpit a fervid preacher. It was his sermon at the ordination of the Rev. Jared Sparks in Baltimore, in 1819, that made him the acknowledged head of the Unitarian separation from the Congregational churches, that had taken place in 1812. His passion for freedom was intense. Whether as to the negro, or woman, or religious thinking, or political economy, or literary traditions, or any domain where he saw fetters on body, mind, or spirit, he was roused to protest and plea for enlargement.

Dr. CHANNING'S writings were received with marked respect, both here and in England. All things akin to man's highest interests were his themes. Among his best-known essays were those on Self-culture, on Milton, Napoleon Bonaparte, Fénelon, and an appeal for a National American Literature, freed from the trammels of European influence in form and spirit. Of this last (originally an Oration before the American Philosophical Society, in Philadelphia, October 18, 1823) is here given the first part, arguing the importance and value of such a literature; the rest of the paper discusses methods for securing it, — good counsels, but now happily no longer needed.

REMARKS ON NATIONAL LITERATURE

WE begin with stating what we mean by national literature. We mean the expression of a nation's mind in writing. We mean the production among a people of important works in philosophy, and in the departments of imagination and taste. We mean the contributions of new truths to the stock of human knowledge. We mean the thoughts of profound and original minds, elaborated by the toil of composition, and fixed and made immortal in books. We mean the manifestation of a nation's intellect in the only forms by which it can multiply itself at home, and send itself abroad. We mean that a nation shall take a place, by its authors, among the lights of the world. It will be seen that we include under literature all the writings of superior minds, be the subjects what they may. We are aware that the term is often confined to compositions which relate to human nature and human life; that it is not generally extended to physical science; that mind, not matter, is regarded as its main subject and sphere. But the worlds of matter and mind are too intimately connected to admit of exact partition. All the objects of human thought flow into one another. Moral and physical truths have many bonds and analogies, and, whilst the former are the chosen and noblest themes of literature, we are not anxious to divorce them from the latter, or to shut them up in a separate department. The expression of superior mind in writing we regard, then, as a nation's literature. We regard its gifted men, whether devoted to the exact sciences, to mental and ethical philosophy, to history and legislation, or to fiction and poetry, as forming a noble intellectual brotherhood; and it is for the purpose of quickening all to join their labors for the public good that we offer the present plea in behalf of a national literature.

To show the importance which we attach to the subject, we begin with some remarks on what we deem the distinction which a nation should most earnestly covet. We believe that more distinct apprehensions on this point are needed, and that, for want of them, the work of improvement is carried on with less energy, consistency, and wisdom, than may and should be brought to bear upon it. The great distinction of a country, then, is, that it produces superior men. Its natural advantages are not to be disdained. But they are of secondary importance. No matter what races of animals a country breeds, the great question is, Does it breed a noble race of men ? No matter what its soil may be, the great question is, How far is it prolific of moral and intellectual power ? No matter how stern its climate

is, if it nourish force of thought and virtuous purpose.
These are the products by which a country is to be
tried, and institutions have value only by the impulse
which they give to the mind. It has sometimes
been said that the noblest men grow where nothing
else will grow. This we do not believe, for mind is
not the creature of climate or soil. But were it
true, we should say that it were better to live among
rocks and sands than in the most genial and pro-
ductive region on the face of the earth.

As yet, the great distinction of a nation on which
we have insisted has been scarcely recognized. The
idea of forming a superior race of men has entered
little into schemes of policy. Invention and effort
have been expended on matter much more than on
mind. Lofty piles have been reared; the earth has
groaned under pyramids and palaces. The thought
of building up a nobler order of intellect and character has hardly crossed the most adventurous statesman. We beg that we may not be misapprehended.
We offer these remarks to correct what we deem a
disproportioned attention to physical good, and not
at all to condemn the expenditure of ingenuity and
strength on the outward world. There is a harmony between all our great interests, between inward
and outward improvements; and by establishing
among them a wise order, all will be secured. We
have no desire to shut up man in his own spiritual
nature. The mind was made to act on matter, and

it grows by expressing itself in material forms. We believe, too, that in proportion as it shall gain intellectual and moral power, it will exert itself with increased energy and delight on the outward creation; will pour itself forth more freely in useful and ornamental arts; will rear more magnificent structures, and will call forth new beauties in nature. An intelligent and resolute spirit in a community perpetually extends its triumphs over matter. It can even subject to itself the most unpromising region. Holland, diked from the ocean, — Venice, rising amidst the waves, — and New England, bleak and rock-bound New England, converted by a few generations from a wilderness into smiling fields and opulent cities, — point us to the mind as the great source of physical good, and teach us that, in making the culture of man our highest end, we shall not retard but advance the cultivation of nature.

The question which we most solicitously ask about this country is, what race of men it is likely to produce. We consider its liberty of value only as far as it favors the growth of men. What is liberty? The removal of restraint from human powers. Its benefit is, that it opens new fields for action and a wider range for the mind. The only freedom worth possessing is that which gives enlargement to a people's energy, intellect, and virtues. The savage makes his boast of freedom. But what is its worth?

Free as he is, he continues for ages in the same ignorance, leads the same comfortless life, sees the same untamed wilderness spread around him.   He is indeed free from what he calls the yoke of civil institutions.   But other and worse chains bind him. The very privation of civil government is in effect a chain; for, by withholding protection from property, it virtually shackles the arm of industry, and forbids exertion for the melioration of his lot.   Progress, the growth of power, is the end and boon of liberty; and, without this, a people may have the name, but want the substance and spirit of freedom. . . .

These views will explain the vast importance which we attach to a national literature.   By this, as we have said, we understand the expression of a nation's mind in writing.   It is the action of the most gifted understandings on the community.   It throws into circulation through a wide sphere the most quickening and beautiful thoughts which have grown up in men of laborious study or creative genius.   It is a much higher work than the communication of a gifted intellect in discourse.   It is the mind giving to multitudes, whom no voice can reach, its compressed and selected thoughts in the most lucid order and attractive forms which it is capable of inventing.   In other words, literature is the concentration of intellect for the purpose of spreading itself abroad and multiplying its energy.

Such being the nature of literature, it is plainly among the most powerful methods of exalting the character of a nation, of forming a better race of men; in truth, we apprehend that it may claim the first rank among the means of improvement. We know nothing so fitted to the advancement of society as to bring its higher minds to bear upon the multitude; as to establish close connections between the more or less gifted; as to spread far and wide the light which springs up in meditative, profound, and sublime understandings. It is the ordinance of God, and one of his most benevolent laws, that the human race should be carried forward by impulses which originate in a few minds, perhaps in an individual; and in this way the most interesting relations and dependencies of life are framed. When a great truth is to be revealed, it does not flash at once on the race, but dawns and brightens on a superior understanding, from which it is to emanate and to illumine future ages. On the faithfulness of great minds to this awful function, the progress and happiness of men chiefly depend. The most illustrious benefactors of the race have been men who, having risen to great truths, have held them as a sacred trust for their kind, and have borne witness to them amid general darkness, under scorn and persecution, perhaps in the face of death. Such men, indeed, have not always made contributions to literature, for their condition has not allowed them to be authors; but we owe the transmission, perpetuity, and immortal power of their new and high thoughts to kindred spirits, which have concentrated and fixed them in books.

The quickening influences of literature need not be urged on those who are familiar with the history of modern Europe, and who of course know the spring given to the human mind by the revival of ancient learning. Through their writings, the great men of antiquity have exercised a sovereignty over these later ages not enjoyed in their own. It is more important to observe that the influence of literature is perpetually increasing; for, through the press and the spread of education, its sphere is indefinitely enlarged. Reading, once the privilege of a few, is now the occupation of multitudes, and is to become one of the chief gratifications of all. Books penetrate everywhere, and some of the works of genius find their way to obscure dwellings which, a little while ago, seemed barred against all intellectual light. Writing is now the mightiest instrument on earth. Through this the mind has acquired a kind of omnipresence. To literature we then look, as the chief means of forming a better race of human beings. To superior minds, which may act through this, we look for the impulses by which their country is to be carried forward. We would teach them that they are the depositaries of the highest power on earth, and that on them the best hopes of society rest.

We are aware that some may think that we are

exalting intellectual above moral and religious influence. They may tell us that the teaching of moral
and religious truth, not by philosophers and boasters
of wisdom, but by the comparatively weak and foolish, is the great means of renovating the world. This
truth we indeed regard as "the power of God unto
salvation." But let none imagine that its chosen
temple is an uncultivated mind, and that it selects,
as its chief organs, the lips of the unlearned. Religious and moral truth is indeed appointed to carry
forward mankind; but not as conceived and ex-
pounded by narrow minds, not as darkened by the
ignorant, not as debased by the superstitious, not as
subtilized by the visionary, not as thundered out by
the intolerant fanatic, not as turned into a driveling
cant by the hypocrite. Like all other truths, it
requires for its full reception and powerful communication a free and vigorous intellect. Indeed, its
grandeur and infinite connections demand a more
earnest and various use of our faculties than any other
subject. . . . Religion has been wronged by nothing more than by being separated from intellect;
than by being removed from the province of reason
and free research into that of mystery and authority,
of impulse and feeling. Hence it is that the prevalent
forms of exhibitions of Christianity are comparatively inert, and that most which is written on the
subject is of little or no worth. Christianity was
given, not to contradict and degrade the rational

nature, but to call it forth, to enlarge its range and its powers. It admits of endless development. It is the last truth which should remain stationary. It ought to be so explored and so expressed as to take the highest place in a nation's literature, as to exalt and purify all other literature. From these remarks it will be seen that the efficacy which we have ascribed to literary or intellectual influence in the work of human improvement is consistent with the supreme importance of moral and religious truth.

If we have succeeded in conveying the impressions which we have aimed to make, our readers are now prepared to inquire with interest into the condition and prospects of literature among ourselves. Do we possess, indeed, what may be called a national literature? Have we produced eminent writers in the various departments of intellectual effort? Are our chief resources of instruction and literary enjoyment furnished from ourselves? We regret that the reply to these questions is so obvious. The few standard works which we have produced, and which promise to live, can hardly, by any courtesy, be denominated a national literature. On this point, if marks and proofs of our real condition were needed, we should find them in the current apologies for our deficiencies. Our writers are accustomed to plead in our excuse our youth, the necessities of a newly settled country, and the direction of our best

talents to practical life. Be the pleas sufficient or
not, one thing they prove, and that is, our consciousness of having failed to make important contributions to the interests of the intellect. . . .

With these views, we do and must lament that,
however we surpass other nations in providing for,
and spreading elementary instruction, we fall behind
many in provision for the liberal training of the
intellect, for forming great scholars, for communicat-
ing that profound knowledge, and that thirst for
higher truths, which can alone originate a com-
manding literature. The truth ought to be known.
There is among us much superficial knowledge,
but little severe, persevering research; little of that
consuming passion for new truth which makes outward things worthless; little resolute devotion
to a high intellectual culture. There is nowhere
a literary atmosphere, or such an accumulation
of literary influence, as determines the whole strength
of the mind to its own enlargement, and to the manifestation of itself in enduring forms. Few among
us can be said to have followed out any great subject
of thought patiently, laboriously, so as to know
thoroughly what others have discovered and taught
concerning it, and thus to occupy a ground from which
new views may be gained. . . . We grant that
there is primary necessity for that information and
skill by which subsistence is earned and life is preserved; for it is plain that we must live in order to

act and improve. But life is the means; action and improvement the end; and who will deny that the noblest utility belongs to that knowledge by which the chief purpose of our creation is accomplished?

According to these views, a people should honor and cultivate, as unspeakably useful, that literature which corresponds to, and calls forth, the highest faculties; which expresses and communicates energy of thought, fruitfulness of invention, force of moral purpose, a thirst for the true, and a delight in the beautiful. According to these views, we attach special importance to those branches of literature which relate to human nature, and which give it a consciousness of its own powers. History has a noble use, for it shows us human beings in various and opposite conditions, in their strength and weakness, in their progress and relapses, and thus reveals the causes and means by which the happiness and virtue of the race may be enlarged. Poetry is useful, by touching deep springs in the human soul; by giving voice to its more delicate feelings; by breathing out, and making more intelligible, the sympathy which subsists between the mind and the outward universe; by creating beautiful forms of manifestations for great moral truths. Above all, that higher philosophy, which treats of the intellectual and moral constitution of man, of the foundation of knowledge, of duty, of perfection, of our relations to the spiritual world, and especially to God — this has a usefulness so peculiar as to throw other departments of knowledge into obscurity; and a people among whom this does not find honor has little ground to boast of its superiority to uncivilized tribes.

It will be seen from these remarks that utility, with us, has a broad meaning. In truth, we are slow to condemn as useless any researches or discoveries of original and strong minds, even when we discern in them no bearing on any interests of mankind; for all truth is of a prolific nature, and has connections not immediately perceived; and it may be that what we call vain speculations may, at no distant period, link themselves with some new facts or theories, and guide a profound thinker to the most important results. The ancient mathematician, when absorbed in solitary thought, little imagined that his theorems, after the lapse of ages, were to be applied by the mind of Newton to the solution of the mysteries of the universe, and not only to guide the astronomer through the heavens, but the navigator through the pathless ocean. For ourselves, we incline to hope much from truths which are particularly decried as useless; for the noblest and most useful truth is of an abstract or universal nature; and yet the abstract, though susceptible of infinite application, is generally, as we know, opposed to the practical. . . .

Let us not be misunderstood. We have no desire to rear in our country a race of pedants, of solemn triflers, of laborious commentators on the mysteries of a Greek accent or a rusty coin. We would have men explore antiquity, not to bury themselves in its dust, but to learn its spirit, and so to commune with its superior minds as to accumulate on the present age the influences of whatever was great and wise in former times. What we want is, that those among us whom God has gifted to comprehend whatever is now known, and to rise to new truths, may find aids and institutions to fit them for their high calling, and may become at once springs of a higher intellectual life to their own country, and joint workers with the great of all nations and times in carrying forward their race.

We know that it will be said that foreign scholars, bred under institutions which this country cannot support, may do our intellectual work, and send us books and learning to meet our wants. To this we have much to answer. In the first place, we reply that, to avail ourselves of the higher literature of other nations, we must place ourselves on a level with them. The products of foreign machinery we can use without any portion of the skill that produced them. But works of taste and genius, and profound investigations of philosophy, can only be estimated and enjoyed through a culture and power corresponding to that from which they sprung. . . . We mean not to be paradoxical, but we believe that it would be better to admit no books from abroad than to make them substitutes for our own intellectual activity. The more we receive from other countries, the greater the need of an original literature. A people into whose minds the thoughts of foreigners are poured perpetually, needs an energy within itself to resist, to modify this mighty influence, and, without it, will inevitably sink under the worst bondage, will become intellectually tame and enslaved. We have certainly no desire to complete our restrictive system by adding to it a literary non-intercourse law. We rejoice in the increasing intellectual connection between this country and the Old World; but sooner would we rupture it than see our country sitting passively at the feet of foreign teachers. It were better to have no literature than form ourselves unresistingly on a foreign one. The true sovereigns of a country are those who determine its mind, its modes of thinking, its tastes, its principles; and we cannot consent to lodge this sovereignty in the hands of strangers. A country, like an individual, has dignity and power only in proportion as it is self-formed. There is a great stir to secure to ourselves the manufacturing of our own clothing. We say, let others spin and weave for us, but let them not think for us. A people whose government and laws are nothing but the embodying of public opinion, should jealously guard this opinion against foreign dictation. We need a literature to counteract, and to use wisely the literature which we import. . . .

We have hitherto spoken of literature as the

expression, the communication, of the higher minds in a community. We now add that it does much more than is commonly supposed to *form* such minds, so that, without it, a people wants one of the chief means of educating or perfecting talent and genius. One of the great laws of our nature, and a law singularly important to social beings, is, that the intellect enlarges and strengthens itself by expressing worthily its best views. In this, as in other respects, it is more blessed to give than to receive. Superior minds are formed, not merely by solitary thought, but almost as much by communication. Great thoughts are never fully possessed till he who has conceived them has given them fit utterance. One of the noblest and most invigorating labors of genius is to clothe its conceptions in clear and glorious forms, to give them existence in other souls. Thus literature creates, as well as manifests, intellectual power, and, without it, the highest minds will never be summoned to the most invigorating action.

We doubt whether a man ever brings his faculties to bear with their whole force on a subject until he writes upon it for the instruction or gratification of others. . . .

We come now to our last — and what we deem a weighty — argument in favor of a native literature. We desire and would cherish it, because we hope from it important aids to the cause of truth and human nature. We believe that a literature, springing up in this new soil, would bear new fruits, and, in some respects, more precious fruits, than are elsewhere produced. . . . The great distinction of our country is, that we enjoy some peculiar advantages for understanding our own nature. Man is the great subject of literature, and juster and profounder views of man may be expected here than elsewhere.

In Europe, political and artificial distinctions have, more or less, triumphed over and obscured our common nature. In Europe, we meet kings, nobles, priests, peasants. How much rarer is it to meet *men;* by which we mean human beings conscious of their own nature, and conscious of the utter worthlessness of all outward distinctions compared with what is treasured up in their own souls. Man does not value himself as man. It is for his blood, his rank, or some artificial distinction, and not for the attributes of humanity, that he holds himself in respect. The institutions of the Old World all tend to throw obscurity over what we most need to know, and that is, the worth and claims of a human being. We know that great improvements in this respect are going on abroad. Still, the many are too often postponed to the few. The mass of men are regarded as instruments to work with, as materials to be shaped for the use of their superiors. That consciousness of our own nature which contains, as a germ, all nobler thoughts, which teaches us at once self-respect and respect for others, and which binds us to God

by filial sentiment and hope, — this has been re-
pressed, kept down by establishments founded in
force; and literature, in all its departments, bears,
we think, the traces of this inward degradation. . . .

We have no thought of speaking contemptuously
of the literature of the Old World. It is our daily
nutriment. We feel our debt to be immense to the
glorious company of pure and wise minds which
foreign lands have bequeathed us in writing their
choicest thoughts and holiest feelings. Still, we
feel that all existing literature has been produced
under influences which have necessarily mixed with
it much error and corruption; and that the whole
of it ought to pass, and must pass, under rigorous
review. For example, we think that the history of
the human race is to be rewritten. Men imbued
with the prejudices which thrive under aristocracies
and state religions cannot understand it. Past ages,
with their great events and great men, are to undergo,
we think, a new trial, and to yield new results. It is
plain that history is already viewed under new as-
pects, and we believe that the true principles for
studying and writing it are to be unfolded here, at
least as rapidly as in other countries. It seems to
us that in literature an immense work is yet to be
done. The most interesting questions to mankind
are yet in debate. Great principles are yet to be
settled in criticism, in morals, in politics; and, above
all, the true character of religion is to be rescued

from the disguises and corruptions of ages.   We want
a reformation.   We want a literature, in which
genius will pay supreme if not undivided homage
to truth and virtue; in which the childish admiration of what has been called greatness will give place
to a wise moral judgment; which will breathe reverence for the mind, and elevating thoughts of God.

The part which this country is to bear in this great
intellectual reform we presume not to predict.   We
feel, however, that, if true to itself, it will have the
glory and happiness of giving new impulses to the
human mind.   This is our cherished hope.   We
should have no heart to encourage native literature,
did we not hope that it would become instinct with
a new spirit.   We cannot admit the thought that this
country is to be only a repetition of the Old World.
We delight to believe that God, in the fullness of time,
has brought a new continent to light, in order that the
human mind should move here with a new freedom,
should frame new social institutions, should explore
new paths, and reap new harvests.   We are accustomed to estimate nations by their creative
energies; and we shall blush for our country if, in
circumstances so peculiar, original, and creative,
it shall satisfy itself with a passive reception and
mechanical reiteration of the thoughts of strangers.

WASHINGTON IRVING

1783–1859

THIS writer, so identified with American literature, was born in New York City, his father being Scotch, and his mother, English. Before he was twenty years old he began writing newspaper dramatic and social criticisms; then studied law, when his health enforced a two years' absence in European travel. He never practiced law, gravitating naturally to literary pursuits, writing with PAULDING the amusing "Salmagundi," papers, and in 1809 publishing the famous "History of New York, by Diedrich Knickerbocker," which made IRVING known on both sides the Atlantic, and to such men abroad as SCOTT, CAMPBELL, MOORE, and other literary lights. The word "Knickerbocker," too, became a name for the older and better grade of New Yorkers, and for the group of writers — PAULDING, DRAKE, HALLECK, BRYANT, etc. — who soon arose in that city. IRVING shortly after went abroad again, was received enthusiastically in England, wrote and published there his "Sketch-Book," "Bracebridge Hall," and "Tales of a Traveler," while after some years' residence in Spain he produced his "Columbus," "Conquest of Granada," "The Alhambra," and other Spanish works. After his return home in 1832, he wrote sundry works on American themes, and several notable biographies. In 1842 IRVING again went abroad, as United States minister to Spain. After four years he returned to his pleasant home of "Sunnyside," at Tarrytown on the Hudson River — a region he had made famous with "Sleepy Hollow" and "Rip Van Winkle" — and there prepared his last and most elaborate work, the "Life of Washington."

Delightful in personality, graceful, genial, elevating, and felicitous in his literary career, IRVING was a product of the finer qualities of the three countries of his parentage and origin — one of the earliest bonds of affection between the Old World and the New.

THE MUTABILITY OF LITERATURE

A COLLOQUY IN WESTMINSTER ABBEY

I know that all beneath the moon decays,
And what by mortals in this world is brought
In time's great period shall return to nought.
I know that all the muse's heavenly lays,
With toil of sprite which are so dearly bought,
As idle sounds, of few or none are sought;
That there is nothing lighter than mere praise.
— DRUMMOND OF HAWTHORNDEN.

THERE are certain half-dreaming moods of mind, in which we naturally steal away from noise and glare, and seek some quiet haunt, where we may indulge our reveries and build our air-castles undisturbed. In such a mood I was loitering about the old gray cloisters of Westminster Abbey, enjoying that luxury of wandering thought which one is apt to dignify with the name of reflection; when suddenly an interruption of madcap boys from Westminster School, playing at football, broke in upon the monastic stillness of the place, making the vaulted passages and moldering tombs echo with their merriment. I sought to take refuge from their noise by penetrating still deeper into the solitudes of the pile, and applied to one of the vergers for admission to the library. He conducted me through a portal rich with the crumbling sculpture of former ages, which opened upon a gloomy passage leading to the chapter-house and the chamber in which Dooms-day-book is deposited. Just within the passage is a small door on the left. To this the verger applied a key; it was double-locked, and opened with some difficulty, as if seldom used. We now ascended a dark, narrow staircase, and, passing through a second door, entered the library.

I found myself in a lofty antique hall, the roof supported by massive joists of old English oak. It was soberly lighted by a row of Gothic windows at a considerable height from the floor, and which apparently opened upon the roofs of the cloisters. An ancient picture of some reverend dignitary of the church in his robes hung over the fireplace. Around the hall and in a small gallery were the books, arranged in carved oaken cases. They consisted principally of old polemical writers, and were much more worn by time than use. In the center of the library was a solitary table with two or three books on it, an inkstand without ink, and a few pens parched by long disuse. The place seemed fitted for quiet study and profound meditation. It was buried deep among the massive walls of the abbey, and shut up from the tumult of the world. I could only hear now and then the shouts of the school-boys faintly swelling from the cloisters, and the sound of a bell tolling for prayers, echoing soberly along the roofs of the abbey. By degrees the shouts of merriment grew fainter and fainter, and at length died away; the bell ceased to toll, and a profound silence reigned through the dusky hall.

I had taken down a little thick quarto, curiously bound in parchment, with brass clasps, and seated myself at the table in a venerable elbow-chair. Instead of reading, however, I was beguiled by the solemn monastic air, and lifeless quiet of the place, into a train of musing. As I looked around upon the old volumes in their moldering covers, thus ranged on the shelves, and apparently never disturbed in their repose, I could not but consider the library a kind of literary catacomb, where authors, like mummies, are piously entombed, and left to blacken and molder in dusty oblivion.

How much, thought I, has each of these volumes, now thrust aside with such indifference, cost some aching head! how many weary days! how many sleepless nights! How have their authors buried themselves in the solitude of cells and cloisters; shut themselves up from the face of man, and the still more blessed face of nature: and devoted themselves to painful research and intense reflection! And all for what? to occupy an inch of dusty shelf, — to have the title of their works read now and then in a future age, by some drowsy churchman or casual straggler like myself; and in another age to be lost, even to remembrance. Such is the amount of this boasted immortality. A mere temporary rumor, a local sound; like the tone of that bell which has just tolled among these towers, filling the ear for a moment — lingering transiently in echo — and then passing away like a thing that was not!

While I sat half murmuring, half meditating these unprofitable speculations, with my head resting on my hand, I was thrumming with the other hand upon the quarto, until I accidentally loosened the clasps; when, to my utter astonishment, the little book gave two or three yawns, like one awaking from a deep sleep; then a husky hem; and at length began to talk. At first its voice was very hoarse and broken, being much troubled by a cobweb which some studious spider had woven across it; and having probably contracted a cold from long exposure to the chills and damps of the abbey. In a short time, however, it became more distinct, and I soon found it an exceedingly fluent, conversable little tome. Its language, to be sure, was rather quaint and obsolete, and its pronunciation, what, in the present day, would be deemed barbarous; but I shall endeavor, as far as I am able, to render it in modern parlance.

It began with railings about the neglect of the world — about merit being suffered to languish in obscurity, and other such commonplace topics of literary repining, and complained bitterly that it had not been opened for more than two centuries.

That the dean only looked now and then into the library, sometimes took down a volume or two, trifled with them for a few moments, and then returned them to their shelves. "What a plague do they mean," said the little quarto, which I began to perceive was somewhat choleric, — "what a plague do they mean by keeping several thousand volumes of us shut up here, and watched by a set of old vergers, like so many beauties in a harem, merely to be looked at now and then by the dean ? Books were written to give pleasure and to be enjoyed; and I would have a rule passed that the dean should pay each of us a visit at least once a year; or, if he is not equal to the task, let them once in a while turn loose the whole School of Westminster among us, that at any rate we may now and then have an airing."

"Softly, my worthy friend," replied I; "you are not aware how much better you are off than most books of your generation. By being stored away in this ancient library, you are like the treasured remains of those saints and monarchs which lie enshrined in the adjoining chapels; while the remains of your contemporary mortals, left to the ordinary course of nature, have long since returned to dust."

"Sir," said the little tome, ruffling his leaves and looking big, "I was written for all the world, not for the bookworms of an abbey. I was intended to circulate from hand to hand, like other great contemporary works; but here have I been clasped

up for more than two centuries, and might have
silently fallen a prey to these worms that are playing
the very vengeance with my intestines, if you had
not by chance given me an opportunity of uttering
a few last words before I go to pieces."

"My good friend," rejoined I, "had you been left
to the circulation of which you speak, you would
long ere this have been no more. To judge from
your physiognomy, you are now well stricken in
years; very few of your contemporaries can be at
present in existence; and those few owe their lon-
gevity to being immured like yourself in old libraries;
which, suffer me to add, instead of likening to harems,
you might more properly and gratefully have compared to those infirmaries attached to religious
establishments, for the benefit of the old and de-
crepit, and where, by quiet fostering and no employment, they often endure to an amazingly good-for-
nothing old age. You talk of your contemporaries
as if in circulation, — where do we meet with their
works ? What do we hear of Robert Groteste, of
Lincoln ? No one could have toiled harder than he
for immortality. He is said to have written nearly
two hundred volumes. He built, as it were, a pyramid of books to perpetuate his name; but, alas!
the pyramid has long since fallen, and only a few
fragments are scattered in various libraries, where
they are scarcely disturbed even by the antiquarian.
What do we hear of Giraldus Cambrensis, the

historian, antiquary, philosopher, theologian, and poet ? He declined two bishoprics, that he might shut himself up and write posterity; but posterity never inquires after his labors. What of Henry of Huntingdon, who, besides a learned history of England, wrote a treatise on the contempt of the world, which the world has revenged by forgetting him ? What is quoted of Joseph of Exeter, styled the miracle of his age in classical composition ? Of his three great heroic poems one is lost forever, excepting a mere fragment; the others are known only to a few of the curious in literature; and as to his love-verses and epigrams, they have entirely disappeared. What is in current use of John Wallis, the Franciscan, who acquired the name of the tree of life ? Of William of Malmsbury; — of Simeon of Durham; — of Benedict of Peterborough; — of John Hanvill of St. Albans; — of ——"

"Prithee, friend," cried the quarto, in a testy tone, "how old do you think me ? You are talking of authors that lived long before my time, and wrote either in Latin or French, so that they in a manner expatriated themselves, and deserved to be forgotten ;[1]

---

[1] In Latin and French hath many soueraine wittes had great delyte to endite, and have many noble thinges fulfilde, but certes there ben some that speaken their poisye in French, of which speche the Frenchmen have as good a fantasye as we have in hearying of Frenchmen's Englishe. — *Chaucer's Testament of Love.*

but I, sir, was ushered into the world from the press of the renowned Wynkyn de Worde. I was written in my own native tongue, at a time when the language had become fixed; and indeed I was considered a model of pure and elegant English."

(I should observe that these remarks were couched in such intolerably antiquated terms, that I have had infinite difficulty in rendering them into modern phraseology.)

"I cry your mercy," said I, "for mistaking your age; but it matters little: almost all the writers of your time have likewise passed into forgetfulness; and De Worde's publications are mere literary rarities among book-collectors. The purity and stability of language, too, on which you found your claims to perpetuity, have been the fallacious dependence of authors of every age, even back to the times of the worthy Robert of Gloucester, who wrote his history in rhymes of mongrel Saxon.[1] Even now many talk of Spenser's 'Well of pure English

---

[1] Holinshed, in his Chronicle, observes: "Afterwards, also, by deligent travell of Geffry Chaucer and of John Gowre, in the time of Richard the Second, and after them of John Scogan and John Lydgate, monke of Berrie, our said toong was brought to an excellent passe, notwithstanding that it never came unto the type of perfection until the time of Queen Elizabeth, wherein John Jewell, Bishop of Sarum, John Fox, and sundrie learned and excellent writers, have fully accomplished the ornature of the same, to their great praise and immortal commendation."

undefiled' as if the language ever sprang from a
well or fountain-head, and was not rather a mere
confluence of various tongues, perpetually subject
to changes and intermixtures. It is this which has
made English literature so extremely mutable, and
the reputation built upon it so fleeting. Unless
thought can be committed to something more permanent and unchangeable than such a medium,
even thought must share the fate of everything else,
and fall into decay. This should serve as a check
upon the vanity and exultation of the most popular
writer. He finds the language in which he has
embarked his fame gradually altering, and subject
to the dilapidations of time and the caprice of fashion.
He looks back and beholds the early authors of his
country, once the favorites of their day, supplanted
by modern writers. A few short ages have covered
them with obscurity, and their merits can only be
relished by the quaint taste of the bookworm.
And such, he anticipates, will be the fate of his own
work, which, however it may be admired in its day,
and held up as a model of purity, will in the course
of years grow antiquated and obsolete; until it
shall become as unintelligible in its native land as
an Egyptian obelisk, or one of those Runic inscrip-
tions said to exist in the deserts of Tartary. I
declare," added I, with some emotion, "when I
contemplate a modern library, filled with new works,
in all the bravery of rich gilding and binding, I feel

disposed to sit down and weep; like the good Xerxes, when he surveyed his army, pranked out in all the splendor of military array, and reflected that in one hundred years not one of them would be in existence!"

"Ah," said the little quarto, with a heavy sigh, "I see how it is; these modern scribblers have superseded all the good old authors. I suppose nothing is read nowadays but Sir Philip Sydney's 'Arcadia,' Sackville's stately plays, and 'Mirror for Magistrates,' or the fine-spun euphuisms of the 'unparalleled John Lyly.'"

"There you are again mistaken," said I; "the writers whom you suppose in vogue, because they happened to be so when you were last in circulation, have long since had their day. Sir Philip Sydney's 'Arcadia,' the immortality of which was so fondly predicted by his admirers,[1] and which, in truth, is full of noble thoughts, delicate images, and graceful turns of language, is now scarcely ever mentioned. Sackville has strutted into obscurity; and even Lyly, though his writings were once the delight of a court, and apparently perpetuated by a proverb,

[1] Live ever sweete booke; the simple image of his gentle witt, and the golden-pillar of his noble courage; and ever notify unto the world that thy writer was the secretary of eloquence, the breath of the muses, the honey-bee of the daintyest flowers of witt and arte, the pith of morale and intellectual virtues, the arme of Bellona in the field, the tongue of Suada in the chamber, the sprite of Practise in esse, and the paragon of excellency in print. — *Harvey Pierce's Supererogation.*

is now scarcely known even by name. A whole crowd of authors who wrote and wrangled at the time, have likewise gone down, with all their writings and their controversies. Wave after wave of succeeding literature has rolled over them, until they are buried so deep, that it is only now and then that some industrious diver after fragments of antiquity brings up a specimen for the gratification of the curious.

"For my part," I continued, "I consider this mutability of language a wise precaution of Providence for the benefit of the world at large, and of authors in particular. To reason from analogy, we daily behold the varied and beautiful tribes of vegetables springing up, flourishing, adorning the fields for a short time, and then fading into dust, to make way for their successors. Were not this the case, the fecundity of nature would be a grievance instead of a blessing. The earth would groan with rank and excessive vegetation, and its surface become a tangled wilderness. In like manner the works of genius and learning decline, and make way for subsequent productions. Language gradually varies, and with it fade away the writings of authors who have flourished their allotted time; otherwise, the creative powers of genius would overstock the world, and the mind would be completely bewildered in the endless mazes of literature. Formerly there were some restraints on this excessive multiplication. Works had to be transcribed by hand, which was

a slow and laborious operation; they were written
either on parchment, which was expensive, so that
one work was often erased to make way for another;
or on papyrus, which was fragile and extremely
perishable. Authorship was a limited and unprofitable craft, pursued chiefly by monks in the leisure
and solitude of their cloisters. The accumulation
of manuscripts was slow and costly, and confined
almost entirely to monasteries. To these circumstances it may, in some measure, be owing that we
have not been inundated by the intellect of antiquity; that the fountains of thought have not been
broken up, and modern genius drowned in the deluge. But the inventions of paper and the press
have put an end to all these restraints. They have
made every one a writer, and enabled every mind
to pour itself into print, and diffuse itself over the
whole intellectual world. The consequences are
alarming. The stream of literature has swollen into
a torrent — augumented into a river — expanded
into a sea. A few centuries since, five or six hundred
manuscripts constituted a great library; but what
would you say to libraries such as actually exist
containing three or four hundred thousand volumes;
legions of authors at the same time busy; and the
press going on with activity, to double and quadruple
the number. Unless some unforeseen mortality
should break out among the progeny of the Muse,
now that she has become so prolific, I tremble for

posterity. I fear the mere fluctuation of language
will not be sufficient. Criticism may do much.
It increases with the increase of literature, and
resembles one of those salutary checks on population
spoken of by economists. All possible encouragement, therefore, should be given to the growth of
critics, good or bad. But I fear all will be in vain;
let criticism do what it may, writers will write,
printers will print, and the world will inevitably
be overstocked with good books. It will soon be the
employment of a lifetime merely to learn their names.
Many a man of passable information, at the present
day, reads scarcely anything but reviews; and before long a man of erudition will be little better than
a mere walking catalogue."

"My very good sir," said the little quarto, yawn-
ing most drearily in my face, "excuse my interrupting
you, but I perceive you are rather given to prose.
I would ask the fate of an author who was making
some noise just as I left the world. His reputation,
however, was considered quite temporary. The
learned shook their heads at him, for he was a poor,
half-educated varlet, that knew little of Latin,
and nothing of Greek, and had been obliged to run
the country for deer-stealing. I think his name was
Shakespeare. I presume he soon sunk into oblivion."

"On the contrary," said I, "it is owing to that
very man that the literature of his period has experienced a duration beyond the ordinary term of

English literature. There rise authors now and
then, who seem proof against the mutability of
language, because they have rooted themselves in
the unchanging principles of human nature. They
are like gigantic trees that we sometimes see on the
banks of a stream; which, by their vast and deep
roots, penetrating through the mere surface, and
laying hold of the very foundations of the earth,
preserve the soil around them from being swept away
by the ever-flowing current, and hold up many a
neighboring plant, and, perhaps, worthless weed,
to perpetuity. Such is the case with Shakespeare,
whom we behold defying the encroachments of time,
retaining in modern use the language and literature
of his day, and giving duration to many an indifferent
author, merely from having flourished in his vicinity.
But even he, I grieve to say, is gradually assuming
the tint of age, and his whole form is overrun by
a profusion of commentators, who, like clambering
vines and creepers, almost bury the noble plant
that upholds them."

Here the little quarto began to heave his sides
and chuckle, until at length he broke out in a plethoric
fit of laughter that had well-nigh choked him, by
reason of his excessive corpulency. "Mighty well!"
cried he, as soon as he could recover breath; "mighty
well! and so you would persuade me that the literature of an age is to be perpetuated by a vagabond
deer-stealer! by a man without learning; by a poet,

forsooth — a poet!" And here he wheezed forth
another fit of laughter.

I confess that I felt somewhat nettled at this
rudeness, which, however, I pardoned on account of
his having flourished in a less polished age. I determined, nevertheless, not to give up my point.

"Yes," resumed I, positively, "a poet; for of all
writers he has the best chance for immortality.
Others may write from the head, but he writes from
the heart, and the heart will always understand him.
He is the faithful portrayer of nature, whose features
are always the same, and always interesting. Prose
writers are voluminous and unwieldy; their pages
are crowded with commonplaces, and their thoughts
expanded into tediousness. But with the true
poet everything is terse, touching, or brilliant.
He gives the choicest thoughts in the choicest language. He illustrates them by everything that he
sees most striking in nature and art. He enriches
them by pictures of human life, such as it is passing
before him. His writings, therefore, contain the
spirit, the aroma, if I may use the phrase, of the age
in which he lives. They are caskets which enclose
within a small compass the wealth of the language,
— its family jewels, which are thus transmitted in
a portable form to posterity. The setting may
occasionally be antiquated, and require now and
then to be renewed, as in the case of Chaucer; but
the brilliancy and intrinsic value of the gems con-

tinue unaltered. Cast a look back over the long reach of literary history. What vast valleys of dullness, filled with monkish legends and academical controversies! what bogs of theological speculations! what dreary wastes of metaphysics! Here and there only do we behold the heaven-illuminated bards, elevated like beacons on their widely separated heights, to transmit the pure light of poetical intelligence from age to age."

I was just about to launch forth into eulogiums upon the poets of the day, when the sudden opening of the door caused me to turn my head. It was the verger, who came to inform me that it was time to close the library. I sought to have a parting word with the quarto, but the worthy little tome was silent; the clasps were closed; and it looked perfectly unconscious of all that had passed. I have been to the library two or three times since, and have endeavored to draw it into further conversation, but in vain; and whether all this rambling colloquy actually took place, or whether it was another of those odd day-dreams to which I am subject, I have never to this moment been able to discover.

EDGAR ALLAN POE

1811–1849

THIS noted Southern genius was the son of a Baltimorean of good family who had become an actor, and who with his wife, an actress, was fulfilling engagements in Boston when the boy was born. The parents both dying shortly after, their three children were adopted by generous friends in Richmond, Virginia, EDGAR by Mr. JOHN ALLAN. The boy was educated, in school, by tutors, and in the University of Virginia, until, despite his brilliant scholarship, waywardness brought expulsion.

The publication of a slight volume of poems, two years' enlistment in the army, an appointment to West Point and dismissal within a year, brought POE to literary labor for a livelihood. In Baltimore he lived and wrought, becoming editor of the *Southern Literary Messenger*, in which his criticisms, poems, and tales gained quick public recognition. At this time, too (1836), he married his cousin, Miss VIRGINIA CLEMM, whom he devotedly loved. But POE's irregularities threw him out again. After this he found editorial work in Philadelphia, and then in New York, always doing brilliant service but never steadily. And thus he struggled on until his distressing death.

POE's home life was ideally devoted and lovely; but a native melancholy temperament seemed to draw him to drink, which crazed his abnormally sensitive nerves. He was faithful and efficient, but periodically revolted from the restraint of work. As critic he was incisive, even caustic, yet sympathetically recognized the fineness of such men as HAWTHORNE and LONGFELLOW in their beginnings. As poet, he was highly imaginative, although in a strange, unnatural fashion, which, however, his exquisite rhythmic gift and tireless patience of elaboration wrought into melodies and harmonies that will not die. His talent in the short story was a marvel, his ingenuity astonishing; but, like his poems, his tales are brooded with fantasies of gloom and at times of positively thrilling horror.

A strange, unhappy man, the very conditions of whose genius made him erratic: but he has left literature that will endure.

THE PHILOSOPHY OF COMPOSITION

CHARLES DICKENS, in a note now lying before me, alluding to an examination I once made of the mechanism of "Barnaby Rudge," says — "By the way, are you aware that Godwin wrote his 'Caleb Williams' backwards ? He first involved his hero in a web of difficulties, forming the second volume, and then, for the first, cast about him for some mode of accounting for what had been done."

I cannot think this the *precise* mode of procedure on the part of Godwin, — and indeed what he himself acknowledges is not altogether in accordance with Mr. Dickens' idea, — but the author of "Caleb Williams" was too good an artist not to perceive the advantage derivable from at least a somewhat similar process. Nothing is more clear than that every plot, worth the name, must be elaborated to its *dénouement* before anything be attempted with the pen. It is only with the *dénouement* constantly in view that we can give a plot its indispensable air of consequence, or causation, by making the incidents, and especially the tone at all points, tend to the development of the intention.

There is a radical error, I think, in the usual mode of constructing a story. Either history affords a thesis — or one is suggested by an incident of the day,— or, at best, the author sets himself to work in the combination of striking events to form merely the basis of his narrative — designing, generally, to fill in with description, dialogue, or autorial comment, whatever crevices of fact, or action, may, from page to page, render themselves apparent.

I prefer commencing with the consideration of an *effect*. Keeping originality *always* in view — for he is false to himself who ventures to dispense with so obvious and so easily attainable a source of interest — I say to myself, in the first place, "Of the innumerable effects, or impressions, of which the heart, the intellect, or (more generally) the soul is susceptible, what one shall I, on the present occasion, select?" Having chosen a novel, first, and secondly a vivid effect, I consider whether it can be best wrought by incident or tone — whether by ordinary incidents and peculiar tone, or the converse, or by peculiarity both of incident and tone — afterward looking about me (or rather within) for such combinations of event, or tone, as shall best aid me in the construction of the effect.

I have often thought how interesting a magazine paper might be written by any author who would — that is to say who could — detail, step by step, the processes by which any one of his compositions

attained its ultimate point of completion. Why
such a paper has never been given to the world, I am
much at a loss to say — but, perhaps, the autorial
vanity has had more to do with the omission than any
one other cause. Most writers — poets in especial
— prefer having it understood that they compose by
a species of fine frenzy — an ecstatic intuition —
and would positively shudder at letting the public
take a peep behind the scenes, at the elaborate and
vacillating crudities of thought — at the true purposes seized only at the last moment — at the innumerable glimpses of idea that arrived not at the
maturity of full view — at the fully matured fancies
discarded in despair as unmanageable — at the cautious selections and rejections — at the painful
erasures and interpolations — in a word, at the
wheels and pinions — the tackle for scene-shifting
— the step-ladders and demon-traps — the cock's
feathers, the red paint and the black patches, which,
in ninety-nine cases out of the hundred, constitute
the properties of the literary *histrio*.

I am aware, on the other hand, that the case is by
no means common, in which an author is at all in
condition to retrace the steps by which his conclusions
have been attained. In general suggestions, having
arisen pell-mell, are pursued and forgotten in a
similar manner.

For my own part, I have neither sympathy with
the repugnance alluded to, nor at any time the least

difficulty in recalling to mind the progressive steps of any of my compositions; and, since the interest of an analysis, or reconstruction, such as I have considered a *desideratum*, is quite independent of any real or fancied interest in the thing analyzed, it will not be regarded as a breach of decorum on my part to show the *modus operandi* by which some one of my own works was put together. I select "The Raven," as most generally known. It is my design to render it manifest that no one point in its composition is referable either to accident or intuition — that the work proceeded, step by step, to its completion with the precision and rigid consequence of a mathematical problem.

Let us dismiss, as irrelevant to the poem, *per se*, the circumstance — or say the necessity — which, in the first place, gave rise to the intention of composing *a* poem that should suit at once the popular and the critical taste.

We commence, then, with this intention.

The initial consideration was that of extent. If any literary work is too long to be read at one sitting, we must be content to dispense with the immensely important effect derivable from unity of impression — for, if two sittings be required, the affairs of the world interfere, and everything like totality is at once destroyed. But since, *ceteris paribus*, no poet can afford to dispense with *anything* that may advance his design, it but remains to be seen whether there is, in extent, any advantage to counterbalance the loss of unity which attends it. Here I say no, at once. What we term a long poem is, in fact, merely a succession of brief ones — that is to say, of brief poetical effects. It is needless to demonstrate that a poem is such, only inasmuch as it intensely excites, by elevating, the soul; and all intense excitements are, through a psychal necessity, brief. For this reason, at least one-half of the "Paradise Lost" is essentially prose — a succession of poetical excitements interspersed, *inevitably*, with corresponding depressions — the whole being deprived, through the extremeness of its length, of the vastly important artistic element, totality, or unity, of effect.

It appears evident, then, that there is a distinct limit, as regards length, to all works of literary art — the limit of a single sitting — and that, although in certain classes of prose composition, such as "Robinson Crusoe," (demanding no unity,) this limit may be advantageously overpassed, it can never properly be overpassed in a poem. Within this limit, the extent of a poem may be made to bear mathematical relation to its merit — in other words, to the excitement or elevation — again in other words, to the degree of the true poetical effect which it is capable of inducing; for it is clear that the brevity must be in direct ratio of the intensity of the intended effect; — this, with one proviso — that a certain degree of duration is absolutely requisite for the production of any effect at all.

Holding in view these considerations, as well as that degree of excitement which I deemed not above the popular, while not below the critical, taste, I reached at once what I conceived the proper *length* for my intended poem — a length of about one hundred lines. It is, in fact, a hundred and eight.

My next thought concerned the choice of an impression, or effect, to be conveyed: and here I may as well observe that, throughout the construction, I kept steadily in view the design of rendering the work *universally* appreciable. I should be carried too far out of my immediate topic were I to demonstrate a point upon which I have repeatedly insisted, and which, with the poetical, stands not in the slightest need of demonstration — the point, I mean, that Beauty is the sole legitimate province of the poem. A few words, however, in elucidation of my real meaning, which some of my friends have evinced a disposition to misrepresent. That pleasure which is at once the most intense, the most elevating, and the most pure, is, I believe, found in the contemplation of the beautiful. When, indeed, men speak of Beauty, they mean, precisely, not a quality, as is supposed, but an effect — they refer, in short, just to that intense and pure elevation of *soul — not* of intellect, or of heart — upon which I have commented, and which is experienced in consequence of contemplating "the beautiful." Now I designate Beauty as the province of the poem, merely because it is an obvious rule of Art that effects should be made to spring from direct causes — that objects should be attained through means best adapted for their attainment — no one as yet having been weak enough to deny that the peculiar elevation alluded to is *most readily* attained in the poem. Now the object, Truth, or the satisfaction of the intellect, and the object, Passion, or the excitement of the heart, are, although attainable, to a certain extent, in poetry, far more readily attainable in prose. Truth, in fact, demands a precision, and Passion a *homeliness* (the truly passionate will comprehend me) which are absolutely antagonistic to that Beauty which, I maintain, is the excitement, or pleasurable elevation, of the soul. It by no means follows from anything here said, that passion, or even truth, may not be introduced, and even profitably introduced, into a poem, — for they may serve in elucidation, or aid the general effect, as do discords in music, by contrast, — but the true artist will always contrive, first, to tone them into proper subservience to the predominant aim, and, secondly, to enveil them, as far as possible, in that Beauty which is the atmosphere and the essence of the poem.

Regarding, then, Beauty, as my province, my next question referred to the *tone* of its highest manifestation — and all experience has shown that this tone is one of *sadness*. Beauty of whatever kind, in its supreme development, invariably excites the sensitive soul to tears. Melancholy is thus the most legitimate of all the poetical tones.

The length, the province, and the tone, being thus determined, I betook myself to ordinary induction, with the view of obtaining some artistic piquancy which might serve me as a key-note in the construction of the poem — some pivot upon which the whole structure might turn. In carefully thinking over all the usual artistic effects — or more properly *points*, in the theatrical sense — I did not fail to perceive immediately that no one had been so universally employed as that of the *refrain*. The universality of its employment sufficed to assure me of its intrinsic value, and spared me the necessity of submitting it to analysis. I considered it, however, with regard to its susceptibility of improvement, and soon saw it to be in a primitive condition. As commonly used, the *refrain*, or burden, not only is limited to lyric verse, but depends for its impression upon the force of monotone — both in sound and thought. The pleasure is deduced solely from the sense of identity — of repetition. I resolved to diversify, and so heighten, the effect, by adhering, in general, to the monotone of sound, while I continually varied that of thought: that is to say, I determined to produce continuously novel effects, by the variation *of the application* of the *refrain* — the *refrain* itself remaining, for the most part, unvaried.

These points being settled, I next bethought me of the *nature* of my *refrain*. Since its application was to be repeatedly varied, it was clear that the *refrain* itself must be brief, for there would have been an insurmountable difficulty in frequent variations of application in any sentence of length. In proportion to the brevity of the sentence, would, of course, be the facility of the variation. This led me at once to a single word as the best *refrain*.

The question now arose as to the *character* of the word. Having made up my mind to a *refrain*, the division of the poem into stanzas was, of course, a corollary: the *refrain* forming the close of each stanza. That such a close, to have force, must be sonorous and susceptible of protracted emphasis, admitted no doubt: and these considerations inevitably led me to the long *o* as the most sonorous vowel, in connection with *r* as the most producible consonant.

The sound of the *refrain* being thus determined, it became necessary to select a word embodying this sound, and at the same time in the fullest possible keeping with that melancholy which I had predetermined as the tone of the poem. In such a search it would have been absolutely impossible to overlook the word "Nevermore." In fact, it was the very first which presented itself.

The next *desideratum* was a pretext for the continuous use of the one word "nevermore." In observing the difficulty which I at once found in inventing a sufficiently plausible reason for its continuous repetition, I did not fail to perceive that this difficulty arose solely from the pre-assumption that the word was to be so continuously or monotonously spoken by *a human* being — I did not fail to perceive, in short, that the difficulty lay in the reconciliation of this monotony with the exercise of reason on the part of the creature repeating the word. Here, then, immediately arose the idea of a *non*-reasoning creature capable of speech; and, very naturally, a parrot, in the first instance, suggested itself, but was superseded forthwith by a Raven, as equally capable of speech, and infinitely more in keeping with the intended *tone.*

I had now gone so far as the conception of a Raven — the bird of ill omen — monotonously repeating the one word, "Nevermore," at the conclusion of each stanza, in a poem of melancholy tone, and in length about one hundred lines. Now, never losing sight of the object *supremeness,* or perfection, at all points, I asked myself — "Of all melancholy topics, what, according to the *universal* understanding of mankind, is the *most* melancholy?" Death—was the obvious reply. "And when," I said, "is this most melancholy of topics most poetical?" From what I have already explained at some length, the answer, here also, is obvious — "When it most closely allies itself to *Beauty:* the death, then, of a beautiful woman is, unquestionably, the most poetical topic in the world — and equally is it beyond doubt that the lips best suited for such topic are those of a bereaved lover."

I had now to combine the two ideas, of a lover lamenting his deceased mistress and a Raven continuously repeating the word "Nevermore." — I had to combine these, bearing in mind my design of varying, at every turn, the *application* of the word repeated; but the only intelligible mode of such combination is that of imagining the Raven employing the word in answer to the queries of the lover. And here it was that I saw at once the opportunity afforded for the effect on which I had been depending — that is to say, the effect of the *variation of application.* I saw that I could make the first query propounded by the lover — the first query to which the Raven should reply "Nevermore" — that I could make this first query a commonplace one — the second less so — the third still less, and so on — until at length the lover, startled from his original *nonchalance* by the melancholy character of the word itself — by its frequent repetition — and by a consideration of the ominous reputation of the fowl that uttered it — is at length excited to superstition, and wildly propounds queries of a far different character — queries whose solution he has passionately at heart — propounds them half in superstition and half in that species of despair which delights in self-torture — propounds them

not altogether because he believes in the prophetic
or demoniac character of the bird (which, reason
assures him, is merely repeating a lesson learned by
rote), but because he experiences a phrenzied pleasure
in so modeling his questions as to receive from the
expected "Nevermore" the most delicious because
the most intolerable of sorrow. Perceiving the
opportunity thus afforded me — or, more strictly,
thus forced upon me in the progress of the construction — I first established in mind the climax, or concluding query — that query to which "Nevermore"
should be in the last place an answer — that in reply
to which this word "Nevermore" should involve the
utmost conceivable amount of sorrow and despair.

Here then the poem may be said to have its beginning, — at the end, where all works of art should begin,
— for it was here, at this point of my preconsidera-
tions, that I first put pen to paper in the composition
of the stanza: —

"Prophet," said I, "thing of evil! prophet still if bird or
    devil!
By that heaven that bends above us — by that God we both
    adore,
Tell this soul with sorrow laden, if within the distant Aidenn,
It shall clasp a sainted maiden whom the angels name
    Lenore —
Clasp a rare and radiant maiden whom the angels name
    Lenore."
        Quoth the raven, "Nevermore."

I composed this stanza, at this point, first that, by establishing the climax, I might the better vary and graduate, as regards seriousness and importance, the preceding queries of the lover — and, secondly, that I might definitely settle the rhythm, the meter, and the length and general arrangement of the stanza — as well as graduate the stanzas which were to precede, so that none of them might surpass this in rhythmical effect. Had I been able, in the subsequent composition, to construct more vigorous stanzas, I should, without scruple, have purposely enfeebled them, so as not to interfere with the climacteric effect.

And here I may as well say a few words of the versification. My first object (as usual) was originality. The extent to which this has been neglected, in versification, is one of the most unaccountable things in the world. Admitting that there is little possibility of variety in mere *rhythm*, it is still clear that the possible varieties of meter and stanza are absolutely infinite — and yet, *for centuries, no man, in verse, has ever done, or ever seemed to think of doing, an original thing*. The fact is, that originality (unless in minds of very unusual force) is by no means a matter, as some suppose, of impulse or intuition. In general, to be found, it must be elaborately sought, and although a positive merit of the highest class, demands in its attainment less of invention than negation.

Of course, I pretend to no originality in either the

rhythm or meter of the "Raven." The former is trochaic — the latter is octameter acatalectic, alternating with heptameter catalectic repeated in the *refrain* of the fifth verse, and terminating with tetrameter catalectic. Less pedantically — the feet employed throughout (trochees) consist of a long syllable followed by a short: the first line of the stanza consists of eight of these feet — the second of seven and a half (in effect two-thirds) — the third of eight — the fourth of seven and a half — the fifth the same — the sixth three and a half. Now, each of these lines, taken individually, has been employed before, and what originality the "Raven" has, is in their *combination into stanza;* nothing even remotely approaching this combination has ever been attempted. The effect of this originality of combination is aided by other unusual, and some altogether novel effects, arising from an extension of the application of the principles of rhyme and alliteration.

The next point to be considered was the mode of bringing together the lover and the Raven — and the first branch of this consideration was the *locale.* For this the most natural suggestion might seem to be a forest, or the fields — but it has always appeared to me that a close *circumscription of space* is absolutely necessary to the effect of insulated incident: — it has the force of a frame to a picture. It has an indisputable moral power in keeping concentrated the

attention, and, of course, must not be confounded
with mere unity of place.

I determined, then, to place the lover in his chamber — in a chamber rendered sacred to him by memories of her who had frequented it. The room is
represented as richly furnished — this in mere pursu-
ance of the ideas I have already explained on the subject of Beauty, as the sole true poetical thesis.

The *locale* being thus determined, I had now to
introduce the bird — and the thought of introducing
him through the window was inevitable. The idea
of making the lover suppose, in the first instance, that
the flapping of the wings of the bird against the
shutter, is a "tapping" at the door, originated in a
wish to increase, by prolonging, the reader's curi-
osity, and in a desire to admit the incidental effect
arising from the lover's throwing open the door,
finding all dark, and thence adopting the half
fancy that it was the spirit of his mistress that
knocked.

I made the night tempestuous, first, to account for
the Raven's seeking admission, and secondly, for the
effect of contrast with the (physical) serenity within
the chamber.

I made the bird alight on the bust of Pallas, also for
the effect of contrast between the marble and the plu-
mage — it being understood that the bust was absolutely *suggested* by the bird — the bust of *Pallas*
being chosen, first, as most in keeping with the schol-

arship of the lover, and, secondly, for the sonorousness of the word, Pallas, itself.

About the middle of the poem, also, I have availed myself of the force of contrast, with a view of deepening the ultimate impression. For example, an air of the fantastic — approaching as nearly to the ludicrous as was admissible — is given to the Raven's entrance. He comes in "with many a flirt and flutter."

Not the *least obeisance made he;* not a moment stopped or stayed he,
But with mien of lord or lady, perched above my chamber door.

In the two stanzas which follow, the design is more obviously carried out: —

Then this ebon bird beguiling my sad fancy into smiling
By the *grave and stern decorum of the countenance it wore*,
"Though thy *crest be shorn and shaven*, thou," I said, "art sure no craven;
Ghastly, grim, and ancient Raven, wandering from the nightly shore —
Tell me what thy lordly name is on the Night's Plutonian shore?"
        Quoth the Raven, "Nevermore."

Much I marveled *this ungainly fowl* to hear discourse so plainly
Though its answer little meaning, little relevancy bore;
For we cannot help agreeing that no living human being

Ever yet was blessed with seeing bird above his chamber door,
Bird or beast upon the sculptured bust above his chamber door,
With such name as "Nevermore."

The effect of the *dénouement* being thus provided for, I immediately drop the fantastic for a tone of the most profound seriousness : — his tone commencing in the stanza directly following the one last quoted, with the line,

But the Raven, sitting lonely on the placid bust, spoke only, etc.

From this epoch the lover no longer jests — no longer sees anything even of the fantastic in the Raven's demeanor. He speaks of him as a "grim, ungainly, ghastly, gaunt, and ominous bird of yore," and feels the "fiery eyes" burning into his "bosom's core." This revolution of thought, or fancy, on the lover's part, is intended to induce a similar one on the part of the reader — to bring the mind into a proper frame for the *dénouement* — which is now brought about as rapidly and as *directly* as possible.

With the *dénouement* proper — with the Raven's reply, "Nevermore," to the lover's final demand if he shall meet his mistress in another world — the poem, in its obvious phase, that of a simple narrative, may be said to have its completion. So far, everything is within the limits of the accountable — of the real. A raven, having learned by rote the single word "Nevermore," and having escaped from the custody of its owner, is driven at midnight, through the violence of a storm, to seek admission at a window from which a light still gleams — the chamber-window of a student, occupied half in poring over a volume, half in dreaming of a beloved mistress deceased. The casement being thrown open at the fluttering of the bird's wings, the bird itself perches on the most convenient seat out of the immediate reach of the student, who, amused by the incident and the oddity of the visitor's demeanor, demands of it, in jest and without looking for a reply, its name. The raven addressed, answers with its customary word, "Nevermore" — a word which finds immediate echo in the melancholy heart of the student, who, giving utterance aloud to certain thoughts suggested by the occasion, is again startled by the fowl's repetition of "Nevermore." The student now guesses the state of the case, but is impelled, as I have before explained, by the human thirst for self-torture, and in part by superstition, to propound such queries to the bird as will bring him, the lover, the most of the luxury of sorrow, through the anticipated answer "Nevermore." With the indulgence, to the extreme, of this self-torture, the narration, in what I have termed its first or obvious phase, has a natural termination, and so far there has been no overstepping of the limits of the real.

But in subjects so handled, however skillfully, or with however vivid an array of incident, there is always a certain hardness or nakedness, which repels the artistical eye. Two things are invariably required — first, some amount of complexity, or more properly, adaptation; and, secondly, some amount of suggestiveness — some under-current, however indefinite, of meaning. It is this latter, in especial, which imparts to a work of art so much of that *richness* (to borrow from colloquy a forcible term) which we are too fond of confounding with *the ideal*. It is the *excess* of the suggested meaning — it is the rendering this the upper instead of the under current of the theme — which turns into prose (and that of the very flattest kind) the so-called poetry of the so-called transcendentalists.

Holding these opinions, I added the two concluding stanzas of the poem — their suggestiveness being thus made to pervade all the narrative which has preceded them. The under-current of meaning is rendered first apparent in the lines —

"Take thy beak from out *my heart*, and take thy form from off my door!"
　　　Quoth the Raven "Nevermore!"

It will be observed that the words, "from out my heart," involve the first metaphorical expression in the poem. They, with the answer, "Nevermore," dispose the mind to seek a moral in all that has been previously narrated. The reader begins now to regard the Raven as emblematical — but it is not

until the very last line of the very last stanza, that
the intention of making him emblematical of *Mournful and Never-ending Remembrance* is permitted distinctly to be seen:

And the Raven, never flitting, still is sitting, still is sitting,
On the pallid bust of Pallas, just above my chamber door;
And his eyes have all the seeming of a demon's that is
    dreaming,
And the lamplight o'er him streaming throws his shadow
    on the floor;
And my soul *from out that shadow* that lies floating on the
    floor
       Shall be lifted — *nevermore!*

RALPH WALDO EMERSON

1803–1882

DESCENDANT of a long line of clergymen, EMERSON was for a few years a minister in Boston, but retired to a greater freedom, as writer and lecturer. After some European wandering, during which began his friendship with CARLYLE, he found in Concord an atmosphere of quiet for contemplation and work. He lectured in various places on science, biography, history; but in 1836 he issued a little book entitled "Nature," which startled readers with a new idealism. The next year his address on "The American Scholar" struck a fresh note, scorning dependence on tradition and European influences. And the year after that he made an address to the senior class of the Divinity School of Harvard, which aroused religionists with a fresh breeze of reality in the stimulating thought, "that God is, not was; that he speaketh, not spake." From that time Emerson gave forth, in lectures, essays, poems, addresses, thoughts on all the pursuits and interests of man, that, while mystical in expression, became clear with study; while called "transcendental," were founded in sense and sanity; while labeled "dangerous" by religious formalists, brought light to the perplexed, courage to the disheartened, and to earnest souls weary of the husks of dogmatism gave a new and radiant faith in the Divine.

To select one of EMERSON'S multitudinous essays is like wandering in Aladdin's cave of splendor; but the one on "Compensation" seems to combine as much of his lofty thinking on lowly, common things, his ideal philosophy and Yankee shrewdness, his hard sense and noble sentiment, as could be packed into so brief a space. He was unquestionably America's most original thinker, and, more than any other one, gave the impulse which has developed into the enlargement of the Christian consciousness of the present day.

COMPENSATION

EVER since I was a boy I have wished to write a
discourse on Compensation; for it seemed to me
when very young that on this subject Life was ahead
of theology and the people knew more than the
preachers taught. The documents, too, from which
the doctrine is to be drawn, charmed my fancy by
their endless variety, and lay always before me, even
in sleep; for they are the tools in our hands, the bread
in our basket, the transactions of the street, the farm
and the dwelling-house; the greetings, the relations,
the debts and credits, the influence of character,
the nature and endowment of all men. It seemed
to me also that in it might be shown men a ray of
divinity, the present action of the Soul of this world,
clean from all vestige of tradition; and so the heart
of man might be bathed by an inundation of eternal
love, conversing with that which he knows was always
and always must be, because it really is now. It
appeared moreover that if this doctrine could be
stated in terms with any resemblance to those bright
intuitions in which this truth is sometimes revealed
to us, it would be a star in many dark hours and

crooked passages in our journey, that would not
suffer us to lose our way.

I was lately confirmed in these desires by hearing
a sermon at church. The preacher, a man esteemed
for his orthodoxy, unfolded in the ordinary manner
the doctrine of the Last Judgment. He assumed
that judgment is not executed in this world; that the
wicked are successful; that the good are miserable;
and then urged from reason and from Scripture a
compensation to be made to both parties in the next
life. No offense appeared to be taken by the con-
gregation at this doctrine. As far as I could observe
when the meeting broke up, they separated without
remark on the sermon.

Yet what was the import of this teaching? What
did the preacher mean by saying that the good are
miserable in the present life? Was it that houses
and lands, offices, wine, horses, dress, luxury, are
had by unprincipled men, whilst the saints are poor
and despised; and that a compensation is to be made
to these last hereafter, by giving them the like gratifications another day, — bank-stock and doubloons,
venison and champagne? This must be the compensation intended; for what else? Is it that they
are to have leave to pray and praise? to love and
serve men? Why, that they can do now. The
legitimate inference the disciple would draw was,
"We are to have *such* a good time as the sinners
have now"; — or, to push it to its extreme import, —

"You sin now, we shall sin by-and-by; we would sin now, if we could; not being successful, we expect our revenge to-morrow."

The fallacy lay in the immense concession that the bad are successful; that justice is not done now. The blindness of the preacher consisted in deferring to the base estimate of the market of what constitutes a manly success, instead of confronting and convicting the world from the truth; announcing the Presence of the Soul; the omnipotence of the Will; and so establishing the standard of good and ill, of success and falsehood, and summoning the dead to its present tribunal.

I find a similar base tone in the popular religious works of the day and the same doctrines assumed by the literary men when occasionally they treat the related topics. I think that our popular theology has gained in decorum, and not in principle, over the superstitions it has displaced. But men are better than this theology. Their daily life gives it the lie. Every ingenuous and aspiring soul leaves the doctrine behind him in his own experience, and all men feel sometimes the falsehood which they cannot demonstrate. For men are wiser than they know. That which they hear in schools and pulpits without afterthought, if said in conversation would probably be questioned in silence. If a man dogmatize in a mixed company on Providence and the divine laws, he is answered by a silence which conveys well enough to an observer the dissatisfaction of the hearer, but his incapacity to make his own statement.

I shall attempt in this and the following chapter to record some facts that indicate the path of the law of Compensation; happy beyond my expectation if I shall truly draw the smallest arc of this circle.

POLARITY, or action and reaction, we meet in every part of nature; in darkness and light, in heat and cold; in the ebb and flow of waters; in male and female; in the inspiration and expiration of plants and animals; in the systole and diastole of the heart; in the undulations of fluids and of sound; in the centrifugal and centripetal gravity; in electricity, galvanism, and chemical affinity. Superinduce magnetism at one end of a needle, the opposite magnetism takes place at the other end. If the south attracts, the north repels. To empty here, you must condense there. An inevitable dualism bisects nature, so that each thing is a half, and suggests another thing to make it whole; as, spirit, matter; man, woman; subjective, objective; in, out; upper, under; motion, rest; yea, nay.

Whilst the world is thus dual, so is every one of its parts. The entire system of things gets represented in every particle. There is somewhat that resembles the ebb and flow of the sea, day and night, man and woman, in a single needle of the pine, in a kernel of corn, in each individual of every animal tribe. The reaction, so grand in the elements, is repeated within these small boundaries. For example, in the animal kingdom the physiologist has observed that no creatures are favorites, but a certain compensation balances every gift and every defect. A surplusage given to one part is paid out of a reduction from another part of the same creature. If the head and neck are enlarged, the trunk and extremities are cut short.

The theory of the mechanic forces is another example. What we gain in power is lost in time, and the converse. The periodic or compensating errors of the planets is another instance. The influences of climate and soil in political history are another. The cold climate invigorates. The barren soil does not breed fevers, crocodiles, tigers, or scorpions.

The same dualism underlies the nature and condition of man. Every excess causes a defect; every defect an excess. Every sweet hath its sour; every evil its good. Every faculty which is a receiver of pleasure has an equal penalty put on its abuse. It is to answer for its moderation with its life. For every grain of wit there is a grain of folly. For everything you have missed, you have gained something else; and for everything you gain, you lose something. If riches increase, they are increased that use them. If the gatherer gathers too much, nature takes out of the man what she puts into his chest; swells the estate, but kills the owner. Nature hates monopolies and exceptions. The waves of the sea do not more speedily seek a level from their loftiest tossing than the varieties of condition tend to equalize themselves. There is always some leveling circumstance that puts down the overbearing, the strong, the rich, the fortunate, substantially on the same ground with all others. Is a man too strong and fierce for society and by temper and position a bad citizen, — a morose ruffian, with a dash of the pirate in him? — nature sends him a troop of pretty sons and daughters who are getting along in the dame's classes at the village school, and love and fear for them smooths his grim scowl to courtesy. Thus she contrives to intenerate the granite and felspar, takes the boar out and puts the lamb in, and keeps her balance true.

The farmer imagines power and place are fine things. But the President has paid dear for his White House. It has commonly cost him all his peace, and the best of his manly attributes. To preserve for a short time so conspicuous an appearance before the world, he is content to eat dust before the real masters who stand erect behind the throne. Or do men desire the more substantial and permanent grandeur of genius? Neither has this an immunity. He who by force of will or of thought is great and overlooks thousands, has the responsibility of overlooking. With every influx of light comes new danger. Has he light? he must bear

witness to the light, and always outrun that sympathy which gives him such keen satisfaction, by
his fidelity to new revelations of the incessant soul.
He must hate father and mother, wife and child.
Has he all that the world loves and admires and
covets? — he must cast behind him their admiration
and afflict them by faithfulness to his truth and become a byword and a hissing.

This Law writes the laws of the cities and nations.
It will not be balked of its end in the smallest iota.
It is in vain to build or plot or combine against it.
Things refuse to be mismanaged long. *Res nolunt
diu male administrari.* Though no checks to a new
evil appear, the checks exist, and will appear. If
the government is cruel, the governor's life is not
safe. If you tax too high, the revenue will yield
nothing. If you make the criminal code sanguinary,
juries will not convict. Nothing arbitrary, nothing
artificial can endure. The true life and satisfactions
of men seem to elude the utmost rigors or felicities
of condition and to establish themselves with great
indifference under all varieties of circumstance. Under all governments the influence of character remains the same, — in Turkey and New England
about alike. Under the primeval despots of Egypt,
history honestly confesses that man must have been
as free as culture could make him.

These appearances indicate the fact that the universe is represented in every one of its particles.

Every thing in nature contains all the powers of
nature. Every thing is made of one hidden stuff;
as the naturalist sees one type under every meta-
morphosis, and regards a horse as a running man,
a fish as a swimming man, a bird as a flying man,
a tree as a rooted man. Each new form repeats
not only the main character of the type, but part
for part all the details, all the aims, furtherances,
hindrances, energies, and whole system of every
other. Every occupation, trade, art, transaction, is
a compend of the world and a correlative of every
other. Each one is an entire emblem of human life;
of its good and ill, its trials, its enemies, its course,
and its end. And each one must somehow accom-
modate the whole man and recite all his destiny.

The world globes itself in a drop of dew. The
microscope cannot find the animalcule which is less
perfect for being little. Eyes, ears, taste, smell,
motion, resistance, appetite, and organs of reproduc-
tion that take hold on eternity, — all find room to
consist in the small creature. So do we put our
life into every act. The true doctrine of omnipresence is that God reappears with all his parts in every
moss and cobweb. The value of the universe contrives to throw itself into every point. If the good
is there, so is the evil; if the affinity, so the repul-
sion; if the force, so the limitation.

Thus is the universe alive. All things are moral.
That soul which within us is a sentiment, outside

of us is a law. We feel its inspirations; out there in history we can see its fatal strength. It is almighty. All nature feels its grasp. "It is in the world, and the world was made by it." It is eternal, but it enacts itself in time and space. Justice is not postponed. A perfect equity adjusts its balance in all parts of life. Οἱ κύβοι Διὸς ἀεὶ εὐπίπτουσι. The dice of God are always loaded. The world looks like a multiplication-table, or a mathematical equation, which, turn it how you will, balances itself. Take what figure you will, its exact value, nor more nor less, still returns to you. Every secret is told, every crime is punished, every virtue rewarded, every wrong redressed, in silence and certainty. What we call retribution is the universal necessity by which the whole appears wherever a part appears. If you see smoke, there must be fire. If you see a hand or a limb, you know that the trunk to which it belongs is there behind.

Every act rewards itself, or in other words integrates itself, in a twofold manner: first in the thing, or in real nature; and secondly in the circumstance, or in apparent nature. Men call the circumstance the retribution. The casual retribution is in the thing and is seen by the soul. The retribution in the circumstance is seen by the understanding; it is inseparable from the thing, but is often spread over a long time and so does not become distinct until after many years. The specific stripes may follow late after the offense, but they follow because they accompany it. Crime and punishment grow out of one stem. Punishment is a fruit that unsuspected ripens within the flower of the pleasure which concealed it. Cause and effect, means and ends, seed and fruit, cannot be severed; for the effect already blooms in the cause, the end preëxists in the means, the fruit in the seed.

Whilst thus the world will be whole and refuses to be disparted, we seek to act partially, to sunder, to appropriate; for example, — to gratify the senses we sever the pleasure of the senses from the needs of the character. The ingenuity of man has been dedicated to the solution of one problem, — how to detach the sensual sweet, the sensual strong, the sensual bright, etc., from the moral sweet, the moral deep, the moral fair; that is, again, to contrive to cut clean off this upper surface so thin as to leave it bottomless; to get a *one end*, without an *other end*. The soul says, Eat; the body would feast. The soul says, The man and woman shall be one flesh and one soul; the body would join the flesh only. The soul says, Have dominion over all things to the ends of virtue; the body would have the power over things to its own ends.

The soul strives amain to live and work through all things. It would be the only fact. All things shall be added unto it, — power, pleasure, knowledge, beauty. The particular man aims to be some-

body; to set up for himself; to truck and higgle for
a private good; and, in particulars, to ride that he
may ride; to dress that he may be dressed; to eat
that he may eat; and to govern, that he may be seen.
Men seek to be great; they would have offices,
wealth, power, and fame. They think that to be
great is to get only one side of nature, — the sweet,
without the other side, — the bitter.

Steadily is this dividing and detaching counter-
acted. Up to this day it must be owned no projector
has had the smallest success. The parted water re-
unites behind our hand. Pleasure is taken out of
pleasant things, profit out of profitable things, power
out of strong things, the moment we seek to separate
them from the whole. We can no more halve things
and get the sensual good, by itself, than we can get
an inside that shall have no outside, or a light without a shadow. "Drive out nature with a fork, she
comes running back."

Life invests itself with inevitable conditions, which
the unwise seek to dodge, which one and another
brags that he does not know, brags that they do not
touch him; — but the brag is on his lips, the conditions are in his soul. If he escapes them in one part
they attack him in another more vital part. If he
has escaped them in form and in the appearance, it
is because he has resisted his life and fled from himself, and the retribution is so much death. So signal
is the failure of all attempts to make this separation

of the good from the tax, that the experiment would
not be tried, — since to try it is to be mad, — but for
the circumstance that when the disease began in the
will, of rebellion and separation, the intellect is at
once infected, so that the man ceases to see God
whole in each object, but is able to see the sensual
allurement of an object and not see the sensual hurt;
he sees the mermaid's head but not the dragon's tail,
and thinks he can cut off that which he would have
from that which he would not have.   "How secret
art thou who dwellest in the highest heavens in
silence, O thou only great God, sprinkling with an
unwearied providence certain penal blindnesses upon
such as have unbridled desires!" [1]

The human soul is true to these facts in the painting of fable, of history, of law, of proverbs, of conversation.   It finds a tongue in literature unawares.
Thus the Greeks called Jupiter, Supreme Mind; but
having traditionally ascribed to him many base actions, they involuntarily made amends to Reason by
tying up the hands of so bad a god.   He is made as
helpless as a king of England.   Prometheus knows
one secret which Jove must bargain for; Minerva,
another.   He cannot get his own thunders; Minerva
keeps the key of them: —

> Of all the gods, I only know the keys
> That ope the solid doors within whose vaults
> His thunders sleep.

[1] St. Augustine, Confessions, B. I.

A plain confession of the in-working of the All and of its moral aim. The Indian mythology ends in the same ethics; and indeed it would seem impossible for any fable to be invented and get any currency which was not moral. Aurora forgot to ask youth for her lover, and though so Tithonus is immortal, he is old. Achilles is not quite invulnerable; for Thetis held him by the heel when she dipped him in the Styx and the sacred waters did not wash that part. Siegfried, in the Nibelungen, is not quite immortal, for a leaf fell on his back whilst he was bathing in the Dragon's blood, and that spot which it covered is mortal. And so it always is. There is a crack in every thing God has made. Always it would seem there is this vindictive circumstance stealing in at unawares even into the wild poesy in which the human fancy attempted to make bold holiday and to shake itself free of the old laws, — this back-stroke, this kick of the gun, certifying that the law is fatal; that in nature nothing can be given, all things are sold.

This is that ancient doctrine of Nemesis, who keeps watch in the Universe and lets no offense go unchastised. The Furies they said are attendants on Justice, and if the sun in heaven should transgress his path they would punish him. The poets related that stone walls and iron swords and leathern thongs had an occult sympathy with the wrongs of their owners; that the belt which Ajax gave Hec-

tor dragged the Trojan hero over the field at the
wheels of the car of Achilles, and the sword which
Hector gave Ajax was that on whose point Ajax
fell. They recorded that when the Thasians erected
a statue to Theogenes, a victor in the games, one of
his rivals went to it by night and endeavored to
throw it down by repeated blows, until at last he
moved it from its pedestal and was crushed to death
beneath its fall.

This voice of fable has in it somewhat divine. It
came from thought above the will of the writer.
That is the best part of each writer which has nothing private in it; that is the best part of each which
he does not know; that which flowed out of his constitution and not from his too active invention; that
which in the study of a single artist you might not
easily find, but in the study of many you would abstract as the spirit of them all. Phidias it is not,
but the work of man in that early Hellenic world
that I would know. The name and circumstance
of Phidias, however convenient for history, embar-
rasses when we come to the highest criticism. We
are to see that which man was tending to do in a
given period, and was hindered, or, if you will, modified in doing, by the interfering volitions of Phidias,
of Dante, of Shakespeare, the organ whereby man at
the moment wrought.

Still more striking is the expression of this fact
in the proverbs of all nations, which are always the

literature of Reason, or the statements of an absolute truth without qualification. Proverbs, like the sacred books of each nation, are the sanctuary of the Intuitions. That which the droning world, chained to appearances, will not allow the realist to say in his own words, it will suffer him to say in proverbs without contradiction. And this law of laws, which the pulpit, the senate and the college deny, is hourly preached in all markets and all languages by flights of proverbs, whose teaching is as true and as omnipresent as that of birds and flies.

All things are double, one against another. — Tit for tat; an eye for an eye; a tooth for a tooth; blood for blood; measure for measure; love for love. — Give, and it shall be given you. — He that watereth shall be watered himself. — What will you have? quoth God; pay for it and take it. — Nothing venture, nothing have. — Thou shalt be paid exactly for what thou hast done, no more, no less. — Who doth not work shall not eat. — Harm watch, harm catch. — Curses always recoil on the head of him who imprecates them. — If you put a chain around the neck of a slave, the other end fastens itself around your own. — Bad counsel confounds the adviser. — The devil is an ass.

It is thus written, because it is thus in life. Our action is overmastered and characterized above our will by the law of nature. We aim at a petty end quite aside from the public good, but our act arranges itself by irresistible magnetism in a line with the poles of the world.

A man cannot speak but he judges himself. With his will or against his will he draws his portrait to the eye of his companions by every word. Every opinion reacts on him who utters it. It is a thread-ball thrown at a mark, but the other end remains in the thrower's bag. Or, rather, it is a harpoon thrown at the whale, unwinding, as it flies, a coil of cord in the boat, and, if the harpoon is not good, or not well thrown, it will go nigh to cut the steersman in twain or to sink the boat.

You cannot do wrong without suffering wrong. "No man had ever a point of pride that was not injurious to him," said Burke. The exclusive in fashionable life does not see that he excludes himself from enjoyment, in the attempt to appropriate it. The exclusionist in religion does not see that he shuts the door of heaven on himself, in striving to shut out others. Treat men as pawns and nine-pins and you shall suffer as well as they. If you leave out their heart, you shall lose your own. The senses would make things of all persons; of women, of children, of the poor. The vulgar proverb, "I will get it from his purse or get it from his skin," is sound philosophy.

All infractions of love and equity in our social relations are speedily punished. They are punished by Fear. Whilst I stand in simple relations to my fellow-man, I have no displeasure in meeting him. We meet as water meets water, or as two currents of air mix, with perfect diffusion and interpenetration of nature. But as soon as there is any departure from simplicity and attempt at halfness, or good for me that is not good for him, my neighbor feels the wrong; he shrinks from me as far as I have shrunk from him; his eyes no longer seek mine; there is war between us; there is hate in him and fear in me.

All the old abuses in society, the great and universal and the petty and particular, all unjust accumulations of property and power, are avenged in the same manner. Fear is an instructor of great sagacity and the herald of all revolutions. One thing he always teaches, that there is rottenness where he appears. He is a carrion crow, and though you see not well what he hovers for, there is death somewhere. Our property is timid, our laws are timid, our cultivated classes are timid. Fear for ages has boded and mowed and gibbered over government and property. That obscene bird is not there for nothing. He indicates great wrongs which must be revised.

Of the like nature is that expectation of change which instantly follows the suspension of our voluntary activity. The terror of cloudless noon, the emerald of Polycrates, the awe of prosperity, the instinct which leads every generous soul to impose on itself tasks of a noble asceticism and vicarious virtue, are the tremblings of the balance of justice through the heart and mind of man.

Experienced men of the world know very well that it is best to pay scot and lot as they go along, and that a man often pays dear for a small frugality. The borrower runs in his own debt. Has a man gained any thing who has received a hundred favors and rendered none ? Has he gained by borrowing, through indolence or cunning, his neighbor's wares, or horses, or money ? There arises on the deed the instant acknowledgment of benefit on the one part and of debt on the other; that is, of superiority and inferiority. The transaction remains in the memory of himself and his neighbor; and every new transaction alters according to its nature their relation to each other. He may soon come to see that he had better have broken his own bones than to have ridden in his neighbor's coach, and that " the highest price he can pay for a thing is to ask for it."

A wise man will extend this lesson to all parts of life, and know that it is always the part of prudence to face every claimant and pay every just demand on your time, your talents, or your heart. Always pay; for first or last you must pay your entire debt. Persons and events may stand for a time between you and justice, but it is only a postponement. You must pay at last your own debt. If you are wise you will dread a prosperity which only loads you with

more. Benefit is the end of nature. But for every
benefit which you receive, a tax is levied. He is
great who confers the most benefits. He is base, —
and that is the one base thing in the universe, — to
receive favors and render none. In the order of
nature we cannot render benefits to those from whom
we receive them, or only seldom. But the benefit we
receive must be rendered again, line for line, deed
for deed, cent for cent, to somebody. Beware of too
much good staying in your hand. It will fast corrupt
and worm worms. Pay it away quickly in some sort.

Labor is watched over by the same pitiless laws.
Cheapest, says the prudent, is the dearest labor.
What we buy in a broom, a mat, a wagon, a knife,
is some application of good sense to a common want.
It is best to pay in your land a skillful gardener, or to
buy good sense applied to gardening; in your sailor,
good sense applied to navigation; in the house, good
sense applied to cooking, sewing, serving; in your
agent, good sense applied to accounts and affairs.
So do you multiply your presence, or spread yourself
throughout your estate. But because of the dual
constitution of things, in labor as in life there can be
no cheating. The thief steals from himself. The
swindler swindles himself. For the real price of
labor is knowledge and virtue, whereof wealth and
credit are signs. These signs, like paper money,
may be counterfeited or stolen, but that which they
represent, namely, knowledge and virtue, cannot be

counterfeited or stolen. These ends of labor cannot
be answered but by real exertions of the mind, and
in obedience to pure motives. The cheat, the de-
faulter, the gambler, cannot extort the benefit, cannot
extort the knowledge of material and moral nature
which his honest care and pains yield to the opera-
tive. The law of nature is, Do the thing, and you
shall have the power; but they who do not the thing
have not the power.

Human labor, through all its forms, from the sharp-
ening of a stake to the construction of a city or an
epic, is one immense illustration of the perfect compensation of the universe. Everywhere and always
this law is sublime. The absolute balance of Give
and Take, the doctrine that every thing has its price,
and if that price is not paid, not that thing but something else is obtained, and that it is impossible to get
anything without its price, is not less sublime in the
columns of a ledger than in the budgets of states, in
the laws of light and darkness, in all the action and reaction of nature. I cannot doubt that the high laws
which each man sees ever implicated in those processes with which he is conversant, the stern ethics
which sparkle on his chisel-edge, which are measured
out by his plumb and foot-rule, which stand as manifest in the footing of the shop-bill as in the history of a
state,—do recommend to him his trade, and though
seldom named, exalt his business to his imagination.

The league between virtue and nature engages all

things to assume a hostile front to vice. The beautiful laws and substances of the world persecute and whip the traitor. He finds that things are arranged for truth and benefit, but there is no den in the wide world to hide a rogue. Commit a crime, and the earth is made of glass. There is no such thing as concealment. Commit a crime, and it seems as if a coat of snow fell on the ground, such as reveals in the woods the track of every partridge and fox and squirrel and mole. You cannot recall the spoken word, you cannot wipe out the foot-track, you cannot draw up the ladder, so as to leave no inlet or clew. Always some damning circumstance transpires. The laws and substances of nature, water, snow, wind, gravitation, become penalties to the thief.

On the other hand the law holds with equal sureness for all right action. Love, and you shall be loved. All love is mathematically just, as much as the two sides of an algebraic equation. The good man has absolute good, which like fire turns every thing to its own nature, so that you cannot do him any harm; but as the royal armies sent against Napoleon, when he approached cast down their colors and from enemies became friends, so do disasters of all kinds, as sickness, offense, poverty, prove benefactors.

> Winds blow and waters roll
> Strength to the brave and power and deity,
> Yet in themselves are nothing.

The good are befriended even by weakness and defect. As no man had ever a point of pride that was not injurious to him, so no man had ever a defect that was not somewhere made useful to him. The stag in the fable admired his horns and blamed his feet, but when the hunter came, his feet saved him, and afterwards, caught in the thicket, his horns destroyed him. Every man in his lifetime needs to thank his faults. As no man thoroughly understands a truth until first he has contended against it, so no man has a thorough acquaintance with the hindrances or talents of men until he has suffered from the one and seen the triumph of the other over his own want of the same. Has he a defect of temper that unfits him to live in society? Thereby he is driven to entertain himself alone and acquire habits of self-help; and thus, like the wounded oyster, he mends his shell with pearl.

Our strength grows out of our weakness. Not until we are pricked and stung and sorely shot at, awakens the indignation which arms itself with secret forces. A great man is always willing to be little. Whilst he sits on the cushion of advantages, he goes to sleep. When he is pushed, tormented, defeated, he has a chance to learn something; he has been put on his wits, on his manhood; he has gained facts; learns his ignorance; is cured of the insanity of conceit; has got moderation and real skill. The wise man always throws himself on the side of his

assailants. It is more his interest than it is theirs to
find his weak point. The wound cicatrizes and falls
off from him like a dead skin, and when they would
triumph, lo! he has passed on invulnerable. Blame
is safer than praise. I hate to be defended in a
newspaper. As long as all that is said is said against
me, I feel a certain assurance of success. But as
soon as honied words of praise are spoken for me I
feel as one that lies unprotected before his enemies.
In general, every evil to which we do not succumb
is a benefactor. As the Sandwich Islander believes
that the strength and valor of the enemy he kills
passes into himself, so we gain the strength of the
temptation we resist.

The same guards which protect us from disaster,
defect and enmity, defend us, if we will, from selfish-
ness and fraud. Bolts and bars are not the best
of our institutions, nor is shrewdness in trade a mark
of wisdom. Men suffer all their life long under the
foolish superstition that they can be cheated. But
it is as impossible for a man to be cheated by any
one but himself, as for a thing to be and not to be
at the same time. There is a third silent party to all
our bargains. The nature and soul of things takes
on itself the guaranty of the fulfillment of every contract, so that honest service cannot come to loss.
If you serve an ungrateful master, serve him the
more. Put God in your debt. Every stroke shall
be repaid. The longer the payment is withholden,

the better for you, for compound interest on compound interest is the rate and usage of this exchequer.

The history of persecution is a history of endeavors to cheat nature, to make water run up hill, to twist a rope of sand. It makes no difference whether the actors be many or one, a tyrant or a mob. A mob is a society of bodies voluntarily bereaving themselves of reason and traversing its work. The mob is man voluntarily descending to the nature of the beast. Its fit hour of activity is night. Its actions are insane, like its whole constitution. It persecutes a principle; it would whip a right; it would tar and feather justice, by inflicting fire and outrage upon the houses and persons of those who have these. It resembles the prank of boys, who run with fire-engines to put out the ruddy aurora streaming to the stars. The inviolate spirit turns their spite against the wrongdoers. The martyr cannot be dishonored. Every lash inflicted is a tongue of fame; every prison a more illustrious abode; every burned book or house enlightens the world: every suppressed or expunged word reverberates through the earth from side to side. The minds of men are at last aroused; reason looks out and justifies her own, and malice finds all her work in vain. It is the whipper who is whipped and the tyrant who is undone.

Thus do all things preach the indifferency of circumstances. The man is all. Every thing has two

sides, a good and an evil. Every advantage has its
tax. I learn to be content. But the doctrine of
compensation is not the doctrine of indifferency.
The thoughtless say, on hearing these representa-
tions, — What boots it to do well? there is one
event to good and evil; if I gain any good I must
pay for it; if I lose any good I gain some other;
all actions are indifferent.

There is a deeper fact in the soul than compensation, to wit, its own nature. The soul is not a compensation, but a life. The soul *is*. Under all this
running sea of circumstance, whose waters ebb and
flow with perfect balance, lies the aboriginal abyss
of real Being. Existence, or God, is not a relation
or a part, but the whole. Being is the vast affirmative, excluding negation, self-balanced, and swallow-
ing up all relations, parts and times within itself.
Nature, truth, virtue, are the influx from thence.
Vice is the absence or departure of the same. . . .

[Man's] life is a progress, and not a station. His
instinct is trust. Our instinct uses "more" and
"less" in application to man, always of the *presence
of the soul*, and not of its absence; the brave man
is greater than the coward; the true, the benevolent,
the wise, is more a man and not less, than the fool
and knave. There is therefore no tax on the good
of virtue, for that is the incoming of God himself,
or absolute existence, without any comparative. All
external good has its tax, and if it came without

desert or sweat, has no root in me, and the next wind will blow it away. But all the good of nature is the soul's, and may be had if paid for in nature's lawful coin, that is, by labor which the heart and the head allow. I no longer wish to meet a good I do not earn, for example to find a pot of buried gold, knowing that it brings with it new responsibility. I do not wish more external goods, — neither possessions, nor honors, nor powers, nor persons. The gain is apparent; the tax is certain. But there is no tax on the knowledge that the compensation exists and that it is not desirable to dig up treasure. Herein I rejoice with a serene eternal peace. . . .

Such also is the natural history of calamity. The changes which break up at short intervals the prosperity of men are advertisements of a nature whose law is growth. Evermore it is the order of nature to grow, and every soul is by this intrinsic necessity quitting its whole system of things, its friends and home and laws and faith, as the shellfish crawls out of its beautiful but stony case, because it no longer admits of its growth, and slowly forms a new house. In proportion to the vigor of the individual these revolutions are frequent, until in some happier mind they are incessant and all worldly relations hang very loosely about him, becoming as it were a transparent fluid membrane through which the living form is always seen, and not, as in most men, an indurated heterogeneous fabric of many dates and of no settled character, in which the man is imprisoned. Then there can be enlargement, and the man of to-day scarcely recognizes the man of yesterday. And such should be the outward biography of man in time, a putting off of dead circumstances day by day, as he renews his raiment day by day. But to us, in our lapsed estate, resting, not advancing, resisting, not coöperating with the divine expansion, this growth comes by shocks.

We cannot part with our friends. We cannot let our angels go. We do not see that they only go out that archangels may come in. We are idolators of the old. We do not believe in the riches of the soul, in its proper eternity and omnipresence. We do not believe there is any force in to-day to rival or re-create that beautiful yesterday. We linger in the ruins of the old tent where once we had bread and shelter and organs, nor believe that the spirit can feed, cover, and nerve us again. We cannot again find aught so dear, so sweet, so graceful. But we sit and weep in vain. The voice of the Almighty saith, "Up and onward forevermore!" We cannot stay amid the ruins. Neither will we rely on the New; and so we walk ever with reverted eyes, like those monsters who look backwards.

And yet the compensations of calamity are made apparent to the understanding also, after long intervals of time. A fever, a mutilation, a cruel disappointment, a loss of wealth, a loss of friends, seems

at the moment unpaid loss, and unpayable. But
the sure years reveal the deep remedial force that
underlies all facts.   The death of a dear friend, wife,
brother, lover, which seemed nothing but privation,
somewhat later assumes the aspect of a guide or
genius; for it commonly operates revolutions in our
way of life, terminates an epoch of infancy or of
youth which was waiting to be closed, breaks up a
wonted occupation, or a household, or style of living,
and allows the formation of new ones more friendly
to the growth of character.   It permits or constrains
the formation of new acquaintances and the reception of new influences that prove of the first importance to the next years; and the man or woman who
would have remained a sunny garden-flower, with no
room for its roots and too much sunshine for its head,
by the falling of the walls and the neglect of the gardener is made the banian of the forest, yielding shade
and fruit to wide neighborhoods of men.

SARAH MARGARET FULLER OSSOLI

1810–1850

A woman of marked native ability, and culture both wide and deep, MARGARET FULLER, born in Cambridgeport, Massachusetts, became early a friend of EMERSON, THOREAU, and the others of the Transcendental School of writers. She worked with EMERSON as editor of *The Dial*, their organ for some years, and in 1844–1846, having interested HORACE GREELEY, became literary critic for the *New York Tribune*. In the latter year she went to Europe, and in 1847 was married to the Marquis D'OSSOLI. Returning to America, with her husband and child, in 1850, she and they perished by shipwreck off Fire Island, having nearly reached New York. Her principal aim in life was the enlargement of the rights and privileges of woman; and, while she left considerable critical work in the realms of art and literature, her most representative performance was her essay on "Woman in the Nineteenth Century," the chief points of which — without her scholarly illustrations and arguments — are given herewith.

GROWTH: IN MAN; IN WOMAN

"Frailty, thy name is WOMAN."
"The Earth waits for her Queen."

THE connection between these quotations may not
be obvious, but it is strict. Yet would any contradict
us, if we made them applicable to the other side,
and began also,

Frailty, thy name is MAN.
The Earth waits for its King?

Yet Man, if not yet fully installed in his powers, has
given much earnest of his claims. Frail he is indeed,
— how frail! how impure! Yet often has the vein
of gold displayed itself amid the baser ores, and Man
has appeared before us in princely promise, worthy
of his future.

If, oftentimes, we see the prodigal son feeding on
the husks in the fair field no more his own, anon we
raise the eyelids, heavy from bitter tears, to behold
in him the radiant apparition of genius and love,
demanding not less than the all of goodness, power,
and beauty. We see that in him the largest claim
finds a due foundation. That claim is for no par-

tial sway, no exclusive possession. He cannot be
satisfied with any one gift of life, any one department of knowledge or telescopic peep at the heavens.
He feels himself called to understand and aid Nature,
that she may, through this intelligence, be raised and
interpreted; to be a student of, and servant to, the
universe-spirit; and king of his planet, that, as an
angelic minister, he may bring it into conscious harmony with the law of that spirit.

In clear, triumphant moments, many times, has
rung through the spheres the prophecy of his jubilee;
and those moments, though past in time, have been
translated into eternity by thought. . . .

Sages and lawgivers have bent their whole nature
to the search for truth, and thought themselves happy
if they could buy, with the sacrifice of all temporal
ease and pleasure, one seed for the future Eden.
Poets and priests have strung the lyre with the heart-
strings, poured out their best blood upon the altar,
which, reared anew from age to age, shall at last
sustain the flame pure enough to rise to highest
heaven. Shall we not name with as deep a benedic-
tion those who, if not so immediately, or so consciously, in connection with the eternal truth, yet,
led and fashioned by a divine instinct, serve no less
to develop and interpret the open secret of love
passing into life, energy creating for the purpose of
happiness; the artist whose hand, drawn by a pre-
existent harmony to a certain medium, molds it to

forms of life more highly and completely organized than are seen elsewhere, and, by carrying out the intention of nature, reveals her meaning to those who are not yet wise enough to divine it; the philosopher who listens steadily for laws and causes, and from those obvious infers those yet unknown; the historian who, in faith that all events must have their reason and their aim, records them, and thus fills archives from which the youth of prophets may be fed; the man of science dissecting the statements, testing the facts and demonstrating order, even where he cannot its purpose?

Lives, too, which bear none of these names, have yielded tones of no less significance. The candle-stick set in a low place has given light as faithfully, where it was needed, as that upon the hill. In close alleys, in dismal nooks, the Word has been read as distinctly as when shown by angels to holy men in the dark prison. Those who till a spot of earth scarcely larger than is wanted for a grave, have deserved that the sun should shine upon its sod till violets answer.

So great has been, from time to time, the promise, that, in all ages, men have said the gods themselves came down to dwell with them; that the All-Creating wandered on the earth to taste, in a limited nature, the sweetness of virtue; that the All-Sustaining incarnated himself to guard, in space and time, the destinies of this world; that heavenly genius dwelt among the shepherds, to sing to them and teach them how to sing. . . .

These were the triumphant moments; but soon the lower nature took its turn, and the era of a truly human life was postponed.

Thus is man still a stranger to his inheritance, still a pleader, still a pilgrim. Yet his happiness is secure in the end. And now, no more a glimmering consciousness, but assurance begins to be felt and spoken, that the highest ideal Man can form of his own powers is that which he is destined to attain. Whatever the soul knows how to seek, it cannot fail to obtain. This is the Law and the Prophets. Knock and it shall be opened; seek and ye shall find. It is demonstrated; it is a maxim. . . .

Meanwhile, not a few believe, and men themselves have expressed the opinion, that the time is come when Eurydice is to call for an Orpheus, rather than Orpheus for Eurydice; that the idea of Man, however imperfectly brought out, has been far more so than that of Woman; that she, the other half of the same thought, the other chamber of the heart of life, needs now take her turn in the full pulsation, and that improvement in the daughters will best aid in the reformation of the sons of this age.

It should be remarked that, as the principle of liberty is better understood, and more nobly interpreted, a broader protest is made in behalf of Woman. As men become aware that few men have had a fair

chance, they are inclined to say that no women have
had a fair chance.   The French revolution, that
strangely disguised angel, bore witness in favor of
Woman, but interpreted her claims no less ignorantly
than those of Man.   Its idea of happiness did not
rise beyond outward enjoyment, unobstructed by
the tyranny of others.   The title it gave was "ci-
toyen," "citoyenne"; and it is not unimportant to
Woman that even this species of equality was awarded
her.   Before, she could be condemned to perish on
the scaffold for treason, not as a citizen, but as a
subject.   The right with which this title then invested a human being was that of bloodshed and
license.   The Goddess of Liberty was impure.   As
we read the poem addressed to her, not long since,
by Béranger, we can scarcely refrain from tears as
painful as the tears of blood that flowed when "such
crimes were committed in her name."   Yes!   Man,
born to purify and animate the unintelligent and
the cold, can, in his madness, degrade and pollute
no less the fair and the chaste.   Yet truth was
prophesied in the ravings of that hideous fever,
caused by long ignorance and abuse.   Europe is
conning a valued lesson from the blood-stained page.
The same tendencies, further unfolded, will bear
good fruit in this country. . . .

Here, as elsewhere, the gain of creation consists
always in the growth of individual minds, which
live and aspire, as flowers bloom and birds sing, in the

midst of morasses; and in the continual development of that thought, the thought of human destiny,
which is given to eternity adequately to express, and
which ages of failure only seemingly impede. Only
seemingly; and whatever seems to the contrary, this
country is as surely destined to elucidate a great
moral law, as Europe was to promote the mental
culture of Man.

Though the national independence be blurred by
the servility of individuals; though freedom and
equality have been proclaimed only to leave room for
a monstrous display of slave-dealing and slave-keep-
ing; though the free American so often feels himself
free, like the Roman, only to pamper his appetites
and his indolence through the misery of his fellow-
beings; still it is not in vain that the verbal statement has been made, "All men are born free and
equal." There it stands, a golden certainty where-
with to encourage the good, to shame the bad. . . .

Of all its banners [those of the triumphal procession
of Freedom], none has been more steadily upheld,
and under none have more valor and willingness for
real sacrifices been shown, than that of the champions
of the enslaved African. And this band it is, which,
partly from a natural following out of principles,
partly because many women have been prominent
in that cause, makes, just now, the warmest appeal
in behalf of Woman. . . .

The numerous party, whose opinions are already

labeled and adjusted too much to their mind to admit
of any new light, strive, by lectures on some model-
woman of bride-like beauty and gentleness, by writing
and lending little treatises, intended to mark out with
precision the limits of Woman's sphere, and Woman's
mission, to prevent other than the rightful shepherd
from climbing the wall, or the flock from using any
chance to go astray.

Without enrolling ourselves at once on either side,
let us look upon the subject from the best point of
view to-day which offers; no better, it is to be feared,
than a high house-top. A high hill-top, or at least
a cathedral spire, would be desirable.

It may well be an Anti-Slavery party that pleads for
Woman, if we consider merely that she does not hold
property on equal terms with men; so that, if a
husband dies without making a will, the wife, instead of taking at once his place as head of the family,
inherits only a part of his fortune, often brought him
by herself, as if she were a child, or ward only, not
an equal partner.

We will not speak of the innumerable instances in
which profligate and idle men live upon the earnings
of industrious wives; or if the wives leave them, and
take with them the children, to perform the double
duty of mother and father, follow from place to place,
and threaten to rob them of the children, if deprived
of the rights of a husband, as they call them, planting
themselves in their poor lodgings, frightening them

into paying tribute by taking from them the children, running into debt at the expense of these otherwise so overtasked helots. Such instances count up by scores within my own memory. I have seen the husband who had stained himself by a long course of low vice, till his wife was wearied from her heroic forgiveness, by finding that his treachery made it useless, and that if she would provide bread for herself and her children, she must be separate from his ill fame — I have known this man come to install himself in the chamber of a woman who loathed him, and say she should never take food without his company. I have known these men steal their children, whom they knew they had no means to maintain, take them into dissolute company, expose them to bodily danger, to frighten the poor woman, to whom, it seems, the fact that she alone had borne the pangs of their birth, and nourished their infancy, does not give an equal right to them. I do believe that this mode of kidnapping — and it is frequent enough in all classes of society — will be by the next age viewed as it is by Heaven now, and that the man who avails himself of the shelter of men's laws to steal from a mother her own children, or arrogate any superior right in them, save that of superior virtue, will bear the stigma he deserves, in common with him who steals grown men from their motherland, their hopes, and their homes. . . .

But to return to the historical progress of this

matter. Knowing that there exists in the minds
of men a tone of feeling toward women as toward
slaves, such as is expressed in the common phrase,
"Tell that to women and children"; that the infinite soul can only work through them in already
ascertained limits; that the gift of reason, Man's
highest prerogative, is allotted to them in much
lower degree; that they must be kept from mischief and melancholy by being constantly engaged in
active labor, which is to be furnished and directed by
those better able to think, etc., etc., — we need not
multiply instances, for who can review the experience
of last week without recalling words which imply,
whether in jest or earnest, these views or views like
these, — knowing this, can we wonder that many
reformers think that measures are not likely to be
taken in behalf of women, unless their wishes could
be publicly represented by women?

"That can never be necessary," cry the other side.
"All men are privately influenced by women; each
has his wife, sister, or female friends, and is too much
biased by these relations to fail of representing their
interests; and, if this is not enough, let them pro-
pose and enforce their wishes with the pen. The
beauty of home would be destroyed, the delicacy
of the sex be violated, the dignity of halls of legislation degraded, by an attempt to introduce them
there. Such duties are inconsistent with those of
a mother;" and then we have ludicrous pictures

of ladies in hysterics at the polls, and senate-chambers filled with cradles.

But if, in reply, we admit as truth that Woman seems destined by nature rather for the inner circle, we must add that the arrangements of civilized life have not been, as yet, such as to secure it to her. Her circle, if the duller, is not the quieter. If kept from "excitement," she is not from drudgery. Not only the Indian squaw carries the burdens of the camp, but the favorites of Louis XIV. accompany him in his journeys, and the washerwoman stands at her tub, and carries home her work at all seasons, and in all states of health. Those who think the physical circumstances of Woman would make a part in the affairs of national government unsuitable, are by no means those who think it impossible for negresses to endure field-work, even during pregnancy, or for sempstresses to go through their killing labors.

As to the use of the pen, there was quite as much opposition to Woman's possessing herself of that help to free agency as there is now to her seizing on the rostrum or the desk; and she is likely to draw, from a permission to plead her cause that way, opposite inferences to what might be wished by those who now grant it.

As to the possibility of her filling with grace and dignity any such position, we should think those who had seen the great actresses, and heard the Quaker preachers of modern times, would not doubt that

Woman can express publicly the fullness of thought
and creation, without losing any of the peculiar
beauty of he: sex. What can pollute and tarnish,
is to act thus from any motive except that something needs to be said or done. Woman could take
part in the processions, the songs, the dances of old
religion; no one fancied her delicacy was impaired
by appearing in public for such a cause.

As to her home, she is not likely to leave it more
than she now does for balls, theaters, meetings for
promoting missions, revival meetings, and others
to which she flies, in hope of an animation for her
existence commensurate with that she sees enjoyed
by men. Governors of ladies' fairs are no less engrossed by such a charge, than the governor of a
state by his; presidents of Washingtonian societies
no less away from home than presidents of conven-
tions. If men look straitly to it, they will find that,
unless their lives are domestic, those of the women
will not be. A house is no home unless it contain
food and fire for the mind as well as for the body.
The female Greek, of our day, is as much in the street
as the male to cry, "What news?" We doubt not it
was the same in Athens of old. The women, shut
out from the market-place, made up for it at the
religious festivals. For human beings are not so
constituted that they can live without expansion.
If they do not get it in one way, they must in another,
or perish.

As to men's representing women fairly at present, while we hear from men who owe to their wives not only all that is comfortable or graceful, but all that is wise, in the arrangement of their lives, the frequent remark, "You cannot reason with a woman," — when from those of delicacy, nobleness, and poetic culture falls the contemptuous phrase "women and children," and that in no light sally of the hour, but in works intended to give a permanent statement of the best experiences, — when not one man, in the million, shall I say? no, not in the hundred million, can rise above the belief that Woman was made *for Man*, — when such traits as these are daily forced upon the attention, can we feel that Man will always do justice to the interests of Woman? Can we think that he takes a sufficiently discerning and religious view of her office and destiny *ever* to do her justice, except when prompted by sentiment, — accidentally or transiently, that is, for the sentiment will vary according to the relations in which he is placed? The lover, the poet, the artist, are likely to view her nobly. The father and the philosopher have some chance of liberality; the man of the world, the legislator for expediency, none.

Under these circumstances, without attaching importance, in themselves, to the changes demanded by the champions of Woman, we hail them as signs of the times. We would have every arbitrary barrier thrown down. We would have every path laid open to Woman as freely as to Man. Were this done, and a slight temporary fermentation allowed to subside, we should see crystallizations more pure and of more various beauty. We believe the divine energy would pervade nature to a degree unknown in the history of former ages, and that no discordant collision, but a ravishing harmony of the spheres, would ensue.

Yet, then and only then will mankind be ripe for this, when inward and outward freedom for Woman as much as for Man shall be acknowledged as a *right*, not yielded as a concession. As the friend of the negro assumes that one man cannot by right hold another in bondage, so should the friend of Woman assume that Man cannot by right lay even well-meant restrictions on Woman. If the negro be a soul, if the woman be a soul, appareled in flesh, to one Master only are they accountable. There is but one law for souls, and if there is to be an interpreter of it, he must come not as man, or son of man, but as son of God.

Were thought and feeling once so far elevated that Man should esteem himself the brother and friend, but nowise the lord and tutor, of Woman, — were he really bound with her in equal worship, — arrangements as to function and employment would be of no consequence. What Woman needs is not as a woman to act or rule, but as a nature to grow, as an intellect to discern, as a soul to live freely and unimpeded, to unfold such powers as were given her when we left our common home. If fewer talents were given her, yet if allowed the free and full employment of these, so that she may render back to the giver his own with usury, she will not complain; nay, I dare to say she will bless and rejoice in her earthly birth-place, her earthly lot. . . . .

It is not Woman, but the law of right, the law of growth, that speaks in us, and demands the perfection of each being in its kind — apple as apple, Woman as Woman. Without adopting your theory, I know that I, a daughter, live through the life of Man; but what concerns me now is, that my life be a beautiful, powerful, in a word, a complete life in its kind. Had I but one more moment to live I must wish the same.

HENRY DAVID THOREAU

1817–1862

THOREAU was one of the Transcendental School of writers. He was born in Concord, Massachusetts. After his graduation at Harvard, and some experience in school-teaching and land-surveying, he settled in his native town and became intimate with EMERSON, ALCOTT, and their circle. A man of intense individuality and a large conceit, he was nevertheless so impressed by EMERSON that in his writings, which became frequent, he took on, perhaps unconsciously, much of the EMERSONIAN style. Yet he was a freakish original, lived for years alone in a lodge he built in the woods, and wrote of his life and experiences there in a delightful book entitled "Walden." From this, the essay or chapter on "Solitude" — the charms of which he had sought in his experiment — is here reprinted.

It has been said that while THOREAU received much from EMERSON, EMERSON owed to THOREAU the unsealing of his eyes to the wonders and beauties of nature; if so, the world also owes much to THOREAU.

THOREAU wrote often for the periodicals, and his writings were gathered into volumes: "A Week on the Concord and Merrimac Rivers," "Cape Cod," "The Maine Woods," and others. His love of nature was sincere, his knowledge of it intimate and almost boundless, his descriptions of it, and of the animated life that peopled its wilds were graphic and picturesque, and the reflections on man, society, government, art, literature, and a multitude of topics, that his philosophic and poetic soul conceived, make his writings unusually suggestive to the thoughtful reader.

154

SOLITUDE

THIS is a delicious evening, when the whole body is one sense, and imbibes delight through every pore. I go and come with a strange liberty in Nature, a part of herself. As I walk along the stony shore of the pond in my shirt-sleeves, though it is cool as well as cloudy and windy, and I see nothing special to attract me, all the elements are unusually congenial to me. The bullfrogs trump to usher in the night, and the note of the whippoorwill is borne on the rippling wind from over the water. Sympathy with the fluttering alder and poplar leaves almost takes away my breath; yet, like the lake, my serenity is rippled but not ruffled. These small waves raised by the evening wind are as remote from storm as the smooth reflecting surface. Though it is now dark, the wind still blows and roars in the wood, the waves still dash, and some creatures lull the rest with their notes. The repose is never complete. The wildest animals do not repose, but seek their prey now; the fox, and skunk, and rabbit now roam the fields and woods without fear. They are Nature's watchmen, — links which connect the days of animated life.

When I return to my house I find that visitors have been there and left their cards, either a bunch of flowers, or a wreath of evergreen, or a name in pencil on a yellow walnut leaf or a chip. They who come rarely to the woods take some little piece of the forest into their hands to play with by the way, which they leave, either intentionally or accidentally. One has peeled a willow wand, woven it into a ring, and dropped it on my table. I could always tell if visitors had called in my absence, either by the bended twigs or grass, or the print of their shoes, and generally of what sex or age or quality they were by some slight trace left, as a flower dropped, or a bunch of grass plucked and thrown away, even as far off as the railroad, half a mile distant, or by the lingering odor of a cigar or pipe. Nay, I was frequently notified of the passage of a traveler along the highway sixty rods off by the scent of his pipe.

There is commonly sufficient space about us. Our horizon is never quite at our elbows. The thick wood is not just at our door, nor the pond, but somewhat is always clearing, familiar and worn by us, appropriated and fenced in some way, and reclaimed from Nature. For what reason have I this vast range and circuit, some square miles of unfrequented forest, for my privacy, abandoned to me by men? My nearest neighbor is a mile distant, and no house is visible from any place but the hilltops within half a mile of my own. I have my horizon bounded by woods all to myself; a distant view of the railroad where it touches the pond on the one hand, and of the fence which skirts the woodland road on the other. But for the most part it is as solitary where I live as on the prairies. It is as much Asia or Africa as New England. ⌉ I have, as it were, my own sun and moon and stars, and a little world all to myself.⌉ At night there was never a traveler passed my house, or knocked at my door, more than if I were the first or last man; unless it were in the spring, when at long intervals some came from the village to fish for pouts, — they plainly fished much more in the Walden Pond of their own natures, and baited their hooks with darkness, — but they soon retreated, usually with light baskets, and left "the world to darkness and to me," and the black kernel of the night was never profaned by any human neighborhood. I believe that men are generally still a little afraid of the dark, though the witches are all hung, and Christianity and candles have been introduced.

⌈Yet I experienced sometimes that the most sweet and tender, the most innocent and encouraging society may be found in any natural object, even for the poor misanthrope and most melancholy man. There can be no very black melancholy to him who lives in the midst of Nature and has his senses still. There was never yet such a storm but it was Æolian music to a healthy and innocent ear.⌉ Nothing can rightly compel a simple and brave man to a vulgar sadness. While I enjoy the friendship of the seasons I trust that nothing can make life a burden to me. The

gentle rain which waters my beans and keeps me in
the house to-day is not drear and melancholy, but
good for me, too. Though it prevents my hoeing
them, it is of far more worth than my hoeing. If it
should continue so long as to cause the seeds to rot
in the ground and destroy the potatoes in the low
lands, it would still be good for the grass on the up-
lands, and, being good for the grass, it would be
good for me. Sometimes, when I compare myself
with other men, it seems as if I were more favored
by the gods than they, beyond any deserts that I am
conscious of; as if I had a warrant and surety at
their hands which my fellows have not, and were
especially guided and guarded.   I do not flatter myself, but if it be possible they flatter me. I have never
felt lonesome, or in the least oppressed by a sense of
solitude, but once, and that was a few weeks after I
came to the woods, when, for an hour, I doubted if the
near neighborhood of man was not essential to a
serene and healthy life.   To be alone was something
unpleasant.   But I was at the same time conscious of
a slight insanity in my mood, and seemed to foresee my
recovery.   In the midst of a gentle rain while these
thoughts prevailed, I was suddenly sensible of such
sweet and beneficent society in Nature, in the very
pattering of the drops, and in every sound and sight
around my house, an infinite and unaccountable
friendliness all at once like an atmosphere sustaining
me, as made the fancied advantages of human neigh-

borhood insignificant, and I have never thought of them since. Every little pine-needle expanded and swelled with sympathy and befriended me. I was so distinctly made aware of the presence of something kindred to me, even in scenes which we are accustomed to call wild and dreary, and also that the nearest of blood to me and humanest was not a person nor a villager, that I thought no place could ever be strange to me again. —

> "Mourning untimely consumes the sad;
> Few are their days in the land of the living,
> Beautiful daughter of Toscar."

Some of my pleasantest hours were during the long rain storms in the spring or fall, which confined me to the house for the afternoon as well as the forenoon, soothed by their ceaseless roar and pelting; when an early twilight ushered in a long evening in which many thoughts had time to take root and unfold themselves. In those driving northeast rains which tried the village houses so, when the maids stood ready with mop and pail in front entries to keep the deluge out, I sat behind my door in my little house, which was all entry, and thoroughly enjoyed its protection. In one heavy thunder shower the lightning struck a large pitch pine across the pond, making a very conspicuous and perfectly regular spiral groove from top to bottom, an inch or more deep, and four or five inches wide, as you would groove a walking-stick.

I passed it again the other day, and was struck with
awe on looking up and beholding that mark, now more
distinct than ever, where a terrific and resistless bolt
came down out of the harmless sky eight years ago.
Men frequently say to me, "I should think you would
feel lonesome down there, and want to be nearer to
folks, rainy and snowy days and nights especially."
I am tempted to reply to such, — This whole earth
which we inhabit is but a point in space. How far
apart, think you, dwell the two most distant inhabitants of yonder star, the breadth of whose disk cannot
be appreciated by our instruments? Why should I
feel lonely? is not our planet in the Milky Way?
This which you put seems to me not to be the most
important question. What sort of space is that
which separates a man from his fellows and makes
him solitary? I have found that no exertion of the
legs can bring two minds much nearer to one another.
What do we want most to dwell near to? Not to
many men surely, the depot, the post-office, the bar-
room, the meeting-house, the school-house, the
grocery, Beacon Hill, or the Five Points, where men
most congregate, but to the perennial source of our
life, whence in all our experience we have found that
to issue, as the willow stands near the water and sends
out its roots in that direction. This will vary with
different natures, but this is the place where a wise
man will dig his cellar.

"How vast and profound is the influence of the subtile powers of Heaven and of Earth!"

"We seek to perceive them, and we do not see them; we seek to hear them, and we do not hear them; identified with the substance of things, they cannot be separated from them."

"They cause that in all the universe men purify and sanctify their hearts, and clothe themselves in their holiday garments to offer sacrifices and oblations to their ancestors. It is an ocean of subtile intelligences. They are everywhere, above us, on our left, on our right; they environ us on all sides." . . .

With thinking, we may be beside ourselves in a sane sense. By a conscious effort of the mind we can stand aloof from actions and their consequences; and all things, good and bad, go by us like a torrent. We are not wholly involved in Nature. I may be either the driftwood in the stream, or Indra in the sky looking down on it. I *may* be affected by a theatrical exhibition; on the other hand, I *may not* be affected by an actual event which appears to concern me much more. I only know myself as a human entity; the scene, so to speak, of thoughts and affections; and am sensible of a certain doubleness by which I can stand as remote from myself as from another. However intense my experience, I am conscious of the presence of and criticism of a part of me, which, as it were, is not a part of me, but spectator, sharing no experience, but taking note of it; and that is no more I than it is you. When the play, it may be the tragedy, of life is over, the spectator goes his way.

It was a kind of fiction, a work of the imagination only, so far as he was concerned. This doubleness may easily make us poor neighbors and friends sometimes. [I find it wholesome to be alone the greater part of the time. To be in company, even with the best, is soon wearisome and dissipating. I love to be alone. I never found the companion that was so companionable as solitude. We are for the most part more lonely when we go abroad among men than when we stay in our chambers. A man thinking or working is always alone, let him be where he will.] Solitude is not measured by the miles of space that intervene between a man and his fellows. The really diligent student in one of the crowded hives of Cambridge College is as solitary as a dervish in the desert. The farmer can work alone in the field or the woods all day, hoeing or chopping, and not feel lonesome, because he is employed; but when he comes home at night he cannot sit down in a room alone, at the mercy of his thoughts, but must be where he can "see the folks," and recreate, and as he thinks remunerate, himself for his day's solitude; and hence he wonders how the student can sit alone in the house all night and most of the day without ennui and "the blues"; but he does not realize that the student, though in the house, is still at work in *his* field, and chopping in *his* woods, as the farmer in his, and in turn seeks the same recreation and society that the latter does, though it may be a more condensed form of it.

⌊ Society is commonly too cheap. We meet at very ✳
short intervals, not having had time to acquire any
new value for each other. We meet at meals three
times a day, and give each other a new taste of that
old musty cheese that we are. We have to agree on
a certain set of rules, called etiquette and politeness,
to make this frequent meeting tolerable and that we
need not come to open war.⌉ We meet at the post-
office, and at the sociable, and about the fireside
every night; ⌊we live thick and are in each other's ✳
way, and stumble over one another, and I think that
we thus lose some respect for one another. Certainly less frequency would suffice for all important
and hearty communications.⌉ Consider the girls in
a factory, — never alone, hardly in their dreams.
It would be better if there were but one inhabitant
to a square mile, as where I live. The value of a
man is not in his skin, that we should touch him.

I have heard of a man lost in the woods and dying
of famine and exhaustion at the foot of a tree,
whose loneliness was relieved by the grotesque visions
with which, owing to bodily weakness, his diseased
imagination surrounded him, and which he believed
to be real. So also, owing to bodily and mental
health and strength, we may be continually cheered
by a like but more normal and natural society, and
come to know that we are never alone.

⌊I have a great deal of company in my house; es- ✳
pecially in the morning, when nobody calls.⌉ Let me

suggest a few comparisons, that some one may convey
an idea of my situation. I am no more lonely than
the loon in the pond that laughs so loud, or than
Walden Pond itself. What company has that lonely
lake, I pray? And yet it has not the blue devils,
but the blue angels in it, in the azure tint of its waters.
The sun is alone, except in thick weather, when there
sometimes appear to be two, but one is a mock sun.
God is alone, — but the devil, he is far from being
alone; he sees a great deal of company; he is legion.
I am no more lonely than a single mullein or dande-
lion in a pasture, or a bean leaf, or sorrel, or a horse-
fly, or a humblebee. I am no more lonely than the
Mill Brook, or a weathercock, or the north star, or
the south wind, or an April shower, or a January
thaw, or the first spider in a new house.

I have occasional visits in the long winter evenings,
when the snow falls fast and the wind howls in the
wood, from an old settler and original proprietor, who
is reported to have dug Walden Pond, and stoned it,
and fringed it with pine woods; who tell me stories
of old time and of new eternity; and between us we
manage to pass a cheerful evening with social mirth
and pleasant views of things, even without apples or
cider, — a most wise and humorous friend, whom I
love much, who keeps himself more secret than ever
did Goffe or Whalley; and though he is thought to be
dead, none can show where he is buried. An elderly
dame, too, dwells in my neighborhood, invisible to

most persons, in whose odorous herb garden I love to stroll sometimes, gathering simples and listening to her fables; for she has a genius of unequaled fertility, and her memory runs back farther than mythology, and she can tell me the original of every fable, and on what fact every one is founded, for the incidents occurred when she was young. A ruddy and lusty old dame, who delights in all weathers and seasons, and is likely to outlive all her children yet.

The indescribable innocence and beneficence of Nature, — of sun and wind and rain, of summer and winter, — such health, such cheer, they afford forever! and such sympathy have they ever with our race, that all Nature would be affected, and the sun's brightness fade, and the winds would sigh humanely, and the clouds rain tears, and the woods shed their leaves and put on mourning in midsummer, if any man should ever for a just cause grieve. Shall I not have intelligence with the earth? Am I not partly leaves and vegetable mold myself?

What is the pill which will keep us well, serene, contented? Not my or thy great-grandfather's, but our great-grandmother Nature's universal, vegetable, botanic medicines, by which she has kept herself young always, outlived so many old Parrs in her day, and fed her health with their decaying fatness. For my panacea, instead of one of those quack vials of a mixture dipped from Acheron and the Dead Sea, which come out of those long, shallow, black-schooner-

looking wagons which we sometimes see made to
carry bottles, let me have a draught of undiluted
morning air. Morning air! If men will not drink of
this at the fountain-head of the day, why, then, we
must even bottle up some and sell it in the shops, for
the benefit of those who have lost their subscription
ticket to morning time in this world. But remember,
it will not keep quite till noonday even in the coolest
cellar, but drive out the stopples long ere that and
follow westward the steps of Aurora. I am no
worshiper of Hygeia, who was the daughter of that
old herb-doctor Æsculapius, and who is represented
on monuments holding a serpent in one hand, and in
the other a cup of which the serpent sometimes
drinks; but rather of Hebe, cupbearer to Jupiter, who
was the daughter of Juno and wild lettuce, and who
had the power of restoring gods and men to the vigor
of youth. She was probably the only thoroughly
sound-conditioned, healthy, and robust young lady
that ever walked the globe, and wherever she came it
was spring.

NATHANIEL HAWTHORNE

1804-1864

BORN in Salem — a town saturated with historical and legendary romance of earlier and darker days — HAWTHORNE was from boyhood shy, sensitive, given to introspection and love of solitude. Even after a college career, he lived for nearly ten years with his mother in her lonely Salem house, considering what profession he was fit for.

Yet here his profession found him: he began writing — sketches, tales, essays — and, although he burned more than he published, he was in training for better work. Many of these writings were printed in obscure periodicals, and formed his first book of gathered fruits, "Twice-told Tales" (1837). In 1841 he joined for a while the Brook Farm Community, his experiences there developing later into "The Blithedale Romance." Marrying, in 1842, he removed to the old EMERSON house in Concord, whence his "Mosses from an Old Manse." The year 1846 interrupted his writing with a position in the Salem Custom House, but when, in 1849, political changes lost him that, he set about a larger and more serious work, one long brooded, "The Scarlet Letter" (1850), that romance of retribution, which put him instantly at the head of American writers of fiction. Then rapidly followed "The House of the Seven Gables" (1851), and "The Blithedale Romance" (1852); and, after seven years in Europe, four as United States Consul at Liverpool and three spent in travel, came his last finished romance "The Marble Faun" (1860), in England called "Transformation." Besides these four strongest works, Hawthorne wrote many mysteriously delightful sketches and tales, and several charming volumes for children — "The Wonder-Book," "Grandfather's Chair," "Tanglewood Tales," etc.

The pure perfection of HAWTHORNE'S style is most alluring, while his brilliant imagination, delicate humor, mastery of the weird and supernatural, and intimate knowledge of the human heart complete his control of the reader.

FIRE-WORSHIP

It is a great revolution in social and domestic life — and no less so in the life of the secluded student — this almost universal exchange of the open fireplace for the cheerless and ungenial stove. On such a morning as now lowers around our old gray parsonage, I miss the bright face of my ancient friend, who was wont to dance upon the hearth, and play the part of a more familiar sunshine. It is sad to turn from the cloudy sky and somber landscape — from yonder hill, with its crown of rusty, black pines, the foliage of which is so dismal in the absence of the sun; that bleak pasture land, and the broken surface of the potato field, with the brown clods partly concealed by the snowfall of last night; the swollen and sluggish river, with ice-incrusted borders, dragging its bluish-gray stream along the verge of our orchard, like a snake half torpid with the cold — it is sad to turn from an outward scene of so little comfort, and find the same sullen influences brooding within the precincts of my study. Where is that brilliant guest — that quick and subtle spirit whom Prometheus lured from Heaven to civilize mankind, and cheer them in their wintry desolation — that comfortable inmate, whose smile, during eight months of the year, was

our sufficient consolation for summer's lingering
advance and early flight? Alas! blindly inhospi-
table, grudging the food that kept him cheery and
mercurial, we have thrust him into an iron prison, and
compel him to smolder away his life on a daily pit-
tance which once would have been too scanty for
his breakfast! Without a metaphor, we now make
our fire in an air-tight stove, and supply it with some
half-a-dozen sticks of wood between dawn and night-
fall.

I never shall be reconciled to this enormity. Truly
may it be said, that the world looks darker for it. In
one way or another, here and there, and all around
us, the inventions of mankind are fast blotting the
picturesque, the poetic, and the beautiful out of
human life. The domestic fire was a type of all these
attributes, and seemed to bring might and majesty,
and wild Nature, and a spiritual essence, into our in-
most home, and yet to dwell with us in such friendliness, that its mysteries and marvels excited no dis-
may. The same mild companion, that smiled so
placidly in our faces, was he that comes roaring out of
Ætna, and rushes madly up the sky, like a fiend
breaking loose from torment, and fighting for a place
among the upper angels. He it is, too, that leaps
from cloud to cloud amid the crashing thunder-
storm. It was he whom the Gheber worshiped, with
no unnatural idolatry; and it was he who devoured
London and Moscow, and many another famous city,

and who loves to riot through our own dark forests, and sweep across our prairies, and to whose ravenous maw, it is said, the universe shall one day be given as a final feast. Meanwhile he is the great artisan and laborer by whose aid men are enabled to build a world within a world, or, at least, to smooth down the rough creation which Nature flung to us. He forges the mighty anchor, and every lesser instrument. He drives the steamboat and drags the rail car. And it was he — this creature of terrible might, and so many-sided utility, and all-comprehensive destructiveness — that used to be the cheerful, homely friend of our wintry days, and whom we have made the prisoner of this iron cage!

How kindly he was, and, though the tremendous agent of change, yet bearing himself with such gentleness, so rendering himself a part of all lifelong and age-coeval associations, that it seemed as if he were the great conservative of Nature! While a man was true to the fireside, so long would he be true to country and law— to the God whom his fathers worshiped—to the wife of his youth — and to all things else which instinct or religion have taught us to consider sacred. With how sweet humility did this elemental spirit perform all needful offices for the household in which he was domesticated! He was equal to the concoction of a grand dinner, yet scorned not to roast a potato, or toast a bit of cheese. How humanely did he cherish the schoolboy's icy fingers,

and thaw the old man's joints with a genial warmth,
which almost equaled the glow of youth! And how
carefully did he dry the cowhide boots that had
trudged through mud and snow, and the shaggy outside garment, stiff with frozen sleet; taking heed,
likewise, to the comfort of the faithful dog who had
followed his master through the storm! When did
he refuse a coal to light a pipe, or even a part of his
own substance to kindle a neighbor's fire? And
then, at twilight, when laborer or scholar, or mortal
of whatever age, sex, or degree, drew a chair beside
him, and looked into his glowing face, how acute, how
profound, how comprehensive was his sympathy
with the mood of each and all! He pictured forth
their very thoughts. To the youthful he showed
the scenes of the adventurous life before them; to
the aged, the shadows of departed love and hope;
and, if all earthly things had grown distasteful, he
could gladden the fireside muser with golden glimpses
of a better world. And, amid this varied communion
with the human soul, how busily would the sym-
pathizer, the deep moralist, the painter of magic
pictures, be causing the tea-kettle to boil!

Nor did it lessen the charm of his soft, familiar
courtesy and helpfulness, that the mighty spirit, were
opportunity offered him, would run riot through the
peaceful house, wrap its inmates in his terrible embrace, and leave nothing of them save their whitened
bones. This possibility of mad destruction only

made his domestic kindness the more beautiful and touching. It was so sweet of him, being endowed with such power, to dwell, day after day, and one long, lonesome night after another, on the dusky hearth, only now and then betraying his wild nature by thrusting his red tongue out of the chimney-top! True, he had done much mischief in the world, and was pretty certain to do more; but his warm heart atoned for all. He was kindly to the race of man; and they pardoned his characteristic imperfections.

The good old clergyman, my predecessor in this mansion, was well acquainted with the comforts of the fireside. His yearly allowance of wood, according to the terms of his settlement, was no less than sixty cords. Almost an annual forest was converted from sound oak logs into ashes, in the kitchen, the parlor, and this little study, where now an unworthy successor — not in the pastoral office, but merely in his earthly abode — sits scribbling beside an air-tight stove. I love to fancy one of those fireside days, while the good man, a contemporary of the Revolution, was in his early prime, some five-and-sixty years ago. Before sunrise, doubtless, the blaze hovered upon the gray skirts of night, and dissolved the frostwork that had gathered like a curtain over the small window-panes. There is something peculiar in the aspect of the morning fireside; a fresher, brisker glare; the absence of that mellowness, which can be produced only by half-consumed logs, and shapeless brands with the white ashes on them, and mighty coals, the remnant of tree trunks that the hungry elements have gnawed for hours. The morning hearth, too, is newly swept, and the brazen andirons well brightened, so that the cheerful fire may see its face in them. Surely it was happiness, when the pastor, fortified with a substantial breakfast, sat down in his armchair and slippers, and opened the Whole Body of Divinity, or the Commentary on Job, or whichever of his old folios or quartos might fall within the range of his weekly sermons. It must have been his own fault, if the warmth and glow of this abundant hearth did not permeate the discourse, and keep his audience comfortable, in spite of the bitterest northern blast that ever wrestled with the church steeple. He reads, while the heat warps the stiff covers of the volume; he writes without numbness either in his heart or fingers; and, with unstinted hand, he throws fresh sticks of wood upon the fire.

A parishioner comes in. With what warmth of benevolence — how should he be otherwise than warm, in any of his attributes? — does the minister bid him welcome, and set a chair for him in so close proximity to the hearth, that soon the guest finds it needful to rub his scorched shins with his great red hands. The melted snow drips from his steaming boots, and bubbles upon the hearth. His puckered forehead unravels its entanglement of crisscross wrinkles.

We lose much of the enjoyment of fireside heat, without such an opportunity of marking its genial effect upon those who have been looking the inclement weather in the face. In the course of the day our clergyman himself strides forth, perchance to pay a round of pastoral visits, or, it may be, to visit his mountain of a wood-pile, and cleave the monstrous logs into billets suitable for the fire. He returns with fresher life to his beloved hearth. During the short afternoon, the western sunshine comes into the study, and strives to stare the ruddy blaze out of countenance, but with only a brief triumph, soon to be succeeded by brighter glories of its rival. Beautiful it is to see the strengthening gleam — the deepening light — that gradually casts distinct shadows of the human figure, the table, and the high-backed chairs, upon the opposite wall, and at length, as twilight comes on, replenishes the room with living radiance, and makes life all rose-color. Afar, the wayfarer discerns the flickering flame, as it dances upon the windows, and hails it as a beacon light of humanity, reminding him, in his cold and lonely path, that the world is not all snow, and solitude, and desolation. At eventide, probably, the study was peopled with the clergyman's wife and family; and children tumbled themselves upon the hearth-rug, and grave Puss sat with her back to the fire, or gazed, with a semblance of human meditation, into its fervid depths. Seasonably, the plenteous ashes of the day were raked

over the moldering brands, and from the heap came
jets of flame, and an incense of night-long smoke,
creeping quietly up the chimney.

Heaven forgive the old clergyman! In his later
life, when, for almost ninety winters, he had been
gladdened by the firelight — when it had gleamed
upon him from infancy to extreme age, and never
without brightening his spirits as well as his visage,
and perhaps keeping him alive so long — he had the
heart to brick up his chimney-place, and bid farewell
to the face of his old friend forever! Why did not he
take an eternal leave of the sunshine too? His sixty
cords of wood had probably dwindled to a far less
ample supply, in modern times; and it is certain that
the parsonage had grown crazy with time and tempest, and pervious to the cold; but still, it was one of
the saddest tokens of the decline and fall of open fire-
places, that the gray patriarch should have deigned
to warm himself at an air-tight stove.

And I, likewise — who have found a home in this
ancient owl's nest, since its former occupant took his
heavenward flight — I, to my shame, have put up
stoves in kitchen, and parlor, and chamber. Wander
where you will about the house, not a glimpse of the
earth-born, heaven-aspiring fiend of Ætna — him
that sports in the thunder-storm — the idol of the
Ghebers — the devourer of cities, the forest-rioter,
and prairie-sweeper — the future destroyer of our
earth — the old chimney-corner companion, who

mingled himself so sociably with household joys and sorrows — not a glimpse of this mighty and kindly one will greet your eyes. He is now an invisible presence. There is his iron cage. Touch it, and he scorches your fingers. He delights to singe a garment, or perpetrate any other little unworthy mischief; for his temper is ruined by the ingratitude of mankind, for whom he cherished such warmth of feeling, and to whom he taught all their arts, even that of making his own prison-house. In his fits of rage, he puffs volumes of smoke and noisome gas through the crevices of the door, and shakes the iron walls of his dungeon, so as to overthrow the ornamental urn upon its summit. We tremble, lest he should break forth amongst us. Much of his time is spent in sighs, burthened with unutterable grief, and long-drawn through the funnel. He amuses himself, too, with repeating all the whispers, the moans, and the louder utterances or tempestuous howls of the wind; so that the stove becomes a microcosm of the aërial world. Occasionally, there are strange combinations of sounds — voices, talking almost articulately — within the hollow chest of iron, insomuch that fancy beguiles me with the idea that my firewood must have grown in that infernal forest of lamentable trees which breathed their complaints to Dante. When the listener is half asleep, he may readily take these voices for the conversation of spirits, and assign them an intelligible meaning. Anon, there is a pattering noise—drip, drip, drip — as if a summer's shower were falling within the narrow circumference of the stove.

These barren and tedious eccentricities are all that the air-tight stove can bestow, in exchange for the invaluable moral influences which we have lost by our desertion of the open fireplace. Alas! is this world so very bright, that we can afford to choke up such a domestic fountain of gladsomeness, and sit down by its darkened source, without being conscious of a gloom?

It is my belief that social intercourse cannot long continue what it has been, now that we have subtracted from it so important and vivifying an element as firelight. The effects will be more perceptible on our children, and the generations that shall succeed them, than on ourselves, the mechanism of whose life may remain unchanged, though its spirit be far other than it was. The sacred trust of the household fire has been transmitted in unbroken succession from the earliest ages, and faithfully cherished, in spite of every discouragement, such as the Curfew law of the Norman conquerors; until, in these evil days, physical science has nearly succeeded in extinguishing it. But we at least have our youthful recollections tinged with the glow of the hearth, and our lifelong habits and associations arranged on the principle of a mutual bond in the domestic fire. Therefore, though the sociable friend be forever departed, yet in a degree he will be spiritually present with us; and still more will the empty forms, which were once full of his rejoicing presence, continue to rule our manners. We shall draw our chairs together, as we and our forefathers have been wont, for thousands of years back, and sit around some blank and empty corner of the room, babbling, with unreal cheerfulness, of topics suitable to the homely fireside. A warmth from the past — from the ashes of bygone years, and the raked-up embers of long ago — will sometimes thaw the ice about our hearts. But it must be otherwise with our successors. On the most favorable supposition, they will be acquainted with the fireside in no better shape than that of the sullen stove; and more probably, they will have grown up amid furnace heat, in houses which might be fancied to have their foundation over the infernal pit, whence sulphurous steams and unbreathable exhalations ascend through the apertures of the floor. There will be nothing to attract these poor children to one center. They will never behold one another through that peculiar medium of vision — the ruddy gleam of blazing wood or bituminous coal — which gives the human spirit so deep an insight into its fellows, and melts all humanity into one cordial heart of hearts. Domestic life — if it may still be termed domestic — will seek its separate corners, and never gather itself into groups. The easy gossip — the merry, yet unambitious jest

— the lifelike, practical discussion of real matters in a casual way — the soul of truth, which is so often incarnated in a simple fireside word — will disappear from earth. Conversation will contract the air of a debate, and all mortal intercourse be chilled with a fatal frost.

In classic times, the exhortation to fight "pro aris et focis" — for the altars and the hearths — was considered the strongest appeal that could be made to patriotism. And it seemed an immortal utterance; for all subsequent ages and people have acknowledged its force, and responded to it with the full portion of manhood that Nature had assigned to each. Wisely were the Altar and the Hearth conjoined in one mighty sentence! For the hearth, too, had its kindred sanctity. Religion sat down beside it, not in the priestly robes which decorated, and perhaps disguised her at the altar, but arrayed in a simple matron's garb, and uttering her lessons with the tenderness of a mother's voice and heart. The holy Hearth! If any earthly and material thing — or rather, a divine idea, embodied in brick and mortar — might be supposed to possess the permanence of moral truth, it was this. All revered it. The man who did not put off his shoes upon this holy ground would have deemed it pastime to trample upon the altar. It has been our task to uproot the hearth. What further reform is left for our children to achieve, unless they overthrow the altar too? And

by what appeal, hereafter, when the breath of hostile
armies may mingle with the pure, cold breezes of our
country, shall we attempt to rouse up native valor ?
Fight for your hearths ?   There will be none throughout the land. FIGHT FOR YOUR STOVES! Not I,
in faith!   If, in such a cause, I strike a blow, it shall
be on the invader's part; and Heaven grant that it
may shatter the abomination all to pieces!

HENRY WADSWORTH LONGFELLOW

1807–1882

It were much for one to be among the early discoverers of foreign literary treasures to his own countrymen; more, to be among the pioneers in creating a national poetical literature: yet both these honors were achieved by LONGFELLOW. Born and educated in Maine, his life was chiefly identified with Cambridge and Harvard, where he labored long.

Even in college (Bowdoin), LONGFELLOW wrote many ballads and other poems. For three years after graduation (1826–1829) he sojourned in European countries, returning to be Professor of Modern Languages and Literatures in Bowdoin. Then two years more of European study, and he held the same chair in Harvard for eighteen years (1836–1854).

It was in 1835 that LONGFELLOW published his first prose work, "Outre-Mer" (Beyond the Sea), travel-sketches from Europe and especially from Spain. Soon after, he began collecting his fugitive poems, and brought out volume after volume: "Voices of the Night" (1839); "Ballads" etc., including Translations (1841); "Poems on Slavery" (1842); "Spanish Student" (1843), etc. In 1847 he published "Evangeline," a pathetic romance of early America, noted for its melodious (though not always faultless) use of the hexameter versification. The Indian legend of "Hiawatha," in 1855, made a great impression. It is impossible here to enumerate LONGFELLOW'S volumes. Whether original poems or sympathetic translations from French, Spanish, Italian, German, Swedish, Danish, etc., the verbal and metrical music, the poetic fancies, delicate or vigorous, the distinct elements both of European history and legend, of American themes, and of the universal human — whatever the note, it was sweet, pure in spiritual intent, and artistically sounded. A devoted student, a finished scholar, LONGFELLOW was, and will long remain, the poet of the hearth and home.

His prose work was much less in amount and importance, but he wrote excellent things in romance and in scholarly literary criticism; among them the "Defense of Poetry."

DEFENSE OF POETRY

"GENTLE Sir Philip Sidney, thou knewest what belonged to a scholar; thou knewest what pains, what toil, what travail, conduct to perfection; well couldest thou give every virtue his encouragement, every art his due, every writer his desert, 'cause none more virtuous, witty, or learned than thyself." [1] This eulogium was bestowed upon one of the most learned and illustrious men that adorned the last half of the sixteenth century. Literary history is full of his praises. He is spoken of as the ripe scholar, the able statesman — "the soldier's, scholar's, courtier's eye, tongue, sword" — the man "whose whole life was poetry put into action." He and the Chevalier Bayard were the connecting links between the ages of chivalry and our own. . . .

The most celebrated productions of Sidney's pen are the "Arcadia" and the "Defence of Poesie." The former was written during the author's retirement at Wilton, the residence of his sister, the Countess of Pembroke. Though so much celebrated in

[1] Nash's "Pierce Penniless."

its day,[1] it is now little known, and still less read. Its very subject prevents it from being popular at present; for now the pastoral reed seems entirely thrown aside. The muses no longer haunt the groves of Arcadia. The shepherd's song — the sound of oaten pipe, — and the scenes of pastoral loves and jealousies, are no becoming themes for the spirit of the age. Few at present take for their motto, "*flumina amo silvasque inglorius,*" and, consequently, few read the "Arcadia."

The "Defence of Poesie" is a work of rare merit. It is a golden little volume, which the scholar may lay beneath his pillow, as Chrysostom did the works of Aristophanes. We do not, however, mean to analyze it in this place; but recommend to our readers to purchase this "sweet food of sweetly uttered knowledge." It will be read with delight by all who have a taste for the true beauties of poetry; and may go far to remove the prejudices of those who have not. To this latter class we address the concluding remarks of the author: —

[1] Many of our readers will recollect the high-wrought eulogium of Harvey Pierce, when he consigned the work to immortality: "Live ever, sweete, sweete booke: the simple image of his gentle witt; and the golden pillar of his noble courage; and ever notify unto the world that thy writer was the secretary of eloquence, the breath of the muses, the honey-bee of the daintyest flowers of witt and arte; the pith of morale and intellectual virtues, the arme of Bellona in the field, the tongue of Suada in the chamber, the sprite of Practice in esse, and the paragon of excellency in print."

"So that since the ever-praiseworthy poesy is full
of virtue, breeding delightfulness, and void of no
gift that ought to be in the noble name of learning;
since the blames laid against it are either false or
feeble; since the cause why it is not esteemed in
England is the fault of poet-apes, not poets; since,
lastly, our tongue is most fit to honor poesy, and to
be honored by poesy; I conjure you all that have
had the evil luck to read this ink-wasting toy of mine,
even in the name of the nine muses, no more to scorn
the sacred mysteries of poesy; no more to laugh at
the name of poets, as though they were next inheritors
to fools; no more to jest at the reverend title of 'a
rhymer'; but to believe, with Aristotle, that they
were the ancient treasurers of the Grecians' divinity;
to believe, with Bembus, that they were the first
bringers in of all civility; to believe, with Scaliger,
that no philosopher's precepts can sooner make you
an honest man, than the reading of Vergil; to believe, with Clauserus, the translator of Cornutus,
that it pleased the heavenly deity by Hesiod and
Homer, under the veil of fables, to give us all knowledge, logic, rhetoric, philosophy, natural and moral,
and '*quid non?*' to believe, with me, that there are
many mysteries contained in poetry, which of purpose
were written darkly, lest by profane wits it should be
abused; to believe, with Landin, that they are so
beloved of the gods, that whatsoever they write
proceeds of a divine fury; lastly, to believe them-

selves, when they tell you they will make you immortal by their verses. . . ."

As no "Apologie for Poetrie" has appeared among
us, we hope that Sir Philip Sidney's "Defence"
will be widely read and long remembered. O that
in our country it might be the harbinger of as bright
an intellectual day as it was in his own! With us,
the spirit of the age is clamorous for utility — for
visible, tangible utility — for bare, brawny, muscular utility. . . . We are swallowed up in schemes
for gain, and engrossed with contrivances for bodily
enjoyments, as if this particle of dust were immortal
— as if the soul needed no aliment, and the mind no
raiment. We glory in the extent of our territory,
in our rapidly increasing population, in our agricul-
tural privileges, and our commercial advantages. We
boast of the magnificence and beauty of our natural
scenery — of the various climates of our sky — the
summers of our northern regions — the salubrious
winters of the south, and of the various products of
our soil, from the pines of our northern highlands
to the palm-tree and aloes of our southern frontier.
We boast of the increase and extent of our physical
strength, the sound of populous cities, breaking the
silence and solitude of our western Territories —
plantations conquered from the forest, and gardens
springing up in the wilderness. Yet the true glory
of a nation consists not in the extent of its territory,
the pomp of its forests, the majesty of its rivers, the

height of its mountains, and the beauty of its sky, but in the extent of its mental power — the majesty of its intellect — the height, and depth, and purity of its moral nature. It consists not in what nature has given to the body, but in what nature and education have given to the mind — not in the world around us, but in the world within us — not in the circumstances of fortune, but in the attributes of the soul — not in the corruptible, transitory, and perishable forms of matter, but in the incorruptible, the permanent, the imperishable mind. True greatness is the greatness of the mind — the true glory of a nation is moral and intellectual preëminence.

But still the main current of education runs in the wide and not well-defined channel of immediate and practical utility. . . . Now, under correction be it said, we are much led astray by this word utility. There is hardly a word in our language whose meaning is so vague, and so often misunderstood and misapplied. We too often limit its application to those acquisitions and pursuits which are of immediate and visible profit to ourselves and the community; regarding as comparatively or utterly useless many others which, though more remote in their effects and more imperceptible in their operation, are, notwithstanding, higher in their aim, wider in their influence, more certain in their results, and more intimately connected with the common weal. We are too apt to think that nothing can be useful but

what is done with a noise, at noonday, and at the
corners of the streets; as if action and utility were
synonymous, and it were not as useless to act without thinking as it is to think without acting. But
the truth is, the word utility has a wider signification
than this. It embraces in its proper definition whatever contributes to our happiness; and thus includes
many of those arts and sciences, many of those secret
studies and solitary avocations which are generally
regarded either as useless or as absolutely injurious
to society. Not he alone does service to the state
whose wisdom guides her councils at home, nor he
whose voice asserts her dignity abroad. A thousand
little rills, springing up in the retired walks of life,
go to swell the rushing tide of national glory and
prosperity; and whoever in the solitude of his
chamber, and by even a single effort of his mind, has
added to the intellectual preëminence of his country,
has not lived in vain, nor to himself alone. Does
not the pen of the historian perpetuate the fame of
the hero and the statesman? Do not their names
live in the song of the bard? Do not the pencil and
the chisel touch the soul while they delight the eye?
Does not the spirit of the patriot and the sage,
looking from the painted canvas, or eloquent from
the marble lip, fill our hearts with veneration for all
that is great in intellect and godlike in virtue? . . .

But against no branch of scholarship is the cry so
loud as against poetry, "the quintessence, or rather

the luxury, of all learning." Its enemies pretend that
it is injurious both to the mind and the heart; that
it incapacitates us for the severer discipline of professional study; and that, by exciting the feelings and misdirecting the imagination, it unfits us
for the common duties of life and the intercourse of
this matter-of-fact world. And yet such men have
lived, as Homer, and Dante, and Milton — poets and
scholars whose minds were bathed in song, and yet
not weakened; men who severally carried forward
the spirit of their age, who soared upward on the wings
of poetry, and yet were not unfitted to penetrate
the deepest recesses of the human soul and search
out the hidden treasures of wisdom and the secret
springs of thought, feeling, and action. None fought
more bravely at Marathon, Salamis, and Platæa
than did the poet Æschylus. Richard Cœur-de-Lion
was a poet; but his boast was in his very song: —

> "Bon guerrier à l'estendart
> Trouvaretz le Roi Richard."

Ercilla and Garcilaso were poets; but the great epic
of Spain was written in the soldier's tent and on the
field of battle, and the descendant of the Incas was
slain in the assault of a castle in the south of France.
Cervantes lost an arm at the battle of Lepanto, and
Sir Philip Sidney was the breathing reality of the
poet's dream, a living and glorious proof that poetry
neither enervates the mind nor unfits us for the
practical duties of life.

Nor is it less true that the legitimate tendency of poetry is to exalt rather than to debase — to purify rather than to corrupt. Read the inspired pages of the Hebrew prophets; the eloquent aspirations of the Psalmist! Where did ever the spirit of devotion bear up the soul more steadily and loftily than in the language of their poetry? And where has poetry been more exalted, more spirit-stirring, more admirable, or more beautiful, than when thus soaring upward on the wings of sublime devotion, the darkness and shadows of earth beneath it, and from above the brightness of an opened heaven pouring around it? It is true the poetic talent may be, for it has been, most lamentably perverted. But when poetry is thus perverted — when it thus forgets its native sky to grovel in what is base, sensual, and depraved — though it may not have lost all its original brightness, nor appear less than "the excess of glory obscured," yet its birthright has been sold, its strength has been blasted, and its spirit wears "deep scars of thunder."

It does not, then, appear to be the necessary nor the natural tendency of poetry to enervate the mind, corrupt the heart, or incapacitate us for performing the private and public duties of life. On the contrary, it may be made, and should be made, an instrument for improving the condition of society, and advancing the great purpose of human happiness. Man must have his hours of meditation as well as of action. The unities of time are not so well preserved

in the great drama but that moments will occur when
the stage must be left vacant, and even the busiest
actors pass behind the scenes. There will be eddies
in the stream of life, though the main current sweeps
steadily onward, till "it pours in full cataract over
the grave." There are times when both mind and
body are worn down by the severity of daily toil;
when the grasshopper is a burden, and, thirsty with
the heat of labor, the spirit longs for the waters of
Shiloah that go softly. At such seasons both mind
and body should unbend themselves; they should
be set free from the yoke of their customary service,
and thought take some other direction than that
of the beaten, dusty thoroughfare of business. And
there are times, too, when the divinity stirs within
us; when the soul abstracts herself from the world,
and the slow and regular motions of earthly business
do not keep pace with the heaven-directed mind.
Then earth lets go her hold; the soul feels herself
more akin to heaven; and soaring upward, the deni-
zen of her native sky, she "begins to reason like herself, and to discourse in a strain above mortality."
Call, if you will, such thoughts and feelings the
dreams of the imagination; yet they are no unprofitable dreams. Such moments of silence and meditation are often those of the greatest utility to ourselves and others. Yes, we would dream awhile,
that the spirit is not always the bondman of the flesh;
that there is something immortal in us, something

which, amid the din of life, urges us to aspire after
the attributes of a more spiritual nature. Let the
cares and business of the world sometimes sleep, for
this sleep is the awakening of the soul. . . .

Popular judgment has seldom fallen into a greater
error than that of supposing that poetry must necessarily, and from its very nature, convey false and
therefore injurious impressions. The error lies in not
discriminating between what is true to nature and
what is true to fact. From the very nature of things,
neither poetry nor any one of the imitative arts can
in itself be false. They can be false no further than,
by the imperfection of human skill, they convey
to our mind imperfect and garbled views of what they
represent. Hence a painting or poetical description
may be true to nature, and yet false in point of fact.
The canvas before you may represent a scene in
which every individual feature of the landscape
shall be true to nature — the tree, the waterfall,
the distant mountain — every object there shall be
an exact copy of an original that has a real existence,
and yet the scene itself may be absolutely false in
point of fact. Such a scene, with the features of
the landscape combined precisely in the way represented, may exist nowhere but in the imagination of
the artist. The statue of the Venus de' Medici is the
perfection of female beauty; and every individual
feature had its living original. Still, the statue itself
had no living archetype. It is true to nature, but

it is not true to fact. So with the stage. The scene represented, the characters introduced, the plot of the piece, and the action of the performers may all be conformable to nature, and yet not be conformable to any preëxisting reality. The characters there personified may never have existed; the events represented may never have transpired. And so, too, with poetry. The scenes and events it describes, the characters and passions it portrays, may all be natural though not real. Thus, in a certain sense, fiction itself may be true — true to the nature of things, and consequently true in the impressions it conveys. And hence the reason why fiction has always been made so subservient to the cause of truth.

Allowing, then, that poetry is nothing but fiction, that all it describes is false in point of fact, still its elements have a real existence, and the impressions we receive can be erroneous so far only as the views presented to the mind are garbled and false to nature. And this is a fault incident to the artist, and not inherent in the art itself. So that we may fairly conclude, from these considerations, that the natural tendency of poetry is to give us correct moral impressions, and thereby advance the cause of truth and the improvement of society.

There is another very important view of the subject arising out of the origin and nature of poetry, and its intimate connection with individual character and the character of society.

The origin of poetry loses itself in the shades of a remote and fabulous age, of which we have only vague and uncertain traditions. Its fountain, like that of the river of the desert, springs up in a distant and unknown region, the theme of visionary story and the subject of curious speculation. Doubtless, however, it originated amid the scenes of pastoral life and in the quiet and repose of a golden age. There is something in the soft melancholy of the groves which pervades the heart and kindles the imagination. Their retirement is favorable to the musings of the poetic mind. The trees that waved their leafy branches to the summer wind or heaved and groaned beneath the passing storm, the shadow moving on the grass, the bubbling brook, the insect skimming on its surface, the receding valley and the distant mountain — these would be some of the elements of pastoral song. Its subject would naturally be the complaint of a shepherd and the charms of some gentle shepherdess —

> "A happy soul, that all the way
> To heaven hath a summer's day."

It is natural, too, that the imagination, familiar with the outward world, and connecting the idea of the changing seasons and the spontaneous fruits of the earth with the agency of some unknown power that regulated and produced them, should suggest the thought of presiding deities, propitious in the smiling sky and adverse in the storm. The fountain that gushed up as if to meet the thirsty lip was made the dwelling of a nymph; the grove that lent its shelter and repose from the heat of noon became the abode of dryads; a god presided over shepherds and their flocks, and a goddess shook the yellow harvest from her lap. These deities were propitiated by songs and festive rites. And thus poetry added new charms to the simplicity and repose of bucolic life, and the poet mingled in his verse the delights of rural ease and the praise of the rural deities which bestowed them.

Such was poetry in those happy ages, when, camps and courts unknown, life was itself an eclogue. But in later days it sang the achievements of Grecian and Roman heroes, and pealed in the war-song of the Gothic Skald. These early essays were rude and unpolished. As nations advanced in civilization and refinement poetry advanced with them. In each successive age it became the image of their thoughts and feelings, of their manners, customs, and characters; for poetry is but the warm expression of the thoughts and feelings of a people, and we speak of it as being national when the character of a nation shines visibly and distinctly through it.

Thus, for example, Castilian poetry is characterized by sounding expressions, and that pomp and majesty so peculiar to Spanish manners and character. On the other hand, English poetry possesses in a high degree the charms of rural and moral feeling; it flows onward like a woodland stream, in which we see the reflection of the sylvan landscape and of the heaven above us.

It is from this intimate connection of poetry with the manners, customs, and characters of nations, that one of its highest uses is drawn. The impressions produced by poetry upon national character, at any period, are again reproduced, and give a more pronounced and individual character to the poetry of a subsequent period. And hence it is that the poetry of a nation sometimes throws so strong a light upon the page of its history, and renders luminous those obscure passages which often baffle the long-searching eye of studious erudition. In this view, poetry assumes new importance with all who search for historic truth. Besides, the view of the various fluctuations of the human mind, as exhibited, not in history, but in the poetry of successive epochs, is more interesting, and less liable to convey erroneous impressions, than any record of mere events. The great advantage drawn from the study of history is not to treasure up in the mind a multitude of disconnected facts, but from these facts to derive some conclusions, tending to illustrate the movements of the general mind, the progress of society, the manners, customs, and institutions, the moral and intellectual character of mankind in different nations, at different times, and under the operation of dif-

ferent circumstances. Historic facts are chiefly
valuable as exhibiting intellectual phenomena. And,
so far as poetry exhibits these phenomena more perfectly and distinctly than history does, so far is it
superior to history. The history of a nation is the
external symbol of its character; from it we reason
back to the spirit of the age that fashioned its shad-
owy outline. But poetry is the spirit of the age itself
—embodied in the forms of language, and speaking
in a voice that is audible to the external as well as
the internal sense. . . .

Besides, there are epochs which have no contem-
poraneous history; but have left in their popular
poetry pretty ample materials for estimating the
character of the times. The events, indeed, therein
recorded may be exaggerated facts, or vague traditions, or inventions entirely apocryphal; yet they
faithfully represent the spirit of the ages which produced them; they contain direct allusions and incidental circumstances, too insignificant in themselves
to have been fictitious, and yet on that very account
the most important parts of the poem in an historical
point of view. Such, for example, are the "Nibelungen Lied" in Germany; the "Poema del Cid"
in Spain; and the "Songs of the Troubadours" in
France. Hence poetry comes in for a large share
in that high eulogy which, in the true spirit of the
scholar, a celebrated German critic has bestowed
upon letters: "If we consider literature in its widest

sense, as the voice which gives expression to human
intellect — as the aggregate mass of symbols, in
which the spirit of an age or the character of a nation
is shadowed forth, then indeed a great and various
literature is, without doubt, the most valuable possession of which any nation can boast." [1]

From all these considerations, we are forced to the
conclusion that poetry is a subject of far greater importance in itself, and in its bearing upon the condition of society, than the majority of mankind would
be willing to allow. . . . It seems every way important that now, while we are forming our literature,
we should make it as original, characteristic, and
national as possible. To effect this, it is not necessary that the warwhoop should ring in every line,
and every page be rife with scalps, tomahawks,
and wampum. Shade of Tecumseh forbid! The
whole secret lies in Sidney's maxim — "Look in
thy heart and write." For —

> "Cantars non pot gaire valer.
> Si d'inz del cor no mov lo chang." [2]

Of this anon. We will first make a few remarks upon
the word national, as applied to the literature of a
country; for when we speak of a national poetry

[1] Schlegel, "Lectures on the History of Literature," vol. i.
lec. vii.

[2]   "The poet's song is little worth,
If it moveth not from within the heart."

we do not employ the term in that vague and indefinite way in which many writers use it.

A national literature, then, in the widest signification of the words, embraces every mental effort made
by the inhabitants of a country, through the medium
of the press. Every book written by a citizen of a
country belongs to its national literature. But the
term has also a more peculiar and appropriate definition; for, when we say that the literature of a
country is national, we mean that it bears upon it the
stamp of national character. We refer to those distinguishing features which literature receives from
the spirit of a nation — from its scenery and climate,
its historic recollections, its government, its various
institutions — from all those national peculiarities
which are the result of no positive institutions; and,
in a word, from the thousand external circumstances,
which either directly or indirectly exert an influence
upon the literature of a nation, and give it a marked
and individual character, distinct from that of the
literature of other nations. . . .

Every one acquainted with the works of the
English poets must have noted that a moral feeling
and a certain rural quiet and repose are among their
most prominent characteristics. The features of
their native landscape are transferred to the printed
page, and as we read we hear the warble of the
skylark — the "hollow murmuring wind, or silver
rain." The shadow of the woodland scene lends a
pensive shadow to the ideal world of poetry.

[Here the writer introduces a number of characteristic rural descriptions from English poems, beautiful in themselves and illustrative of his argument, but not necessary to it.]

Still, with all this taste for the charms of rural description and sylvan song, pastoral poetry has never been much cultivated nor much admired in England. . . . Nor is this remarkable. For though the love of rural ease is characteristic of the English, yet the rigors of their climate render their habits of pastoral life anything but delightful. . . . On the contrary, the poetry of the Italians, the Spaniards, and the Portuguese is redolent of the charms of pastoral indolence and enjoyment; for they inhabit countries in which pastoral life is a reality and not a fiction, where the winter's sun will almost make you seek the shade, and the summer nights are mild and beautiful in the open air. The babbling brook and cooling breeze are luxuries in a southern clime, where you

> "See the sun set, sure he'll rise to-morrow,
> Not through a misty morning twinkling, weak as
> A drunken man's dead eye, in maudlin sorrow,
> But with all heaven t' himself."

A love of indolence and a warm imagination are characteristic of the inhabitants of the South. These are natural effects of a soft, voluptuous climate. It is there a luxury to let the body lie at ease, stretched by a fountain in the lazy stillness of a summer noon, and suffer the dreamy fancy to lose itself in idle reverie and give a form to the wind and a spirit to the shadow and the leaf. Hence the prevalence of personification and the exaggerations of figurative language, so characteristic of the poetry of southern nations. . . .

We repeat, then, that we wish our native poets would give a more national character to their writings. In order to effect this they have only to write more naturally, to write from their own feelings and impressions, from the influence of what they see around them, and not from any preconceived notions of what poetry ought to be, caught by reading many books and imitating many models. This is peculiarly true in descriptions of natural scenery. In these let us have no more skylarks and nightingales. For us they only warble in books. A painter might as well introduce an elephant or a rhinoceros into a New England landscape. We would not restrict our poets in the choice of their subjects or the scenes of their story; but, when they sing under an American sky and describe a native landscape, let the description be graphic, as if it had been seen and not imagined. We wish, too, to see the figures and imagery of poetry a little more characteristic, as if drawn from nature and not from books. . . .

As the human mind is so constituted that all men receive to a greater or less degree a complexion

from those with whom they are conversant, the
writer who means to school himself to poetic composition — we mean so far as regards style and
diction — should be very careful what authors he
studies. He should leave the present age and go
back to the olden time. He should make, not the
writings of an individual, but the whole body of
English classical literature his study. There is a
strength of expression, a clearness, and force and
raciness of thought in the elder English poets which
we may look for in vain among those who flourish in
these days of verbiage. Truly, the degeneracy of
modern poetry is no schoolboy declamation! The
stream, whose fabled fountain gushes from the
Grecian mount, flowed brightly through those ages,
when the souls of men stood forth in the rugged freedom of nature and gave a wild and romantic character to the ideal landscape. But in these practical
days, whose spirit has so unsparingly leveled to the
even surface of utility the bold irregularities of human genius, and lopped off the luxuriance of poetic
feeling which once lent its grateful shade to the
haunts of song, that stream has spread itself into
stagnant pools which exhale an unhealthy atmosphere, while the party-colored bubbles that glitter on
its surface show the corruption from which they
spring.

Another circumstance which tends to give an effem-
inate and unmanly character to our literature is

the precocity of our writers. Premature exhibitions
of talent are an unstable foundation to build a national literature upon. Roger Ascham, the school-
master of princes, and for the sake of antithesis, we
suppose, called the Prince of Schoolmasters, has
well said of precocious minds: "They be like trees
that showe forth faire blossoms and broad leaves
in spring-time, but bring out small and not long-
lasting fruit in harvest-time; and that, only such as
fall and rott before they be ripe, and so never or
seldome come to any good at all." It is natural that
the young should be enticed by the wreaths of literary
fame, whose hues are so passing beautiful even to the
more sober-sighted, and whose flowers breathe around
them such exquisite perfumes. Many are deceived
into a misconception of their talents by the indiscreet
and indiscriminate praise of friends. They think
themselves destined to redeem the glory of their age
and country; to shine as "bright particular stars";
but in reality their genius

"Is like the glow-worm's light the apes so wondered at,
    Which, when they gathered sticks and laid upon 't,
    And blew — and blew — turned tail and went out
    presently."

We have set forth the portrait of modern poetry
in rather gloomy colors; for we really think that the
greater part of what is published in this book-writing
age ought in justice to suffer the fate of the children

of Thetis, whose immortality was tried by fire. We hope, however, that ere long some one of our most gifted bards will throw his fetters off, and, relying in himself alone, fathom the recesses of his own mind, and bring up rich pearls from the secret depths of thought.

OLIVER WENDELL HOLMES

1809-1894

ONE of the most alert intelligences produced in America, Dr. HOLMES — distinctively a Bostonian — filled a wide place. He was a physician, and, besides his practice, was Professor of Anatomy and Physiology in Dartmouth from 1838, and at Harvard from 1847 to 1882, taking high rank as an authority. While still in college he was known as a humorous poet, and later life brought knowledge and wisdom, infusing his verse with beauty, philosophy, and an unaffected pathos.

By 1857 HOLMES had won an enviable place, both in his profession, as poet, and as popular lecturer. But in that year began the *Atlantic Monthly*, LOWELL its first editor, who insisted on prose contributions from HOLMES. Thus came the original, varied, wise, and witty papers called "Autocrat of the Breakfast-Table." In them — as well as in succeeding series, "Professor at the Breakfast-Table" (1859), "Poet at the Breakfast-Table" (1872), and the last and most autobiographical notes, "Over the Tea-cups" (1891) — appeared some of the author's finest poems. "The Chambered Nautilus" was in Number IV of "The Autocrat," most of which is given in this volume, and many others of the most widely known were among them. These papers are considered HOLMES's best work.

The author wrote several novels, — "Elsie Venner," "The Guardian Angel," and "A Mortal Antipathy" — all turning on the mysteries of heredity: profoundly interesting, but rather as studies in the abnormal than as artistic fiction.

The combination of genial fun with pathos, witty scintillation with thoughtful profundity, warm human sympathy with free religious aspiration (his creed, as he said, being "in two words — the two first of the Paternoster"), diffuse an inspiring cheer and delight, while the author's literary felicity, whether in prose or poetry, is altogether admirable.

TABLE TALK

[I AM so well pleased with my boarding-house that I intend to remain there, perhaps for years. Of course I shall have a great many conversations to report, and they will necessarily be of different tone and on different subjects. The talks are like the breakfasts, — sometimes dipped toast, and sometimes dry. You must take them as they come. How can I do what all these letters ask me to? No. 1 wants serious and earnest thought. No. 2 (letter smells of bad cigars) must have more jokes; wants me to tell a "good storey" which he has copied out for me. (I suppose two letters before the word "good" refer to some Doctor of Divinity who told the story.) No. 3 (in female hand) — more poetry. No. 4 wants something that would be of use to a practical man. (*Prahctical mahn* he probably pronounces it.) No. 5. (gilt-edged, sweet-scented) — "more sentiment," — "heart's outpourings."

My dear friends, one and all, I can do nothing but report such remarks as I happen to have made at our breakfast-table. Their character will depend on many accidents, — a good deal on the particular persons in the company to whom they were addressed. It so happens that those which follow

were mainly intended for the divinity-student and
the schoolmistress; though others, whom I need not
mention, saw fit to interfere, with more or less propriety, in the conversation.   This is one of my privileges as a talker; and of course, if I was not talking
for our whole company, I don't expect all the readers
of this periodical to be interested in my notes of what
was said.   Still, I think there may be a few that will
rather like this vein, — possibly prefer it to a livelier
one, — serious young men, and young women generally, in life's roseate parenthesis from —— years of
age to —— inclusive. . . .]

— The more we study the body and the mind, the
more we find both to be governed, not *by*, but *according to* laws, such as we observe in the larger universe. — You think you know all about *walking*, —
don't you, now? Well, how do you suppose your
lower limbs are held to your body? They are sucked
up by two cupping vessels ("cotyloid" — cup-like—
cavities), and held there as long as you live, and
longer.   At any rate, you think you move them backward and forward at such a rate as your will determines, don't you?   On the contrary, they swing just
as any other pendulums swing, at a fixed rate, determined by their length. You can alter this by
muscular power, as you can take hold of the pendulum
of a clock and make it move faster or slower; but
your ordinary gait is timed by the same mechanism
as the movements of the solar system. . . .

Just as we find a mathematical rule at the bottom of many of the bodily movements, just so thought may be supposed to have its regular cycles. Such or such a thought comes round periodically, in its turn. Accidental suggestions, however, so far interfere with the regular cycles, that we may find them practically beyond our power of recognition. Take all this for what it is worth, but at any rate you will agree that there are certain particular thoughts that do not come up once a day, nor once a week, but that a year would hardly go round without your having them pass through your mind. Here is one which comes up at intervals in this way. Some one speaks of it, and there is an instant and eager smile of assent in the listener or listeners. Yes, indeed; they have often been struck by it.

All at once a conviction flashes through us that we have been in the same precise circumstances as at the present instant, once or many times before.

O, dear, yes! — said one of the company, — everybody has had that feeling.

The landlady didn't know anything about such notions; it was an idee in folks' heads, she expected.

The schoolmistress said, in a hesitating sort of way, that she knew the feeling well, and didn't like to experience it; it made her think she was a ghost, sometimes.

The young fellow whom they call John said he knew all about it; he had just lighted a cheroot the

other day, when a tremendous conviction all at once
came over him that he had done just that same thing
ever so many times before. I looked severely at him,
and his countenance immediately fell — *on the side
toward me;* I cannot answer for the other, for he can
wink and laugh with either half of his face without
the other half's knowing it.

— I have noticed — I went on to say — the following circumstances connected with these sudden impressions. First, that the condition which seems
to be the duplicate of a former one is often very
trivial, — one that might have presented itself a
hundred times. Secondly, that the impression is
very evanescent, and that it is rarely, if ever, recalled
by any voluntary effort, at least after any time has
elapsed. Thirdly, that there is a disinclination to
record the circumstances, and a sense of incapacity
to reproduce the state of mind in words. Fourthly,
I have often felt that the duplicate condition had not
only occurred once before, but that it was familiar
and, as it seemed, habitual. Lastly, I have had the
same convictions in my dreams.

How do I account for it? — Why, there are several
ways that I can mention, and you may take your
choice. The first is that which the young lady
hinted at; — that these flashes are sudden recollections of a previous existence. I don't believe that;
for I remember a poor student I used to know told
me he had such a conviction one day when he was

blacking his boots, and I can't think he had ever lived in another world where they use Day and Martin.

Some think that Dr. Wigan's doctrine of the brain's being a double organ, its hemispheres working together like the two eyes, accounts for it. One of the hemispheres hangs fire, they suppose, and the small interval between the perceptions of the nimble and the sluggish half seems an indefinitely long period, and therefore the second perception appears to be the copy of another, ever so old. But even allowing the center of perception to be double, I can see no good reason for supposing this indefinite lengthening of the time, nor any analogy that bears it out. It seems to me most likely that the coincidence of circumstances is very partial, but that we take this partial resemblance for identity, as we occasionally do resemblances of persons. A momentary posture of circumstances is so far like some preceding one that we accept it as exactly the same, just as we accost a stranger occasionally, mistaking him for a friend. The apparent similarity may be owing, perhaps, quite as much to the mental state at the time, as to the outward circumstances.

— Here is another of these curiously recurring remarks. I have said it, and heard it many times, and occasionally met with something like it in books, — somewhere in Bulwer's novels, I think, and in one of the works of Mr. Olmsted, I know.

Memory, imagination, old sentiments and associa-

tions, are more readily reached through the sense of SMELL *than by almost any other channel.*

Of course the particular odors which act upon each person's susceptibilities differ. — O, yes! I will tell you some of mine. The smell of *phosphorus* is one of them. During a year or two of adolescence I used to be dabbling in chemistry a good deal, and as about that time I had my little aspirations and passions like another, some of these things got mixed up with each other: orange-colored fumes of nitrous acid, and visions as bright and transient; reddening litmus-paper, and blushing cheeks; — *eheu!*

"Soles occidere et redire possunt,"

but there is no reagent that will redden the faded roses of eighteen hundred and — spare them! But, as I was saying, phosphorus fires this train of associations in an instant; its luminous vapors with their penetrating odor throw me into a trance; it comes to me in a double sense "trailing clouds of glory." Only the confounded Vienna matches, *ohne phosphorgeruch*, have worn my sensibilities a little.

Then there is the *marigold.* When I was of smallest dimensions, and wont to ride impacted between the knees of fond parental pair, we would sometimes cross the bridge to the next village-town and stop opposite a low, brown, "gambrel-roofed" cottage. Out of it would come one Sally, sister of its swarthy tenant, swarthy herself, shady-lipped, sad-voiced, and, bending over her flower-bed, would gather a "posy," as she called it, for the little boy. Sally lies in the churchyard with a slab of blue slate at her head, lichen-crusted, and leaning a little within the last few years. Cottage, garden-beds, posies, grenadier-like rows of seedling onions, — stateliest of vegetables, — all are gone, but the breath of a marigold brings them all back to me.

Perhaps the herb *everlasting*, the fragrant *immortelle* of our autumn fields, has the most suggestive odor to me of all those that set me dreaming. I can hardly describe the strange thoughts and emotions that come to me as I inhale the aroma of its pale, dry, rustling flowers. A something it has of sepulchral spicery, as if it had been brought from the core of some great pyramid, where it had lain on the breast of a mummied Pharaoh. Something, too, of immortality in the sad, faint sweetness lingering so long in its lifeless petals. Yet this does not tell why it fills my eyes with tears and carries me in blissful thought to the banks of asphodel that border the River of Life.

— I should not have talked so much about these personal susceptibilities, if I had not a remark to make about them which I believe is a new one. It is this. There may be a physical reason for the strange connection between the sense of smell and the mind. The olfactory nerve — so my friend, the Professor, tells me — is the only one directly connected with the hemispheres of the brain, the parts in which, as we have every reason to believe, the intellectual processes are performed. To speak more truly, the olfactory "nerve" is not a nerve at all, he says, but a part of the brain, an intimate connection with its anterior lobes. Whether this anatomical arrangement is at the bottom of the facts I have mentioned, I will not decide, but it is curious enough to be worth remembering. Contrast the sense of taste, as a source of suggestive impressions, with that of smell. Now the Professor assures me that you will find the nerve of taste has no immediate connection with the brain proper, but only with the prolongation of the spinal cord. . . .

Ah me! what strains and strophes of unwritten verse pulsate through my soul when I open a certain closet in the ancient house where I was born! On its shelves used to lie bundles of sweet-marjoram and pennyroyal and lavender and mint and catnip; there apples were stored until their seeds should grow black, which happy period there were sharp little milk-teeth always ready to anticipate; there peaches lay in the dark, thinking of the sunshine they had lost, until, like the hearts of saints that dream of heaven in their sorrow, they grew fragrant as the breath of angels. The odorous echo of a score of dead summers lingers yet in those dim recesses.

— Do I remember Byron's line about "striking the electric chain"? — To be sure I do. I sometimes

think the less the hint that stirs the automatic machinery of association, the more easily this moves us.
What can be more trivial than that old story of
opening the folio Shakespeare that used to lie in some
ancient English hall and finding the flakes of Christmas pastry between its leaves, shut up in them perhaps a hundred years ago?   And, lo! as one looks
on these poor relics of a bygone generation, the universe changes in the twinkling of an eye; old George
the Second is back again, and the elder Pitt is coming
into power, and General Wolfe is a fine, promising
young man, and over the Channel they are pulling
the Sieur Damiens to pieces with wild horses, and
across the Atlantic the Indians are tomahawking
Hirams and Jonathans and Jonases at Fort William
Henry; all the dead people who have been in the
dust so long — even to the stout-armed cook that
made the pastry — are alive again; the planet un-
winds a hundred of its luminous coils, and the pre-
cession of the equinoxes is retraced on the dial of
heaven!   And all this for a bit of pie crust!

— I will thank you for that pie, — said the pro-
voking young fellow whom I have named repeatedly.
He looked at it for a moment, and put his hands to
his eyes as if moved. — I was thinking, — he said
indistinctly —

— How?   What is 't? — said our landlady.

— I was thinking — said he — who was king of
England when this old pie was baked, — and it made

me feel bad to think how long he must have been
dead.

[Our landlady is a decent body, poor, and a
widow, of course; *cela va sans dire.* She told me her
story once; it was as if a grain of corn that had
been ground and bolted had tried to individualize
itself by a special narrative. There was the wooing
and the wedding, — the start in life, — the disappointment, — the children she had buried, — the
struggle against fate, — the dismantling of life, first
of its small luxuries, and then of its comforts, — the
broken spirits, — the altered character of the one on
whom she leaned, — and at last the death that came
and drew the black curtain between her and all her
earthly hopes.

I never laughed at my landlady after she had told
me her story, but I often cried, — not those pattering
tears that run off the eaves upon our neighbors'
grounds, the *stillicidium* of self-conscious sentiment,
but those which steal noiselessly through their con-
duits until they reach the cisterns lying round about
the heart; those tears that we weep inwardly with
unchanging features; — such I did shed for her often
when the imps of the boarding-house Inferno tugged
at her soul with their red-hot pincers.]

Young man, — I said, — the pasty you speak
lightly of is not old, but courtesy to those who labor
to serve us, especially if they are of the weaker sex,
is very old, and yet well worth retaining. May I

recommend to you the following caution, as a guide, whenever you are dealing with a woman, or an artist, or a poet; — if you are handling an editor or politician, it is superfluous advice.   I take it from the back of one of those little French toys which contain pasteboard figures moved by a small running stream of fine sand; Benjamin Franklin will translate it for you: *"Quoiqu'elle soit très solidement montée il faut ne pas* BRUTALISER *la machine."* — I will thank you for the pie, if you please.

[I took more of it than was good for me, — as much as $85°$, I should think, — and had an indigestion in consequence.   While I was suffering from it, I wrote some sadly desponding poems, and a theological essay which took a very melancholy view of creation. When I got better I labeled them all "Pie-crust," and laid them by as scarecrows and solemn warnings. I have a number of books on my shelves that I should like to label with some such title; but, as they have great names on their title-pages, — Doctors of Divinity, some of them, — it wouldn't do.] . . .

— There is no power I envy so much — said the divinity-student — as that of seeing analogies and making comparisons.   I don't understand how it is that some minds are continually coupling thoughts or objects that seem not in the least related to each other, until all at once they are put in a certain light, and you wonder that you did not always see that they were as like as a pair of twins.   It appears to me a sort of miraculous gift.

[He is rather a nice young man, and I think has an appreciation of the higher mental qualities remarkable for one of his years and training. I try his head occasionally as housewives try eggs, — give it an intellectual shake and hold it up to the light, so to speak, to see if it has life in it, actual or potential, or only contains lifeless albumen.]

You call it *miraculous*, — I replied, — tossing the expression with my facial eminence, a little smartly, I fear. — Two men are walking by the polyphlœsbœan ocean, one of them having a small tin cup with which he can scoop up a gill of sea-water when he will, and the other nothing but his hands, which will hardly hold water at all, — and you call the tin cup a miraculous possession! It is the ocean that is the miracle, my infant apostle! Nothing is clearer than that all things are in all things, and that just according to the intensity and extension of our mental being we shall see the many in the one and the one in the many. Did Sir Isaac think what he was saying when he made *his* speech about the ocean, — the child and the pebbles, you know? Did he mean to speak slightingly of a pebble? Of a spherical solid which stood sentinel over its compartment of space before the stone that became the pyramids had grown solid, and has watched it until now! A body which knows all the currents of force that traverse the globe; which holds by invisible threads to the ring of Saturn and the belt of Orion! A body from the

contemplation of which an archangel could infer the
entire inorganic universe as the simplest of corollaries!
A throne of the all-pervading Deity, who has guided
its every atom since the rosary of heaven was strung
with beaded stars!

So, — to return to *our* walk by the ocean, — if all
that poetry has dreamed, all that insanity has raved,
all that maddening narcotics have driven through the
brains of men, or smothered passion nursed in the
fancies of women, — if the dreams of colleges and
convents and boarding-schools, — if every human
feeling that sighs, or smiles, or curses, or shrieks, or
groans, should bring all their innumerable images,
such as come with every hurried heart-beat, — the
epic which held them all, though its letters filled the
zodiac, would be but a cupful from the infinite ocean
of similitudes and analogies that rolls through the
universe.

[The divinity-student honored himself by the way
in which he received this. He did not swallow it at
once, neither did he reject it; but he took it as a
pickerel takes the bait, and carried it off with him to
his hole (in the fourth story) to deal with at his
leisure.] . . .

— I have often seen pianoforte players and singers
make such strange motions over their instruments or
song-books that I wanted to laugh at them. "Where
did our friends pick up all these fine ecstatic airs?"
I would say to myself. Then I would remember **My**

Lady in "Marriage à la Mode," and amuse myself
with thinking how affectation was the same thing in
Hogarth's time and in our own.   But one day I
bought me a canary-bird and hung him up in a cage
at my window.   By and by he found himself at
home, and began to pipe his little tunes; and there he
was, sure enough, swimming and waving about, with
all the droopings and liftings and languishing side-
turnings of the head that I had laughed at.   And now
I should like to ask, WHO taught him all this? — and
me, through him, that the foolish head was not the
one swinging itself from side to side and bowing and
nodding over the music, but that other which was
passing its shallow and self-satisfied judgment on a
creature made of finer clay than the frame which
carried that same head upon its shoulders? . . .

— Weaken moral obligations? — No, not weaken,
but define them.   When I preach that sermon I
spoke of the other day, I shall have to lay down
some principles not fully recognized in some of your
text-books.

I should have to begin with one most formidable
preliminary.   You saw an article the other day in
one of the journals, perhaps, in which some old
Doctor or other said quietly that patients were very
apt to be fools and cowards.   But a great many of
the clergyman's patients are not only fools and
cowards, but also liars.

[Immense sensation at the table. — Sudden retire-

ment of the angular female in oxydated bombazine.
Movement of adhesion — as they say in the Chamber
of Deputies — on the part of the young fellow they
call John. Falling of the old-gentleman-opposite's
lower jaw — (gravitation is beginning to get the
better of him). Our landlady to Benjamin Franklin,
briskly, — Go to school right off, there's a good boy!
Schoolmistress curious, — takes a quick glance at
divinity-student. Divinity-student slightly flushed;
draws his shoulders back a little, as if a big falsehood — or truth — had hit him in the forehead.
Myself calm.] . . .

— If you think I have used rather strong language,
I shall have to read something to you out of the book
of this keen and witty scholar, — the great Erasmus,
— who "laid the egg of the Reformation which
Luther hatched." Oh, you never read his *Naufra-
gium*, or "Shipwreck," did you? Of course not; for,
if you had, I don't think you would have given me
credit — or discredit — for entire originality in that
speech of mine. That men are cowards in the contemplation of futurity he illustrates by the extraor-
dinary antics of many on board the sinking vessel;
that they are fools, by their praying to the sea, and
making promises to bits of wood from the true cross,
and all manner of similar nonsense; that they are
fools, cowards, and liars all at once, by this story:
I will put it into rough English for you. — "I couldn't
help laughing to hear one fellow bawling out, so that

he might be sure to be heard, a promise to Saint Christopher of Paris — the monstrous statue in the great church there — that he would give him a wax taper as big as himself. 'Mind what you promise!' said an acquaintance that stood near him, poking him with his elbow; 'you couldn't pay for it, if you sold all your things at auction.' 'Hold your tongue, you donkey!' said the fellow, — but softly, so that Saint Christopher should not hear him, — 'do you think I'm in earnest? If I once get my foot on dry ground, catch me giving him so much as a tallow candle!'"

Now, therefore, remembering that those who have been loudest in their talk about the great subject of which we were speaking have not necessarily been wise, brave, and true men, but, on the contrary, have very often been wanting in one or two or all of the qualities these words imply, I should expect to find a good many doctrines current in the schools which I should be obliged to call foolish, cowardly, and false.

— So you would abuse other people's beliefs, sir, and yet not tell us your own creed! — said the divinity-student, coloring up with a spirit for which I liked him all the better.

— I have a creed, — I replied; none better, and none shorter. It is told in two words, — the two first of the Paternoster. And when I say these words I mean them. And when I compared the human will to a drop in a crystal, and said I meant to *define*

moral obligations, and not weaken them, this was
what I intended to express: that the fluent, self-
determining power of human beings is a very strictly
limited agency in the universe. The chief planes
of its enclosing solid are, of course, organization,
education, condition. Organization may reduce the
power of the will to nothing, as in some idiots; and
from this zero the scale mounts upwards by slight
gradations. Education is only second to nature.
Imagine all the infants born this year in Boston and
Timbuctoo to change places! Condition does less,
but "Give me neither poverty nor riches" was the
prayer of Agur, and with good reason. If there is
any improvement in modern theology, it is in getting
out of the region of pure abstractions and taking
these everyday working forces into account. The
great theological question now heaving and throbbing
in the minds of Christian men is this: —

No, I won't talk about these things now. My
remarks might be repeated, and it would give my
friends pain to see with what personal incivilities I
should be visited. Besides, what business has a
mere boarder to be talking about such things at a
breakfast-table? Let him make puns. To be sure,
he was brought up among the Christian fathers, and
learned his alphabet out of a quarto "Concilium
Tridentinum." He has also heard many thousand
theological lectures by men of various denomina-
tions; and it is not at all to the credit of these

teachers, if he is not fit by this time to express an opinion on theological matters.

I know well enough that there are some of you who had a great deal rather see me stand on my head than use it for any purpose of thought. . . .

— Well, I can't be savage with you for wanting to laugh, and I like to make you laugh, well enough, when I can. But then observe this: if the sense of the ridiculous is one side of an impressible nature, it is very well; but if that is all there is in a man, he had better have been an ape at once, and so have stood at the head of his profession. Laughter and tears are meant to turn the wheel of the same machinery of sensibility; one is wind-power, and the other water-power; that is all. I have often heard the Professor talk about hysterics as being Nature's cleverest illustration of the reciprocal convertibility of the two states of which these acts are the manifestations; but you may see it every day in children; and if you want to choke with stifled tears a sight of the transition, as it shows itself in older years, go and see Mr. Blake play *Jesse Rural.* . . .

— Oh, indeed, no! — I am not ashamed to make you laugh, occasionally. I think I could read you something I have in my desk which would probably make you smile. Perhaps I will read it one of these days, if you are patient with me when I am sentimental and reflective; not just now. The ludicrous has its place in the universe; it is not a human invention, but one of the Divine ideas, illustrated in the practical jokes of kittens and monkeys long before Aristophanes or Shakespeare.   How curious it is that we always consider solemnity and the absence of all gay surprises and encounter of wits as essential to the idea of the future life of those whom we thus deprive of half their faculties and then call *blessed!*   There are not a few who, even in this life, seem to be preparing themselves for that smileless eternity to which they look forward, by banishing all gayety from their hearts and all joyousness from their countenances. I meet one such in the street not unfrequently, a person of intelligence and education, but who gives me (and all that he passes) such a rayless and chilling look of recognition, — something as if he were one of Heaven's assessors, come down to "doom" every acquaintance he met, — that I have sometimes begun to sneeze on the spot, and gone home with a violent cold, dating from that instant.   I don't doubt he would cut his kitten's tail off, if he caught her playing with it.   Please tell me, who taught her to play with it ?

No, no! — give me a chance to talk to you, my fellow-boarders, and you need not be afraid that I shall have any scruples about entertaining you, if I can do it, as well as giving you some of my serious thoughts, and perhaps my sadder fancies.   I know nothing in English or any other literature more admirable than that sentiment of Sir Thomas Browne:

"EVERY MAN TRULY LIVES, SO LONG AS HE ACTS HIS NATURE, OR SOME WAY MAKES GOOD THE FACULTIES OF HIMSELF."

I find the great thing in this world is not so much where we stand, as in what direction we are moving. To reach the port of heaven, we must sail sometimes with the wind and sometimes against it, — but we must sail, and not drift, nor lie at anchor. There is one very sad thing in old friendships, to every mind that is really moving onward. It is this: that one cannot help using his early friends as the seaman uses the log, to mark his progress. . . .

Don't misunderstand that metaphor of heaving the log, I beg you. It is merely a smart way of saying that we cannot avoid measuring our rate of movement by those with whom we have long been in the habit of comparing ourselves; and when they once become stationary, we can get our reckoning from them with painful accuracy. We see just what we were when they were our peers, and can strike the balance between that and whatever we may feel ourselves to be now. No doubt we may sometimes be mistaken. If we change our last simile to that very old and familiar one of a fleet leaving the harbor and sailing in company for some distant region, we can get what we want out of it. There is one of our companions; — her streamers were torn into rags before she had got into the open sea, then by and by her sails blew out of the ropes one after another, the

waves swept her deck, and as night came on we left
her a seeming wreck, as we flew under our pyramid
of canvas.   But lo! at dawn she is still in sight, — it
may be in advance of us.   Some deep ocean-current
has been moving her on, strong, but silent, — yes,
stronger than these noisy winds that puff our sails
until they are swollen as the cheeks of jubilant cher-
ubim.   And when at last the black steam-tug with
the skeleton arms, which comes out of the mist sooner
or later and takes us all in tow, grapples her and goes
off panting and groaning with her, it is to that harbor
where all wrecks are refitted, and where, alas! we,
towering in our pride, may never come. . . .

— Did I not say to you a little while ago that the
universe swam in an ocean of similitudes and analogies?   I will not quote Cowley, or Burns, or Wordsworth, just now, to show you what thoughts were
suggested to them by the simplest natural objects,
such as a flower or a leaf; but I will read you a few
lines, if you do not object, suggested by looking at
a section of one of those chambered shells to which
is given the name of Pearly Nautilus.   We need not
trouble ourselves about the distinction between this
and the Paper Nautilus, the *Argonauta* of the an-
cients.   The name applied to both shows that each
has long been compared to a ship, as you may see
more fully in Webster's Dictionary, or the "Ency-
clopedia," to which he refers.   If you will look into
Roget's Bridgewater Treatise, you will find a figure of

one of these shells, and a section of it.   The last will
show you the series of enlarging compartments suc-
cessively dwelt in by the animal that inhabits the
shell, which is built in a widening spiral.   Can you
find no lesson in this?

THE CHAMBERED NAUTILUS

This is the ship of pearl, which, poets feign,
    Sails the unshadowed main, —
    The venturous bark that flings
On the sweet summer wind its purpled wings
In gulfs enchanted, where the siren sings,
    And coral reefs lie bare,
Where the cold sea-maids rise to sun their streaming hair.

Its webs of living gauze no more unfurl;
    Wrecked is the ship of pearl!
    And every chambered cell,
Where its dim dreaming life was wont to dwell,
As the frail tenant shaped his growing shell,
    Before thee lies revealed, —
Its irised ceiling rent, its sunless crypt unsealed!

Year after year beheld the silent toil
    That spread his lustrous coil;
    Still, as the spiral grew,
He left the past year's dwelling for the new,
Stole with soft step its shining archway through,
    Built up its idle door,
Stretched in his last-found home, and knew the old no more.

Thanks for the heavenly message brought by thee,
    Child of the wandering sea,
    Cast from her lap forlorn!
From thy dead lips a clearer note is born
Than ever Triton blew from wreathèd horn!
    While on mine ear it rings,
Through the deep caves of thought I hear a voice that sings:—

Build thee more stately mansions, O my soul,
    As the swift seasons roll!
    Leave thy low-vaulted past!
Let each new temple, nobler than the last,
Shut thee from heaven with a dome more vast,
    Till thou at length art free,
Leaving thine outgrown shell by life's unresting sea!

HARRIET BEECHER STOWE

1811–1896

Of New England birth and training, a daughter of the famous Dr. LYMAN BEECHER, this lady went in her twenty-first year (1832) to Cincinnati, when her father became president of Lane Theological Seminary. Shortly after she was married to Professor CALVIN E. STOWE. Amid increasing family cares she was an industrious writer of articles and tales, and in 1849 collected some of these, in "The Mayflower; or Sketches of the Descendants of the Pilgrims." In 1851 the *National Era* of Washington asked her to write a story of slave life. In youth she had visited Kentucky, and her later residence just across the Ohio River in Cincinnati familiarized her with the negro character and with incessant cases of escaping fugitives. She had learned the best and the worst and the average result of slavery; her heart burned; the request fell upon prepared ground. She began " Uncle Tom's Cabin " as a brief tale, but it grew upon her; she was rapt with the power of it. The story seized upon the world; not only in America, where it was potent in arousing anti-slavery sentiment to a passion, but in England, and in twenty or more countries into whose languages it was rapidly translated.

Then came "Dred" (1856) another tale of slavery; and then a series of notable novels of New England life and character in which her keen perception, thoughtful reflection, captivating wit and humor, her intelligence and her ardent religious nature found scope, presented in a style, fluent, graceful, and alluring. The best known of these are: "The Minister's Wooing " (1859), from which a chapter on *Romance* is here given, "The Pearl of Orr's Island" (1862), "Old Town Folks " (1869), and "Sam Lawson's Fireside Stories " (1871). "Agnes of Sorrento " (1864) is a medieval romance, souvenir of a winter spent in Italy, and luminous with its atmosphere.

Mrs. STOWE was slight of person, somewhat quaint but charming in companionship, devotedly unselfish, spiritual in nature, and of a saint-like life. Her place as writer is secure in history, and in the hearts of her readers.

ROMANCE

THERE is no word in the English language more unceremoniously kicked and cuffed about, by what are called sensible people, than the word romance. When Mr. Smith or Mr. Stubbs has brought every wheel of life into such range and order that it is one steady, daily grind, — when they themselves have come into the habits and attitudes of the patient donkey who steps round and round the endlessly turning wheel of some machinery, then they fancy that they have gotten "the victory that overcometh the world."

All but this dead grind, and the dollars that come through the mill, is by them thrown into one waste "catch-all" and labeled *Romance*. Perhaps there was a time in Mr. Smith's youth, — he remembers it now, — when he read poetry, when his cheek was wet with strange tears, when a little song, ground out by an organ-grinder in the street, had power to set his heart beating and bring a mist before his eyes. Ah, in those days he had a vision! — a pair of soft eyes stirred him strangely; a little weak hand was laid on his manhood, and it shook and trembled; and then came all the humility, the aspiration, the fear, the hope, the high desire, the troubling of the waters by the descending angel of love, — and a little more and Mr. Smith might have become a man, instead of a banker! He thinks of it now, sometimes, as he looks across the fireplace after dinner and sees Mrs. Smith asleep, innocently shaking the bouquet of pink bows and Brussels lace that waves over her placid red countenance.

Mrs. Smith wasn't his first love, nor, indeed, any love at all; but they agree reasonably well. And as for poor Nellie, — well, she is dead and buried, — all that was stuff and romance. Mrs. Smith's money set him up in business, and Mrs. Smith is a capital manager, and he thanks God that he isn't romantic, and tells Smith Junior not to read poetry or novels, and to stick to realities.

"This is the victory that overcometh the world," — to learn to be fat and tranquil, to have warm fires and good dinners, to hang your hat on the same peg at the same hour every day, to sleep soundly all night, and never to trouble your head with a thought or imagining beyond.

But there are many people besides Mr. Smith who have gained this victory, — who have strangled their higher nature and buried it, and built over its grave the structure of their life, the better to keep it down. The fascinating Mrs. T., whose life is a whirl between ball and opera, point-lace, diamonds, and schemings of admiration for herself, and of establishments for her daughters, — there was a time, if you will believe me, when that proud, worldly woman was so humbled, under the touch of some mighty power, that she actually thought herself capable of being a poor man's wife. She thought she could live in a little, mean house on no-matter-what-street, with one servant, and make her own bonnets and mend her own clothes, and sweep the house Mondays, while Betty washed, — all for what? All because she thought that there was a man so noble, so true, so good, so high-minded, that to live with him in poverty, to be guided by him in adversity, to lean on him in every rough place of life, was a something nobler, better, purer, more satisfying, than French laces, opera boxes, and Madame Roget's best gowns.

Unfortunately, this was all romance, — there was no such man. There was, indeed, a person of very common, self-interested aims of worldly nature, whom she had credited at sight with an unlimited draft on all her better nature; and when the hour of discovery came, she awoke from her dream with a start and a laugh, and ever since has despised aspiration, and been busy with the realities of life, and feeds poor little Mary Jane, who sits by her in the opera box there, with all the fruit which she has picked from the bitter tree of knowledge. There is no end of the epigrams and witticisms which she can throw out, this elegant Mrs. T., on people who marry for love, lead prosy, worky lives, and put on their best

cap with pink ribbons for Sunday. "Mary Jane
shall never make a fool of herself;" but, even as she
speaks, poor Mary Jane's heart is dying within her
at the vanishing of a pair of whiskers from an opposite box, — which whiskers the poor little fool has
credited with a résumé drawn from her own imaginings of all that is grandest and most heroic, most
worshipful in man. By and by, when Mrs. T. finds
the glamour has fallen on her daughter, she wonders; she has "tried to keep novels out of the girl's
way, — where did she get these notions ?"

All prosaic, and all bitter, disenchanted people talk
as if poets and novelists *made* romance. They do,
— just as much as craters make volcanoes, — no
more. What is romance ? whence comes it ? Plato
spoke to the subject wisely, in his quaint way, some
two thousand years ago, when he said, "Man's soul,
in a former state, was winged, and soared among the
gods, and so it comes to pass that, in this life, when the
soul, by the power of music or poetry, or the sight of
beauty, hath her remembrance quickened, forthwith
there is a struggling and a pricking pain as of wings
trying to come forth, — even as children in teething."
And if an old heathen, two thousand years ago, dis-
coursed thus gravely of the romantic part of our
nature, whence comes it that in Christian lands we
think in so pagan a way of it, and turn the whole care
of it to ballad-makers, romancers, and opera-singers?

Let us look up in fear and reverence and say, "God

is the great maker of romance. He, from whose hand came man and woman, — He who strung the great harp of Existence with all its wild and wonderful and manifold chords, and attuned them to one another, — He is the great Poet of life." Every impulse of beauty, or heroism, and every craving for purer love, fairer perfection, nobler type and style of being than that which closes like a prison-house around us, in the dim, daily walk of life, is God's breath, God's impulse, God's reminder to the soul that there is something higher, sweeter, purer, yet to be attained. Therefore, man or woman, when thy ideal is shattered, — as shattered a thousand times it must be, — when the vision fades, the rapture burns out, turn not away in skepticism and bitterness, saying, "There is nothing better for a man than that he should eat and drink," but rather cherish the revelations of those hours as prophecies and foreshadowings of something real and possible, yet to be attained in the manhood of immortality. The scoffing spirit that laughs at romance is an apple of the Devil's own handling from the bitter tree of knowledge; it opens the eyes only to see eternal nakedness.

If ever you have had a romantic, uncalculating friendship, — a boundless worship and belief in some hero of your soul, — if ever you have so loved, that all cold prudence, all selfish worldly considerations have gone down like driftwood before a river flooded with new rain from heaven, so that you even forgot yourself, and were ready to cast your whole being into the chasm of existence, as an offering before the feet of another, and all for nothing, — if you awoke bitterly betrayed and deceived, still give thanks to God that you have had one glimpse of heaven. The door now shut will open again. Rejoice that the noblest capability of your eternal inheritance has been made known to you; treasure it, as the highest honor of your being, that ever you could so feel, — that so divine a guest ever possessed your soul.

By such experiences are we taught the pathos, the sacredness of life; and if we use them wisely, our eyes will ever after be anointed to see what poems, what romances, what sublime tragedies lie around us in the daily walk of life, "written not with ink, but on fleshly tables of the heart." The dullest street of the most prosaic town has matter in it for more smiles, more tears, more intense excitement, than ever were written in story or sung in poem; the reality is there, of which the romancer is the second-hand recorder.

So much of a plea we put in boldly, because we foresee grave heads beginning to shake over our history, and doubts rising in reverend and discreet minds whether this history is going to prove anything but a love-story, after all.

We do assure you, right reverend sir, and you, most discreet madam, that it is not going to prove anything else; and you will find, if you will follow us, that there is as much romance burning under the snowbanks of cold Puritan preciseness as if Dr. Hopkins had been brought up to attend operas instead of metaphysical preaching, and Mary had been nourished on Byron's poetry instead of "Edwards on the Affections."

The innocent credulities, the subtle deceptions, that were quietly at work under the grave, white curls of the Doctor's wig were exactly of the kind which have beguiled man in all ages, when near the sovereign presence of her who is born for his destiny; and as for Mary, what did it avail her that she could say the Assembly's Catechism from end to end without tripping, and that every habit of her life beat time to practical realities, steadily as the parlor clock? The wildest Italian singer or dancer, nursed on nothing but excitement from her cradle, never was more thoroughly possessed by the awful and solemn mystery of woman's life than this Puritan girl.

It is quite true that, the next morning after James' departure, she rose as usual in the dim gray, and was to be seen opening the kitchen door just at the moment when the birds were giving the first drowsy stir and chirp, — and that she went on setting the breakfast-table for the two hired men, who were bound to the fields with the oxen, — and that then she went on skimming cream for the butter, and getting ready to churn, and making up biscuit for the

Doctor's breakfast, when he and they should sit down together at a somewhat later hour; and as she moved about, doing all these things, she sung various scraps of old psalm-tunes; and the good Doctor, who was then busy with his early exercises of devotion, listened, as he heard the voice, now here, now there, and thought about angels and the millennium. Solemnly and tenderly there floated in at his open study-window, through the breezy lilacs, mixed with low of kine and bleat of sheep and hum of early wakening life, the little silvery ripples of that singing, somewhat mournful in its cadence, as if a gentle soul were striving to hush itself to rest. . . .

The tone of life in New England, so habitually earnest and solemn, breathed itself in the grave and plaintive melodies of the tunes then sung in the churches; and so these words, though in the saddest minor key, did not suggest to the listening ear of the auditor anything more than that pensive religious calm in which he delighted to repose. A contrast indeed they were, in their melancholy earnestness, to the exuberant carolings of a robin, who, apparently attracted by them, perched himself hard by in the lilacs, and struck up such a merry roulade as quite diverted the attention of the fair singer; in fact, the intoxication breathed in the strain of this little messenger, whom God had feathered and winged and filled to the throat with ignorant joy, came in singular contrast with the sadder notes breathed by that

creature of so much higher mold and fairer clay, —
that creature born for an immortal life.

But the good Doctor was inly pleased when she
sung, — and when she stopped, looked up from his
Bible wistfully, as missing something, he knew not
what; for he scarce thought how pleasant the little
voice was, or knew he had been listening to it, —
and yet he was in a manner enchanted by it, so
thankful and happy that he exclaimed with fervor,
"The lines are fallen unto me in pleasant places; yea,
I have a goodly heritage." So went the world with
him, full of joy and praise, because the voice and the
presence wherein lay his unsuspected life were se-
curely near, so certainly and constantly a part of his
daily walk that he had not even the trouble to wish
for them. But in that other heart, how was it? —
how with the sweet saint that was talking to herself
in psalms and hymns and spiritual songs?

The good child had remembered her mother's
parting words the night before, — "Put your mind
upon your duties," — and had begun her first conscious exercise of thought with a prayer that grace
might be given her to do it. But even as she spoke,
mingling and interweaving with that golden thread
of prayer was another consciousness, a life in another
soul, as she prayed that the grace of God might over-
shadow him, shield him from temptation, and lead
him up to heaven; and this prayer so got the start
of the other, that, ere she was aware, she had quite

forgotten self, and was feeling, living, thinking in that other life.

The first discovery she made, when she looked out into the fragrant orchard, whose perfumes steamed in at her window, and listened to the first chirping of birds among the old apple-trees, was one that has astonished many a person before her; it was this: she found that all that had made life interesting to her was suddenly gone.   She herself had not known that, for the month past, since James came from sea, she had been living in an enchanted land, — that New-port harbor, and every rock and stone, and every mat of yellow seaweed on the shore, that the two-mile road between the cottage and the white house of Zebedee Marvyn, every mullein-stalk, every juniper-tree, had all had a light and a charm which were sud-denly gone.   There had not been an hour in the day for the last four weeks that had not had its unsus-pected interest, — because he was at the white house; because, possibly, he might be going by, or coming in; nay, even in church, when she stood up to sing, and thought she was thinking only of God, had she not been conscious of that tenor voice that poured itself out by her side ? and though afraid to turn her head that way, had she not felt that he was there every moment, — heard every word of the sermon and prayer for him ?   The very vigilant care which her mother had taken to prevent private interviews had only served to increase the interest by throwing over it the veil of constraint and mystery. Silent looks, involuntary starts, things indicated, not expressed, — these are the most dangerous, the most seductive aliment of thought to a delicate and sensitive nature. If things were said out, they might not be said wisely, — they might repel by their freedom, or disturb by their unfitness; but what is only looked is sent into the soul through the imagination, which makes of it all that the ideal faculties desire.

In a refined and exalted nature, it is very seldom that the feeling of love, when once thoroughly aroused, bears any sort of relation to the reality of the object. It is commonly an enkindling of the whole power of the soul's love for whatever she considers highest and fairest; it is, in fact, the love of something divine and unearthly, which, by a sort of illusion, connects itself with a personality. Properly speaking, there is but One true, eternal Object of all that the mind conceives, in this trance of its exaltation. Disenchantment must come, of course; and in a love which terminates in happy marriage there is a tender and gracious process, by which, without shock or violence, the ideal is gradually sunk in the real, which, though found faulty and earthly, is still ever tenderly remembered as it seemed under the morning light of that enchantment. . . .

Nor was Mary wrong; for, as to every leaf and every flower there is an ideal to which the growth of the plant is constantly urging, so is there an ideal to every human being, — a perfect form in which it might appear, were every defect removed and every characteristic excellence stimulated to the highest point. Once in an age God sends to some of us a friend who loves in us, not a false imagining, an unreal character, but, looking through all the rubbish of our imperfections, loves in us the divine ideal of our nature, — loves, not the man that we are, but the angel that we may be. Such friends seem inspired by a divine gift of prophecy, — like the mother of St. Augustine, who, in the midst of the wayward, reckless youth of her son, beheld him in a vision, standing, clothed in white, a ministering priest at the right hand of God, — as he has stood for long ages since. Could a mysterious foresight unveil to us this resurrection form of the friends with whom we daily walk, compassed about with formal infirmity, we should follow them with faith and reverence through all the disguises of human faults and weaknesses, "waiting for the manifestation of the sons of God."

HENRY WARD BEECHER

1813–1887

BETWEEN this man and his lovely sister, Mrs. STOWE, there was an intimate comradeship and confidence from babyhood to the end of life; they were twins of noble goodness. And as to his great powers, his personal influence was wider and more potent than that of any other man of his time — not an official influence, of governmental or military or institutional authority, but the result of the man himself. As preacher, pastor, lecturer, orator, editor, writer, citizen, he was very great, and so recognized.

BEECHER'S literary work was chiefly in many volumes of sermons and religious addresses, but he wrote a most inspiring "Life of Jesus the Christ"; a novel of New England life, "Norwood," a genuine Yankee product; and many editorial articles for the papers he edited, — *The Western Farmer and Gardener*, when he was in the West, and the *Independent* and *The Christian Union* when he lived in Brooklyn. Besides these he wrote "Star Papers" (signed with a *) for the *Independent*, and numberless brief essays and sketches for other papers, many of which have been published in book form. In these he gave freer play to the humor which gleamed and laughed under the surface of all his work, occasionally coming out, even in his sermons. Like all real orators, he knew the secret of the kinship between smile and tear, and his great intellect, poetic fancy, and "power of speech to move men's blood" owed not a little to his exuberant sense of humor. But his genius was essentially that of the orator, and the trifle taken to represent him here (one of the "Star Papers") shows his sympathy with nature, his imaginative use of common things, his shrewd sense, his playful mood, and the native religious trend of his spirit rather than his intellectual strength.

DREAM–CULTURE

LENOX, MASS., *August* 10, 1854.

THERE is something in *the owning* of a piece of ground, which affects me as did the old ruins in England. I am free to confess that the value of a farm is not chiefly in its crops of cereal grain, its orchards of fruit, and in its herds; but in those larger and more easily reapt harvests of associations, fancies, and dreamy broodings which it begets. From boyhood I have associated classical civic virtues and old heroic integrity with the soil. No one who has peopled his young brain with the fancies of Grecian mythology, but comes to feel a certain magical sanctity for the earth. The very smell of fresh-turned earth brings up as many dreams and visions of the country as sandal-wood does of oriental scenes. At any rate, I feel, in walking under these trees and about these slopes, something of that enchantment of the vague and mysterious glimpses of the past, which I once felt about the ruins of Kenilworth Castle. For thousands of years this piece of ground hath wrought its tasks. Old slumberous forests used to darken it; innumerable deer have trampled across it; foxes have blinked through its bushes, and wolves have

howled and growled as they pattered along its rustling leaves with empty maws. How many birds; how
many flocks of pigeons, thousands of years ago;
how many hawks dashing wildly among them;
how many insects, nocturnal and diurnal; how
many mailed bugs, and limber serpents, gliding
among mossy stones, have had possession here,
before my day! It will not be long before I too shall
be as wasted and recordless as they.

Doubtless the Indians made this a favorite resort.
Their sense of beauty in natural scenery is proverbial.
Where else, in all this region, could they find a more
glorious amphitheater? But thick-studded forests
may have hidden from them this scenic glory, and
left it to solace another race. I walk over the ground
wondering what lore of wild history I should read if
all that ever lived upon this round and sloping hill
had left an invisible record, unreadable except by
such eyes as mine, that seeing, see not, and not seeing, do plainly see.

Then, while I stand upon the crowning point of the
hill, from which I can behold every foot of the hundred acres, and think what is going on, what gigantic
powers are silently working, I feel as if all the work-
manship that was stored in the Crystal Palace was
not to be compared with the subtle machinery all
over this round. What chemists could find solvents
to liquefy these rocks? But soft rains and roots
small as threads dissolve them and re-compose them

into stems and leaves. What an uproar, as if a hundred stone quarries were being wrought, if one should attempt to crush with hammers all the flint and quartz which the stroke of the dew powders noiselessly! All this turf is but a camp of soldier-roots, that wage their battle upon the elements with endless victory. There is a greater marvel in this defiant thistle, which wearies the farmer's wits, taxed for its extermination, than in all the repositories of New York or London. And these mighty trees, how easily do they pump up and sustain supplies of moisture that it would require scores of rattling engines to lift! This farm, it is a vast laboratory, full of expert chemists. It is a vast shop, full of noiseless machinists. And all this is mine! These rocks, that lie in bulk under the pasture-trees, and all this moss that loves to nestle in its crevices, and clasp the invisible projections with its little clinging hands, and all these ferns and sumach, these springs and trickling issues, are mine!

Let me not be puffed up with sudden wealth! Let me rule discreetly among my tenants. Let me see what tribes are mine. There are the black and glossy crickets, the gray crickets, the grasshoppers of every shape and hue, the silent, prudent toad, type of conservative wisdom, wise-looking, but slow-hopping; the butterflies by day, and the moth and millers by night; all birds — wrens, sparrows, king-birds, bluebirds, robins, and those unnamed warblers that make the forests sad with their melancholy whistle. Besides these, who can register the sappers and miners that are always at work in the soil: angleworms, white grubs, and bugs that carry pick and shovel in the head? Who can muster all the mice that nest in the barn or nibble in the stubble-field, and all the beetles that sing base in the wood's edge to the shrill treble of gnats and myriad musquitoes? These all are mine!

Are they mine? Is it my eye and my hand that mark their paths and circuits? Do they hold their life from me, or do I give them their food in due season? Vastly as my bulk is greater than theirs, am I so much superior that I can despise, or even not admire? Where is the strength of muscle by which I can spring fifty times the length of my body? That grasshopper's thigh lords it over mine. Spring up now in the evening air, and fly toward the lights that wink from yonder hillside! Ten million wings of despised flies and useless insects are mightier than hand or foot of mine. Each mortal thing carries some quality of distinguishing excellence by which it may glory, and say, "In this, I am first in all the world!"

Since the same hand made me that made them, and the same care feeds them that spreads my board, let there be fellowship between us. There is. I have signed articles of peace even with the abdominal spiders, who carry their fleece in their belly, and not

on their back. It is agreed that they shall not cross
the Danube of my doors, and I, on the other hand,
will let them camp down, without wanton disturb-
ance, in my whole domain beside! I, too, am but
an insect on a larger scale. Are there not those who
tread with unsounding feet through the invisible
air, of being so vast, that I seem to them but a mite,
a flitting insect? And of capacities so noble and
eminent, that all the stores which I could bring of
thought and feeling to them would be but as the com-
muning of a grasshopper with me, or the chirp of a
sparrow?

No. It is not in the nature of true greatness to be
exclusive and arrogant. If such noble shadows fill
the realm, it is their nature to condescend and to
spread their power abroad for the loving protection
of those whose childhood is little, but whose immortal
manhood shall yet, through their kind teaching, stand
unabashed, and not ashamed, in the very royalty
of heaven. Only vulgar natures employ their superiority to task and burden weaker natures. He whose
genius and wisdom are but instruments of oppression,
however covered and softened with lying names, is
the beginning of a monster. The line that divides
between the animal and the divine is the line of suffering. The animal, for its own pleasure, inflicts
suffering. The divine endures suffering for another's
pleasure. Not then when he went up to the proportions of original glory was Christ the greatest; but

when he descended, and wore our form, and bore our
sins and sorrows, that by his stripes we might be
healed!

I have no vicarious mission for these populous
insects. But I will at least not despise their little-
ness nor trample upon their lives. Yet, how may I
spare them? At every step I must needs crush scores,
and leave the wounded in my path! Already I have
lost my patience with that intolerable fly, and slapped
him out of being, and breathed out fiery vengeance
against those mean conspirators that, night and day,
suck my blood, hypocritically singing a grace before
their meal!

The chief use of a farm, if it be well selected, and
of a proper soil, is to lie down upon. Mine is an
excellent farm for such uses, and I thus cultivate it
every day. Large crops are the consequence, of great
delight and fancies more than the brain can hold.
My industry is exemplary. Though but a week here,
I have lain down more hours and in more places than
that hard-working brother of mine in the whole year
that he has dwelt here. Strange that industrious
lying down should come so naturally to me, and
standing up and lazing about after the plow or behind
his scythe, so naturally to him! My eyes against his
feet! It takes me but a second to run down that
eastern slope, across the meadow, over the road, up
to that long hillside, (which the benevolent Mr. Dorr
is so beautifully planting with shrubbery for my sake

— blessings on him!) but his feet could not perform the task in less than ten minutes. I can spring from Grey Lock in the north, through the hazy air, over the wide sixty miles to the dome of the Taconic mountains in the south, by a simple roll of the eyeball, a mere contraction of a few muscles. Now let any one try it with their feet, and two days would scant suffice! With my head I can sow the ground with glorious harvests; I can build barns, fill them with silky cows and nimble horses; I can pasture a thousand sheep, run innumerable furrows, sow every sort of seed, rear up forests just wherever the eye longs for them, build my house, like Solomon's Temple, without the sound of a hammer. Ah! mighty worker is the head! These farmers that use the foot and the hand, are much to be pitied. I can change my structures every day, without expense. I can enlarge that gem of a lake that lies yonder, twinkling and rippling in the sunlight. I can pile up rocks where they ought to have been found, for landscape effect, and clothe them with the very pines that ought to grow over them. I can transplant every tree that I meet in my rides, and put it near my house without the drooping of a leaf.

But of what use is all this fanciful using of the head? It is a mere waste of precious time!

Yet, if it gives great delight, if it keeps the soul awake, sweet thoughts alive and sordid thoughts dead, if it brings one a little out of conceit with hard economies, and penurious reality, and stingy self-conceit; if it be like a bath to the soul, in which it washes away the grime of human contacts, and the sweat and dust of life among selfish, sordid men; if it makes the thoughts more supple to climb along the ways where spiritual fruits do grow; and especially, if it introduces the soul to a fuller conviction of the Great Unseen, and teaches it to esteem the visible as less real than things which no eye can see, or hands handle, it will have answered a purpose which is in vain sought among stupid conventionalities.

At any rate, such a discourse of the thoughts with things that are beautiful, and such an opening of the soul to things which are sweet-breathed, will make one joyful at the time and tranquil thereafter. And if one fully believes that the earth is the Lord's, and that God yet walks among leaves, and trees, in the cool of the day, he will not easily be persuaded to cast away the belief that all these vagaries and wild communings are but those of a child in his father's house, and that the secret springs of joy which they open are touched of God!

JAMES RUSSELL LOWELL

1819–1871

BORN in Cambridge, Massachusetts, LOWELL studied law, and passed into literature. His earliest publication was a volume of love-poems, "A Year's Life" (1841), followed by "Poems" (1844), and in 1845 "The Vision of Sir Launfal," an exquisite allegory of the Grail. The Mexican War occasioned his Yankee "Biglow Papers" (begun serially in 1846), sarcastically lashing the crawling before the slave-power which had made the war. His "Fable for Critics" (1848) was a witty satire on contemporary poets — including fun at his own expense.

Meantime he wrote articles and reviews, had wandered in Europe and at home, and issued charming sketches of travel, and in 1857 became Professor of French, Spanish, and Italian in Harvard, while he was editor of the *Atlantic Monthly* during its first nine volumes, — a valuable task, — and from 1863 to 1872 joined CHARLES ELIOT NORTON in editing the *North American Review*. During the Civil War a second series of "Biglow Papers" scourged secession as the first had scored slavery, with satire and fun. In 1865 came his grand "Commemoration Ode." This, and the earlier "Concord Ode" and "Centennial Ode," were his most signal patriotic utterances.

In 1877 LOWELL went as United States Minister to Spain, and in 1879 to Great Britain, remaining till 1885, smoothing difficulties and winning good will. Later years produced admirable volumes of poetry, criticism, political and other essays.

All in all, LOWELL was the best-equipped literary American that has appeared : — as poet, fine-spirited, delicate, in sympathy with man and nature, artistic of touch; as critic, learned, discriminating, brilliant; as teacher, illuminating; as editor, of severe but catholic judgment and unerring taste; as humorist, genial, wittily sarcastic, with sober thought beneath the sparkle, his serious writing being lightened by a rare subtlety of humorous consciousness. As diplomat he was admirable, and as patriot his soul glowed from youth to death.

AT SEA

THE sea was meant to be looked at from shore, as mountains are from the plain. Lucretius made this discovery long ago, and was blunt enough to blurt it forth, romance and sentiment — in other words, the pretense of feeling what we do not feel — being inventions of a later day. To be sure, Cicero used to twaddle about Greek literature and philosophy, much as people do about ancient art nowadays; but I rather sympathize with those stout old Romans who despised both, and believed that to found an empire was as grand an achievement as to build an epic or to carve a statue. But though there might have been twaddle (as why not, since there was a Senate ?), I rather think Petrarch was the first choragus of that sentimental dance which so long led young folks away from the realities of life like the piper of Hamelin, and whose succession ended, let us hope, with Chateaubriand. But for them, Byron, whose real strength lay in his sincerity, would never have talked about the "sea bounding beneath him like a steed that knows his rider," and all that sort of thing. Even if it had been true, steam has been as fatal to that part of the romance of the sea as to hand-loom weaving. But what say you to a twelve days' calm such as we dozed

through in mid-Atlantic and in mid-August? I
know nothing so tedious at once and exasperating
as that regular slap of the wilted sails when the ship
rises and falls with the slow breathing of the sleeping
sea, one greasy, brassy swell following another, slow,
smooth, immitigable as the series of Wordsworth's
"Ecclesiastical Sonnets." Even at his best, Nep-
tune, in a *tête-à-tête*, has a way of repeating himself, an
obtuseness to the *ne quid nimis*, that is stupefying.
It reminds me of organ music and my good friend
Sebastian Bach. A fugue or two will do very well;
but a concert made up of nothing else is altogether
too epic for me. There is nothing so desperately
monotonous as the sea, and I no longer wonder at the
cruelty of pirates. Fancy an existence in which the
coming up of a clumsy finback whale, who says *Pooh!*
to you solemnly as you lean over the taffrail, is an
event as exciting as an election on shore! . . .

The finback whale recorded just above has much
the look of a brown-paper parcel, — the whitish
stripes that run across him answering for the pack-
thread. He has a kind of accidental hole in the top
of his head, through which he *pooh-poohs* the rest of
creation, and which looks as if it had been made by
the chance thrust of a chestnut rail. He was our first
event. Our second was harpooning a sunfish, which
basked dozing on the lap of the sea, looking so much
like the giant turtle of an alderman's dream, that I
am persuaded he would have made mock-turtle-

soup rather than acknowledge his imposture. But he broke away just as they were hauling him over the side, and sank placidly through the clear water, leaving behind him a crimson trail that wavered a moment and was gone.

The sea, though, has better sights than these. When we were up with the Azores, we began to meet flying-fish and Portuguese men-of-war beautiful as the galley of Cleopatra, tiny craft that dared these seas before Columbus. I have seen one of the former rise from the crest of a wave, and, glancing from another some two hundred feet beyond, take a fresh flight of perhaps as long. How Calderon would have similized this pretty creature had he ever seen it! How would he have run him up and down the gamut of simile! If a fish, then a fish with wings; if a bird, then a bird with fins; and so on, keeping up the poor shuttlecock of a conceit as is his wont. Indeed, the poor thing is the most killing bait for a comparison, and I assure you I have three or four in my inkstand; — but be calm, they shall stay there. Moore, who looked on all nature as a kind of *Gradus ad Parnassum*, a *thesaurus* of similitude, and spent his life in a game of What is my thought like? with himself, *did* the flying-fish on his way to Bermuda. So I leave him in peace.

The most beautiful thing I have seen at sea, all the more so that I had never heard of it, is the trail of a shoal of fish through the phosphorescent water. It

is like a flight of silver rockets, or the streaming of
northern lights through that silent nether heaven.   I
thought nothing could go beyond that rustling star-
foam which was churned up by our ship's bows, or
those eddies and disks of dreamy flame that rose and
wandered out of sight behind us.

> 'Twas fire our ship was plunging through,
> Cold fire that o'er the quarter flew;
> And wandering moons of idle flame
> Grew full and waned, and went and came,
> Dappling with light the huge sea snake
> That slid behind us in the wake.

Another sight worth taking a voyage for is that of
the sails by moonlight.   Our course was "south and
by east, half south," so that we seemed bound for the
full moon as she rolled up over our wavering horizon.
Then I used to go forward to the bowsprit and look
back.   Our ship was a clipper, with every rag set,
stunsails, sky-scrapers, and all; nor was it easy to
believe that such a wonder could be built of canvas as
that white many-storied pile of cloud that stooped
over me, or drew back as we rose and fell with the
waves.

In the ocean-horizon I took untiring delight.   It
is the true magic-circle of expectation and conjecture
— almost as good as a wishing-ring.   What will rise
over that edge we sail toward daily and never overtake?   A sail? an island? the new shore of the Old

World? Something rose every day, which I need not have gone so far to see, but at whose levee I was a much more faithful courtier than on shore. A cloudless sunrise in mid-ocean is beyond comparison for simple grandeur. It is like Dante's style, bare and perfect. Naked sun meets naked sea, the true classic of nature. There may be more sentiment in morning on shore, — the shivering fairy-jewelry of dew, the silver point-lace of sparkling hoar-frost, — but there is also more complexity, more of the romantic. The one savors of the elder Edda, the other of the Minnesingers.

> And I thus floating, lonely elf,
> A kind of planet by myself,
> The mists draw up and furl away,
> And in the east a warming gray,
> Faint as the tint of oaken woods
> When o'er their buds May breathes and broods,
> Tells that the golden sunrise-tide
> Is lapsing up earth's thirsty side,
> Each moment purpling on the crest
> Of some stark billow farther west:
> And as the sea-moss droops and hears
> The gurgling flood that nears and nears,
> And then with tremulous content
> Floats out each thankful filament,
> So waited I until it came,
> God's daily miracle, — O shame
> That I had seen so many days
> Unthankful, without wondering praise,

Not recking more this bliss of earth
Than the cheap fire that lights my hearth!
But now glad thoughts and holy pour
Into my heart, as once a year
To San Miniato's open door,
In long procession, chanting clear,
Through slopes of sun, through shadows hoar,
The coupled monks slow-climbing sing,
And like a golden censer swing
From rear to front, from front to rear
Their alternating bursts of praise,
Till the roof's fading seraphs gaze
Down through an odorous mist that crawls
Lingeringly up the darkened walls,
And the dim arches, silent long,
Are startled with triumphant song.

I wrote yesterday that the sea still rimmed our prosy
lives with mystery and conjecture. But one is shut
up on shipboard like Montaigne in his tower, with
nothing to do but to review his own thoughts and
contradict himself. *Dire, redire, et me contredire*,
will be the staple of my journal till I see land. I say
nothing of such matters as the *montagna bruna* on
which Ulysses wrecked; but since the sixteenth century could any man reasonably hope to stumble on
one of those wonders which were cheap as dirt in the
days of St. Saga? Faustus, Don Juan, and Tann-
haüser are the last ghosts of legend, that lingered
almost till the Gallic cock-crow of universal enlighten-

ment and disillusion. The Public School has done
for Imagination. What shall I see in Outre-Mer
or on the way thither, but what can be seen with
eyes? To be sure, I stick by the sea-serpent, and
would fain believe that science has scotched, not
killed him. Nor is he to be lightly given up, for,
like the old Scandinavian snake, he binds together
for us the two hemispheres of Past and Present,
of Belief and Science. He is the link which knits
us seaboard Yankees with our Norse progenitors, in-
terpreting between the age of the dragon and that
of the railroad-train. We have made ducks and
drakes of that large estate of wonder and delight
bequeathed to us by ancestral vikings. . . .

The fault of modern travelers is, that they see
nothing out of sight. They talk of eocene periods
and tertiary formations, and tell us how the world
looked to the plesiosaur. They take science (or
nescience) with them, instead of that soul of generous
trust their elders had. All their senses are skeptics
and doubters, materialists reporting things for other
skeptics to doubt still further upon. Nature becomes
a reluctant witness upon the stand, badgered with
geologist hammers and phials of acid. There have
been no travelers since those included in Hakluyt
and Purchas, except Martin, perhaps, who saw an
inch or two into the invisible at the Orkneys. We
have peripatetic lecturers, but no more travelers.
Travelers' stories are no longer proverbial. We have

picked nearly every apple (wormy or otherwise)
from the world's tree of knowledge, and that without
an Eve to tempt us. Two or three have hitherto
hung luckily beyond reach on a lofty bough shadow-
ing the interior of Africa, but there is a German Doctor at this very moment pelting at them with sticks
and stones. It may be only next week, and these too,
bitten by geographers and geologists, will be thrown
away.

Analysis is carried into everything. Even Deity
is subjected to chemic tests. We must have exact
knowledge, a cabinet stuck full of facts pressed, dried,
or preserved in spirits, instead of the large, vague
world our fathers had. With them, science was
poetry; with us, poetry is science. Our modern
Eden is a *hortus siccus*. Tourists defraud rather
than enrich us. They have not that sense of esthetic
proportion which characterized the elder traveler.
. . . The journals of the elder navigators are prose
Odysseys. The geographies of our ancestors were
works of fancy and imagination. They read poems
where we yawn over items. Their world was a huge
wonder-horn, exhaustless as that which Thor strove
to drain. Ours would scarce quench the small
thirst of a bee. No modern voyager brings back the
magical foundation stones of a Tempest. No Marco
Polo, traversing the desert beyond the city of Lok,
would tell of things able to inspire the mind of Milton
with

"Calling shapes and beckoning shadows dire,
And airy tongues that syllable men's names
On sands and shores and desert wildernesses."

It was easy enough to believe the story of Dante,
when two-thirds of even the upper-world were yet un-
traversed and unmapped. With every step of the
recent traveler our inheritance of the wonderful is
diminished. Those beautifully pictured notes of the
Possible are redeemed at a ruinous discount in the
hard and cumbrous coin of the Actual. How are we
not defrauded and impoverished? Does California
vie with El Dorado? or are Bruce's Abyssinian kings
a set-off for Prester John? A bird in the bush is
worth two in the hand. And if the philosophers have
not even yet been able to agree whether the world
has any existence independent of ourselves, how do
we not gain a loss in every addition to the catalogue
of Vulgar Errors? Where are the fishes which nidi-
ficated in trees? Where the monopodes sheltering
themselves from the sun beneath their single umbrella-like foot, — umbrella-like in everything but
the fatal necessity of being borrowed? Where the
Acephali, with whom Herodotus, in a kind of ecstasy,
wound up his climax of men with abnormal top-
pieces? Where the Roc whose eggs are possibly
boulders, needing no far-fetched theory of glacier or
iceberg to account for them? Where the tails of the
men of Kent? Where the no legs of the bird of paradise? Where the Unicorn, with that single horn of

his, sovereign against all manner of poisons? Where
the Fountain of Youth? Where the Thessalian
spring, which, without cost to the country, convicted
and punished perjurers? Where the Amazons of
Orellana? All these, and a thousand other varieties,
we have lost, and have got nothing instead of them.
And those who have robbed us of them have stolen
that which not enriches themselves. It is so
much wealth cast into the sea beyond all approach
of diving-bells. We owe no thanks to Mr. J. E.
Worcester, whose Geography we studied enforcedly
at school. Yet even he had his relentings, and in
some softer moment vouchsafed us a fine inspiring
print of the Maelstrom, answerable to the twenty-
four mile diameter of its suction. Year by year,
more and more of the world gets disenchanted.
Even the icy privacy of the arctic and antarctic circles
is invaded. Our youth are no longer ingenious, as
indeed no ingenuity is demanded of them. Everything is accounted for, everything cut and dried, and
the world may be put together as easily as the fragments of a dissected map. The Mysterious bounds
nothing now on the North, South, East, or West.
We have played Jack Horner with our earth, till
there is never a plum left in it.

GEORGE WILLIAM CURTIS

1824–1892

A WRITER of grace and force, a polished and effective orator, an editor with both skill and high principle, and a publicist of wide influence, Mr. CURTIS achieved a singularly successful career. In young manhood he entered and soon left mercantile life, came under the Transcendental influence at Brook Farm and Concord, and then made an extended European tour. His early impressions of travel were published in his "Nile Notes" (1851), "Howadji in Syria" and "Lotus-Eating" (1852). "The Potiphar Papers" (1853) were gracefully ironic criticisms of society. "Prue and I" (1856) under guise of an autobiographical narrative was a series of delightful essays and reflections in and about New York — one chapter of which, "My Chateaux," has been selected for this volume. These and other books were his lighter labors. Mr. CURTIS did fine work on the *New York Tribune*, in 1852, and as editor of the "Easy Chair" of *Harper's Magazine* (from 1854), while, as editor of *Harper's Weekly* (from 1863), he became a positive force in municipal and national affairs, especially after the seventies, in advocacy of Civil Service Reform, a cause which engaged his interest and his powers to the end. He was the president of the Civil Service Reform Leagues of New York State and of the nation. Throughout the exciting periods of anti-slavery labors, the Civil War, and Reconstruction, he was a cogent factor in the highest national interests, with voice and pen, gladly listened to and read with respect, while his personality bore the winning charm of the thorough gentleman.

MY CHATEAUX

"In Xanadu did Kubla Khan
A stately pleasure-dome decree."
— COLERIDGE.

I AM the owner of great estates. Many of them lie
in the West; but the greater part are in Spain. You
may see my western possessions any evening at sunset, when their spires and battlements flash against
the horizon.

It gives me a feeling of pardonable importance,
as a proprietor, that they are visible, to my eyes at
least, from any part of the world in which I chance
to be. In my long voyage around the Cape of Good
Hope to India (the only voyage I ever made, when I
was a boy and a supercargo), if I fell homesick, or
sank into a reverie of all the pleasant homes I had left
behind, I had but to wait until sunset, and then, looking toward the west, I beheld my clustering pinnacles
and towers brightly burnished as if to salute and
welcome me.

So in the city, if I get vexed and wearied, and cannot find my wonted solace in sallying forth at dinner-
time to contemplate the gay world of youth and
beauty hurrying to the congress of fashion, — or

if I observe that years are deepening their tracks
around the eyes of my wife, Prue, I go quietly up to the
housetop, toward evening, and refresh myself with
a distant prospect of my estates. It is as dear to
me as that of Eton to the poet Gray; and, if I sometimes wonder at such moments whether I shall find
those realms as fair as they appear, I am suddenly
reminded that the night air may be noxious, and
descending, I enter the little parlor where Prue sits
stitching, and surprise that precious woman by ex-
claiming with the poet's pensive enthusiasm: —

> "Thought would destroy their Paradise.
> No more; — where ignorance is bliss,
> 'Tis folly to be wise."

Columbus, also, had possessions in the West;
and as I read aloud the romantic story of his life,
my voice quivers when I come to the point in which
it is related that sweet odors of the land mingled with
the sea-air, as the admiral's fleet approached the
shores; that tropical birds flew out and fluttered
around the ships, glittering in the sun, gorgeous promises of the new country; that boughs, perhaps with
blossoms not all decayed, floated out to welcome the
strange wood from which the craft were hollowed.
Then I cannot restrain myself. I think of the gorgeous visions I have seen before I have even under-
taken the journey to the West, and I cry aloud to
Prue: —

"What sun-bright birds and gorgeous blossoms and celestial odors will float out to us, my Prue, as we approach our western possessions!"

The placid Prue raises her eyes to mine with a reproof so delicate that it could not be trusted to words; and after a moment she resumes her knitting, and I proceed.

These are my western estates, but my finest castles are in Spain. It is a country famously romantic, and my castles are all of perfect proportions and appropriately set in the most picturesque situations. I have never been to Spain myself, but I have naturally conversed much with travelers to that country; although, I must allow, without deriving from them much substantial information about my property there. The wisest of them told me that there were more holders of real estate in Spain than in any other region he had ever heard of, and they are all great proprietors. Every one of them possesses a multitude of the stateliest castles. From conversation with them you easily gather that each one considers his own castles much the largest and in the loveliest positions. And, after I had heard this said, I verified it by discovering that all my immediate neighbors in the city were great Spanish proprietors.

One day as I raised my head from entering some long and tedious accounts in my books, and began to reflect that the quarter was expiring, and that I must begin to prepare the balance-sheet, I observed my subordinate, in office but not in years (for poor old Titbottom will never see sixty again!), leaning on his hand, and much abstracted.

"Are you not well, Titbottom?" asked I.

"Perfectly, but I was just building a castle in Spain," said he.

I looked at his rusty coat, his faded hands, his sad eye, and white hair, for a moment, in great surprise, and then inquired : —

"Is it possible that you own property there too?"

He shook his head silently; and still leaning on his hand, and with an expression in his eye as if he were looking upon the most fertile estate of Andalusia, he went on making his plans; laying out his gardens, I suppose, building terraces for the vines, determining a library with a southern exposure, and resolving which should be the tapestried chamber.

"What a singular whim," thought I, as I watched Titbottom and filled up a cheque for four hundred dollars, my quarterly salary, "that a man who owns castles in Spain should be deputy bookkeeper at nine hundred dollars a year!"

When I went home I ate my dinner silently, and afterward sat for a long time upon the roof of the house, looking at my western property, and thinking of Titbottom.

It is remarkable that none of the proprietors have ever been to Spain to take possession and report to the rest of us the state of our property there. I, of course, cannot go, I am too much engaged. So is Titbottom. And I find it is the case with all the proprietors. We have so much to detain us at home that we cannot get away. But it is always so with rich men. Prue sighed once as she sat at the window and saw Bourne, the millionaire, the president of innumerable companies, and manager and director of all the charitable societies in town, going by with wrinkled brow and hurried step. I asked her why she sighed.

"Because I was remembering that my mother used to tell me not to desire great riches, for they occasioned great cares," said she.

"They do indeed," answered I, with emphasis, remembering Titbottom, and the impossibility of looking after my Spanish estates.

Prue turned and looked at me with mild surprise; but I saw that her mind had gone down the street with Bourne. I could never discover if he held much Spanish stock. But I think he does. All the Spanish proprietors have a certain expression. Bourne has it to a remarkable degree. It is a kind of look, as if, in fact, a man's mind were in Spain. Bourne was an old lover of Prue's, and he is not married, which is strange for a man in his position.

It is not easy for me to say how I know so much, as I certainly do, about my castles in Spain. The sun always shines upon them. They stand lofty and fair in a luminous, golden atmosphere, a little hazy and dreamy, perhaps, like the Indian summer, but in which no gales blow and there are no tempests. All the sublime mountains, and beautiful valleys, and soft landscape, that I have not yet seen, are to be found in the grounds. They command a noble view of the Alps; so fine, indeed, that I should be quite content with the prospect of them from the highest tower of my castle, and not care to go to Switzerland.

The neighboring ruins, too, are as picturesque as those of Italy, and my desire of standing in the Coliseum, and of seeing the shattered arches of the Aqueducts stretching along the Campagna and melting into the Alban Mount, is entirely quenched. The rich gloom of my orange groves is gilded by fruit as brilliant of complexion and exquisite of flavor as any that ever dark-eyed Sorrento girls, looking over the high plastered walls of southern Italy, hand to the youthful travelers, climbing on donkeys up the narrow lane beneath.

The Nile flows through my grounds. The desert lies upon their edge, and Damascus stands in my garden. I am given to understand, also, that the Parthenon has been removed to my Spanish possessions. The Golden-Horn is my fish-preserve; my flocks of golden fleece are pastured on the plain of Marathon, and the honey of Hymettus is distilled from the flowers that grow in the vale of Enna — all in my Spanish domains.

From the windows of those castles look the beautiful women whom I have never seen, whose portraits the poets have painted. They wait for me there, and chiefly the fair-haired child, lost to my eyes so long ago, now bloomed into an impossible beauty. The lights that never shone, glance at evening in the vaulted halls, upon banquets that were never spread. The bands I have never collected, play all night long, and enchant the brilliant company, that was never assembled, into silence.

In the long summer mornings the children that I never had, play in the gardens that I never planted. I hear their sweet voices sounding low and far away, calling, "Father! father!" I see the lost fair-haired girl, grown now into a woman, descending the stately stairs of my castle in Spain, stepping out upon the lawn, and playing with those children. They bound away together down the garden; but those voices linger, this time airily calling, "Mother! mother!"

But there is a stranger magic than this in my Spanish estates. The lawny slopes on which, when a child, I played, in my father's old country place, which was sold when he failed, are all there, and not a flower faded, nor a blade of grass sere. The green leaves have not fallen from the spring woods of half a century ago, and a gorgeous autumn has blazed undimmed for fifty years among the trees I remember. . . .

Yes, and in those castles in Spain, Prue is not the placid, breeches-patching helpmate, with whom you are acquainted, but her face has a bloom which we both remember, and her movement a grace which my Spanish swans emulate, and her voice a music sweeter than those that orchestras discourse. She is always there what she seemed to me when I fell in love with her, many and many years ago. . . .

So, when I meditate my Spanish castles, I see Prue in them as my heart saw her standing by her father's door. "Age cannot wither her." There is a magic in the Spanish air that paralyzes Time. He glides by, unnoticed and unnoticing. I greatly admire the Alps, which I see so distinctly from my Spanish windows; I delight in the taste of the southern fruit that ripens upon my terraces; I enjoy the pensive shade of the Italian ruins in my gardens; I like to shoot crocodiles, and talk with the Sphinx upon the shores of the Nile, flowing through my domain; I am glad to drink sherbet in Damascus, and fleece my flocks on the plains of Marathon; but I would resign all these forever rather than part with that Spanish portrait of Prue for a day. Nay, have I not resigned them all forever, to live with that portrait's changing original?

I have often wondered how I should reach my castles. The desire of going comes over me very strongly sometimes, and I endeavor to see how I can arrange my affairs, so as to get away. To tell the truth, I am not quite sure of the route, — I mean, to that particular part of Spain in which my estates lie. I have inquired very particularly, but nobody seems to know precisely. . . .

It occurred to me that Bourne, the millionaire, must have ascertained the safest and most expeditious route to Spain; so I stole a few minutes one afternoon and went into his office. He was sitting at his desk, writing rapidly, and surrounded by files of papers and patterns, specimens, boxes, everything that covers the tables of a great merchant. In the outer rooms clerks were writing. Upon high shelves over their heads, were huge chests, covered with dust, dingy with age, many of them, and all marked with the name of the firm, in large black letters — "Bourne & Dye." They were all numbered also with the proper year; some of them with a single capital B, and dates extending back into the last century, when old Bourne made the great fortune, before he went into partnership with Dye. Everything was indicative of immense and increasing prosperity.

There were several gentlemen in waiting to converse with Bourne (we all call him so, familiarly, down town), and I waited until they went out. But others came in. There was no pause in the rush. All kinds of inquiries were made and answered. At length I stepped up.

"A moment, please, Mr. Bourne,"

He looked up hastily, wished me good morning, which he had done to none of the others, and which courtesy I attributed to Spanish sympathy.

"What is it, sir?" he asked blandly, but with wrinkled brow.

"Mr. Bourne, have you any castles in Spain?" said I, without preface.

He looked at me for a few moments without speaking, and without seeming to see me. His brow gradually smoothed, and his eyes, apparently looking into the street, were really, I have no doubt, feasting upon the Spanish landscape.

"Too many, too many," said he at length, musingly, shaking his head, and without addressing me.

I suppose he felt himself too much extended — as we say in Wall Street. He feared, I thought, that he had too much impracticable property, elsewhere, to own so much in Spain, so I asked: —

"Will you tell me what you consider the shortest and safest route thither, Mr. Bourne? for, of course, a man who drives such an immense trade with all parts of the world, will know all that I have come to inquire."

"My dear sir," answered he, wearily, "I have been trying all my life to discover it; but none of my ships have ever been there — none of my captains have any report to make. They bring me, as they brought my father, gold dust from Guinea; ivory, pearls, and precious stones, from every part of the earth ; but not a fruit, not a solitary flower, from one of my castles in Spain. I have sent clerks, agents, and travelers of all kinds, philosophers, pleasure-hunters, and invalids, in all sorts of ships, to all sorts of places, but none of them ever saw or heard of my castles, except one young poet, and he died in a mad-house."

"Mr. Bourne, will you take five thousand at ninety-seven?" hastily demanded a man, whom, as he entered, I recognized as a broker. "We'll make a splendid thing of it."

Bourne nodded assent, and the broker disappeared.

"Happy man!" muttered the merchant, as the broker went out; "he has no castles in Spain."

"I am sorry to have troubled you, Mr. Bourne," said I, retiring.

"I am glad you came," returned he; "but I assure you, had I known the route you hoped to ascertain from me, I should have sailed years and years ago. People sail for the North-west Passage, which is nothing when you have found it. Why don't the English Admiralty fit out expeditions to discover all our castles in Spain?"

He sat lost in thought.

"It's nearly post-time, sir," said the clerk.

Mr. Bourne did not heed him. He was still musing; and I turned to go, wishing him good morning. When I had nearly reached the door, he called me back, saying, as if continuing his remarks: —

"It is strange that you, of all men, should come to ask me this question. If I envy any man, it is you, for I sincerely assure you that I supposed you lived altogether upon your Spanish estates. I once thought I knew the way to mine. I gave directions for furnishing them, and ordered bridal bouquets, which were never used, but I suppose they are there still."

He paused a moment, then said slowly — "How is your wife?"

I told him that Prue was well — that she was always remarkably well. Mr. Bourne shook me warmly by the hand.

"Thank you," said he. "Good morning."

I knew why he thanked me; I knew why he thought that I lived altogether upon my Spanish estates; I knew a little bit about those bridal bouquets. Mr. Bourne, the millionaire, was an old lover of Prue's. There is something very odd about these Spanish castles. When I think of them, I somehow see the fair-haired girl whom I knew when I was not out of short jackets. When Bourne meditates them, he sees Prue and me quietly at home in their best chambers. It is very singular thing that my wife should live in another man's castle in Spain.

At length I resolved to ask Titbottom if he had ever heard of the best route to our estates. He said that he owned castles, and sometimes there was an expression in his face, as if he saw them. I hope he did. I should long ago have asked him if he had ever observed the turrets of my possessions in the West, without alluding to Spain, if I had not feared he would suppose I was mocking his poverty. I hope his poverty has not turned his head, for he is very forlorn.

One Sunday I went with him a few miles into the country. It was a soft, bright day, the fields and hills lay turned to the sky, as if every leaf and blade of grass were nerves, bared to the touch of the sun. I almost felt the ground warm under my feet. The meadows waved and glittered, the lights and shadows were exquisite, and the distant hills seemed only to remove the horizon farther away. As we strolled along, picking wild flowers, for it was in summer, I was thinking what a fine day it was for a trip to Spain, when Titbottom suddenly exclaimed: —

"Thank God! I own this landscape."

"You?" returned I.

"Certainly," said he.

"Why," I answered, "I thought this was part of Bourne's property."

Titbottom smiled.

"Does Bourne own the sun and sky? Does Bourne own that sailing shadow yonder? Does Bourne own the golden luster of the grain, or the motion of the wood, or those ghosts of hills that glide pallid along the horizon? Bourne owns the dirt and fences; I own the beauty that makes the landscape, or otherwise how could I own castles in Spain?"

That was very true. I respected Titbottom more than ever. . . .

When I reached home, my darling Prue was sitting in the small parlor, reading. I felt a little guilty for having been so long away, and upon my only holiday, too. . . .

So we went in to tea. We eat in the back parlor, for our little house and limited means do not allow us to have things upon the Spanish scale. It is better than a sermon to hear my wife Prue talk to the children; and when she speaks to me it seems sweeter than psalm singing; at least, such as we have in our church. I am very happy. . . .

As the years go by, I am not conscious that my interest diminishes. If I see that age is subtly sifting his snow in the dark hair of my Prue, I smile, contented, for her hair, dark and heavy as when I first saw it, is all carefully treasured in my castles in Spain. If I feel her arm more heavily leaning upon mine, as we walk around the squares, I press it closely to my side, for I know that the easy grace of her youth's motion will be restored by the elixir of that Spanish air. If her voice sometimes falls less clearly from her lips, it is no less sweet to me, for the music of her voice's prime fills, freshly as ever, those Spanish halls. If the light I love fades a little from her eyes, I know that the glances she gave me, in our youth, are the eternal sunshine of my castles in Spain.

I defy time and change. Each year laid upon our

heads is a hand of blessing. I have no doubt that I shall find the shortest route to my possessions as soon as need be. Perhaps, when Adoniram is married, we shall all go out to one of my castles to pass the honeymoon. . . . I have considered already what society I should ask to meet the bride. Jephthah's daughter and the Chevalier Bayard, I should say — and fair Rosamond with Dean Swift — King Solomon and the Queen of Sheba would come over, I think, from his famous castle — Shakespeare and his friend the Marquis of Southampton might come in a galley with Cleopatra; and, if any guest were offended by her presence, he should devote himself to the Fair One with Golden Locks. Mephistopheles is not personally disagreeable, and is exceedingly well-bred in society, I am told; and he should come *tête-à-tête* with Mrs. Rawdon Crawley. Spenser should escort his Faerie Queene, who would preside at the tea-table.

Mr. Samuel Weller I should ask as Lord of Misrule, and Dr. Johnson as the Abbot of Unreason. I would suggest to Major Dobbin to accompany Mrs. Fry; Alcibiades would bring Homer and Plato in his purple-sailed galley; and I would have Aspasia, Ninon de l'Enclos, and Mrs. Battle, to make up a table of whist with Queen Elizabeth. I shall order a seat placed in the oratory for Lady Jane Grey and Joan of Arc. I shall invite General Washington to bring some of the choicest cigars from his plantation

for Sir Walter Raleigh; and Chaucer, Browning, and
Walter Savage Landor should talk with Goethe, who is
to bring Tasso on one arm and Iphigenia on the other.

Dante and Mr. Carlyle would prefer, I suppose,
to go down into the dark vaults under the castle,
The Man in the Moon, the Old Harry, and William
of the Wisp would be valuable additions, and the
Laureate Tennyson might compose an official ode
upon the occasion; or I would ask "They" to say
all about it.

Of course there are many other guests whose
names I do not at the moment recall. . . .

And yet, if Adoniram should never marry? — or
if we could not get to Spain? — or if the company
would not come?

What then? Shall I betray a secret? I have
already entertained this party in my humble little
parlor at home; and Prue presided as serenely as
Semiramis over her court. Have I not said that I
defy time, and shall space hope to daunt me? I keep
books by day, but by night books keep me. They
leave me to dreams and reveries. Shall I confess
that sometimes when I have been sitting, reading to
my Prue, Cymbeline, perhaps, or a Canterbury tale,
I have seemed to see clearly before me the broad
highway to my castles in Spain; and as she looked
up from her work, and smiled in sympathy, I have
even fancied that I was already there?

DONALD GRANT MITCHELL

1822-1908

"Ik Marvel," as the author called himself in one of his early books, pursued an unusually long career, being known as an active writer from 1857 to 1897. And he was always a favorite, his grace and ease and refined purity of style commending to a wide circle of readers his fancies and his facts, travel-gleanings and history, farming, fiction, legendary lore, and literary criticisms. He is credited with a score or more of books. Probably the most famous of these are "Reveries of a Bachelor" (1850) and "Dream Life" (1851), from the former of which is presented an example of his delicate and airily humorous imaginings. This book attained a very large circulation when first issued, and is still widely read, especially by young men and women, to whom its sentiment naturally appeals, while older hearts may well find refreshment in memories evoked. It was republished in England and translated into French.

Perhaps "My Farm of Edgewood" (1863), "Doctor Johns" (1866), a novel, "About Old Story-tellers" (1878), "English Lands, Letters, and Kings" (1889), and "American Lands and Letters" (1897), are the best of his work, but the "Reveries" and "Dream Life" will be longest remembered and read.

BESIDE A CITY GRATE

I AM in a garret of the city. From my window I look over a mass of crowded house-tops — moralizing often upon the scene, but in a strain too long and somber to be set down here. In place of the wide country chimney, with its iron fire-dogs, is a snug grate, where the maid makes me a fire in the morning, and rekindles it in the afternoon.

I am usually fairly seated in my chair — a cosily stuffed office chair — by five or six o'clock of the evening. The fire has been newly made, perhaps an hour before: first, the maid drops a withe of paper in the bottom of the grate, then a stick or two of pine-wood, and after it a hod of Liverpool coal; so that by the time I am seated for the evening, the sea-coal is fairly in a blaze.

When this has sunk to a level with the second bar of the grate, the maid replenishes it with a hod of anthracite; and I sit musing and reading, while the new coal warms and kindles — not leaving my place, until it has sunk to the third bar of the grate, which marks my bed-time. . . .

ANTHRACITE

It does not burn freely, so I put on the blower. Quaint and good-natured Xavier de Maistre [1] would have made, I dare say, a pretty epilogue about a sheet-iron blower; but I cannot.

I try to bring back the image that belonged to the lingering bituminous flame, but with my eyes on that dark blower, — how can I ?

It is the black curtain of destiny which drops down before our brightest dreams. How often the phantoms of joy regale us, and dance before us — golden-winged, angel-faced, heart-warming, and make an Elysium in which the dreaming soul bathes, and feels translated to another existence; and then — sudden as night, or a cloud — a word, a step, a thought, a memory will chase them away, like scared deer vanishing over a gray horizon of moor-land!

I know not justly, if it be a weakness or a sin to create these phantoms that we love, and to group them into a paradise — soul-created. But if it is a sin, it is a sweet and enchanting sin; and if it is a weakness, it is a strong and stirring weakness. If this heart is sick of the falsities that meet it at every hand, and is eager to spend that power which nature has ribbed it with, on some object worthy of its fullness and depth, — shall it not feel a rich relief, — nay more, an exercise in keeping with its end, if it flow out — strong as a tempest, wild as a rushing

[1] Voyage autour de Ma Chambre.

river, upon those ideal creations, which imagination invents, and which are tempered by our best sense of beauty, purity, and grace ?

— Useless, do you say ? Aye, it is as useless as the pleasure of looking, hour upon hour, over bright landscapes; it is as useless as the rapt enjoyment of listening, with heart full and eyes brimming, to such music as the Miserere at Rome; it is as useless as the ecstasy of kindling your soul into fervor and love and madness, over pages that reek with genius. . . .

But my fire is in a glow, a pleasant glow, throwing a tranquil, steady light to the farthest corner of my garret. How unlike it is to the flashing play of the sea-coal! — unlike as an unsteady, uncertain-working heart to the true and earnest constancy of one cheerful and right. . . .

But let me distinguish this heart from your clay-cold, luke-warm, half-hearted soul; — considerate, because ignorant; judicious, because possessed of no latent fires that need a curb; prudish, because with no warm blood to tempt. This sort of soul may pass scatheless through the fiery furnace of life; strong, only in its weakness; pure, because of its failings; and good, only by negation. It may triumph over love, and sin, and death; but it will be a triumph of the beast, which has neither passions to subdue, or energy to attack, or hope to quench.

Let us come back to the steady and earnest heart, glowing like my anthracite coal.

I fancy I see such a one now: — the eye is deep
and reaches back to the spirit. . . .

It is full of deep, tender, and earnest feeling. It is
an eye, which looked on once, you long to look on
again; it is an eye which will haunt your dreams, —
an eye which will give a color, in spite of you, to all
your reveries. It is an eye which lies before you in
your future, like a star in the mariner's heaven; by it,
unconsciously, and from force of deep soul-habit, you
take all your observations. It is meek and quiet;
but it is full, as a spring that gushes in flood; an
Aphrodite and a Mercury — a Vaucluse and a
Clitumnus!

The face is an angel face; no matter for curious
lines of beauty; no matter for popular talk of pretti-
ness; no matter for its angles or its proportions; no
matter for its color or its form — the soul is there,
illuminating every feature, burnishing every point,
hallowing every surface. It tells of honesty, sincerity, and worth; it tells of truth and virtue; — and
you clasp the image to your heart, as the received
ideal of your fondest dreams.

The figure may be this or that, may be tall or short,
it matters nothing, — the heart is there. The
talk may be soft or low, serious or piquant — a free
and honest soul is warming and softening it all. As
you speak, it speaks back again; as you think, it
thinks again — (not in conjunction, but in the same
sign of the Zodiac); as you love, it loves in return.

— It is the heart for a sister, and happy is the man who can claim such! The warmth that lies in it is not only generous, but religious, genial, devotional, tender, self-sacrificing, and looking heavenward.

A man without some sort of religion is at best a poor reprobate, the foot-ball of destiny, with no tie linking him to infinity, and the wondrous eternity that is begun with him; but a woman without it is even worse — a flame without heat, a rainbow without color, a flower without perfume!

A man may in some sort tie his frail hopes and honors, with weak, shifting ground-tackle, to business, or to the world; but a woman without that anchor which they call Faith, is adrift, and a-wreck! A man may clumsily contrive a kind of moral responsibility, out of his relations to mankind; but a woman in her comparatively isolated sphere, where affection and not purpose is the controlling motive, can find no basis for any system of right action but that of spiritual faith. A man may craze his thought, and his brain, to trustfulness in such poor harborage as Fame and Reputation may stretch before him; but a woman — where can she put her hope in storms, if not in Heaven?

And that sweet trustfulness — that abiding love — that enduring hope, mellowing every page and scene of life, lighting them with pleasantest radiance, when the world-storms break like an army with smoking cannon — what can bestow it all, but a holy soul-tie to what is above the storms, and to what is stronger than an army with cannon? Who that has enjoyed the counsel and the love of a Christian mother, but will echo the thought with energy, and hallow it with a tear? —— *et moi, je pleurs!*

My fire is now a mass of red-hot coal. The whole atmosphere of my room is warm. The heart that with its glow can light up and warm a garret with loose casements and shattered roof, is capable of the best love — domestic love. I draw farther off, and the images upon the screen change. The warmth, the hour, the quiet, create a home feeling; and that feeling, quick as lightning, has stolen from the world of fancy (a Promethean theft,) a home object, about which my musings go on to drape themselves in luxurious reverie.

— There she sits, by the corner of the fire, in a neat home dress, of sober, yet most adorning color. A little bit of lace ruffle is gathered about the neck, by a blue ribbon; and the ends of the ribbon are crossed under the dimpling chin, and are fastened neatly by a simple, unpretending brooch — your gift. The arm, a pretty, taper arm, lies over the carved elbow of the oaken chair; the hand, white and delicate, sustains a little home volume that hangs from her fingers. The forefinger is between the leaves, and the others lie in relief upon the dark embossed cover. She repeats in a silver voice, a line that has attracted her fancy; and you listen — or at any rate, you seem to listen — with the eyes now on the lips, now on the forehead, and now on the finger, where glitters like a star, the marriage ring — little gold band, at which she does not chafe, that tells you, — she is yours! . . .

It is a strange force of the mind and of the fancy, that can set the objects which are closest to the heart far down the lapse of time. Even now, as the fire fades slightly, and sinks slowly towards the bar, which is the dial of my hours, I seem to see that image of love which has played about the fire-glow of my grate — years hence. It still covers the same warm, trustful, religious heart. Trials have tried it; afflictions have weighed upon it; danger has scared it; and death is coming near to subdue it; but still it is the same.

The fingers are thinner; the face has lines of care and sorrow, crossing each other in a web-work, that makes the golden tissue of humanity. But the heart is fond, and steady; it is the same dear heart, the same self-sacrificing heart, warming, like a fire, all around it. Affliction has tempered joy; and joy adorned affliction. Life and all its troubles have become distilled into an holy incense, rising ever from your fireside, — an offering to your household gods.

Your dreams of reputation, your swift determination, your impulsive pride, your deep uttered vows to win a name, have all sobered into affection — have all blended into that glow of feeling, which finds its

center, and hope, and joy in HOME. From my soul I
pity him whose soul does not leap at the mere utterance of that name.

A home! — it is the bright, blessed, adorable phan-
tom which sits highest on the sunny horizon that
girdeth Life! When shall it be reached? . . .

The town clock is striking midnight. The cold
of the night-wind is urging its way in at the door
and window-crevice; the fire sunk almost to the
third bar of the grate. Still my dream tires not,
but wraps fondly round that image, — now in the far-
off, chilling mists of age, growing sainted. Love has
blended into reverence; passion has subsided into
joyous content.

— And what if age comes, said I, in a new flush
of excitation, — what else proves the wine? What
else gives inner strength, and knowledge, and a steady
pilot-hand, to steer your boat out boldly upon
that shoreless sea, where the river of life is running?
Let the white ashes gather; let the silver hair lie,
where lay the auburn; let the eye gleam farther back,
and dimmer; it is but retreating toward the pure sky-
depths, an usher to the land where you will follow after.

It is quite cold, and I take away the screen altogether; there is a little glow yet, but presently the
coal slips below the third bar, with a rumbling sound,
— like that of coarse gravel falling into a new-dug
grave.

— She is gone!

Well, the heart has burned fairly, evenly, gener-
ously, while there was mortality to kindle it; eternity
will surely kindle it better.

— Tears indeed; but they are tears of thanks
giving, of resignation, and of hope!

And the eyes, full of those tears, which ministering
angels bestow, climb with quick vision, upon the
angelic ladder, and open upon the futurity where she
has entered, and upon the country which she enjoys.

It is midnight, and the sounds of life are dead.

You are in the death chamber of life; but you are
also in the death chamber of care. The world seems
sliding backward; and hope and you are sliding
forward. The clouds, the agonies, the vain expec-
tancies, the braggart noise, the fears, now vanish
behind the curtain of the Past, and of the Night.
They roll from your soul like a load.

In the dimness of what seems the ending Present,
you reach out your prayerful hands toward that
boundless Future, where God's eye lifts over the
horizon, like sunrise on the ocean. Do you recognize it as an earnest of something better? Aye, if
the heart has been pure, and steady, — burning like
my fire — it has learned it without seeming to learn.
Faith has grown upon it, as the blossom grows upon
the bud, or the flower upon the slow-lifting stalk.

Cares cannot come into the dream-land where I
live. They sink with the dying street noise, and
vanish with the embers of my fire. . . .

A little rumbling, and a last plunge of the cinders within my grate, startled me, and dragged back my fancy from my flower chase, beyond the Phlegethon, to the white ashes, that were now thick all over the darkened coals.

— And this — mused I — is only a bachelor-dream about a pure, and loving heart! And to-morrow comes cankerous life again: — is it wished for? Or if not wished for, is the not wishing, wicked? . . .

— I threw myself upon my bed: and as my thoughts ran over the definite, sharp business of the morrow, my Reverie, and its glowing images, that made my heart bound, swept away, like those fleecy rain clouds of August, on which the sun paints rainbows — driven Southward, by a cool, rising wind from the North.

— I wonder, — thought I, as I dropped asleep, — if a married man with his sentiment made actual is, after all, as happy as we poor fellows, in our dreams?

CHARLES DUDLEY WARNER

1829–1900

ESSENTIALLY an essayist, — whatever special form his writings took, — WARNER won a place in the reading world akin to those of IRVING and CURTIS, and not unlike the quiet affection with which CHARLES LAMB is regarded. Massachusetts born, he was graduated at Hamilton College, New York, and for some years followed land-surveying and then the law. But some Western letters of his to the *Hartford* (*Conn.*) *Press* led to his joining that paper (afterward *The Courant*) and, at first with General HAWLEY and later alone, he was for years its editor.

His books (republished articles mainly) attracted much interest from their delicate humor, shrewd perception, and lazy, graceful style. "Being a Boy" (1867) was the first, "My Summer in a Garden" (1870) the next, and that, with "Back-Log Studies" (1872) quite assured his place as a popular favorite. He issued a number of books of foreign travel, each one with its special charm, and in 1884 became associate editor of *Harper's Magazine* and occupied the "Easy Chair." In this delightful and unconventional position he wrote many apt, interesting, inspiring, witty, and substantially useful things which, despite their playful style, were full of admirable thought and counsel. Two of these, on the general theme of "Christmas," are here presented.

WARNER'S novels could not but be of interest, but they were not equal to his discursive essay-work. His lives of IRVING and of Captain JOHN SMITH are fine; but his genial discussions of life, men, women, society, and the infinitude of everyday topics, will always be his best title to remembrance.

CHRISTMAS

JUVENTUS MUNDI

SOMETIMES the world seems very old. It appeared so to Bernard of Cluny in the twelfth century, when he wrote:

> " The world is very evil,
> The times are waxing late."

There was a general impression among the Christians of the first century of our era that the end was near. The world must have seemed very ancient to the Egyptians fifteen hundred years before Christ, when the Pyramid of Cheops was a relic of antiquity, when almost the whole circle of arts, sciences, and literature had been run through, when every nation within reach had been conquered, when woman had been developed into one of the most fascinating of beings, and even reigned more absolutely than Elizabeth or Victoria has reigned since: it was a pretty tired old world at that time. One might almost say that the further we go back the older and more "played out" the world appears, notwithstanding that the poets, who were generally pessimists of the present, kept harping about the youth of the world and the joyous spontaneity of human life in some golden age before their time. In fact, the world *is* old in spots — in Memphis and Boston and Damascus and Salem and Ephesus. Some of these places are venerable in traditions, and some of them are actually worn out and taking a rest from too much civilization — lying fallow, as the saying is. But age is so entirely relative that to many persons the landing of the *Mayflower* seems more remote than the voyage of Jason, and a *Mayflower* chest a more antique piece of furniture than the timbers of the Ark, which some believe can still be seen on top of Mount Ararat.

But, speaking generally, the world is still young and growing, and a considerable portion of it unfinished. The oldest part, indeed, the Laurentian Hills, which were first out of water, is still only sparsely settled; and no one pretends that Florida is anything like finished, or that the delta of the Mississippi is in anything more than the process of formation. Men are so young and lively in these days that they cannot wait for the slow processes of nature, but they fill up and bank up places, like Holland, where they can live; and they keep on exploring and discovering incongruous regions, like Alaska, where they can go and exercise their juvenile exuberance.

In many respects the world has been growing younger ever since the Christian era. A new spirit came into it then which makes youth perpetual, a spirit of living in others, which got the name of universal brotherhood, a spirit that has had a good many discouragements and set-backs, but which, on the whole, gains ground, and generally works in harmony with the scientific spirit, breaking down the exclusive character of the conquests of nature. What used to be the mystery and occultism of the few is now general knowledge, so that all the playing at occultism by conceited people now seems jejune and foolish. A little machine called the instantaneous photograph takes pictures as quickly and accurately as the human eye does, and besides makes them permanent. Instead of fooling credulous multitudes with responses from Delphi, we have a Congress which can enact tariff regulations susceptible of interpretations enough to satisfy the love of mystery of the entire nation. Instead of loafing round Memnon at sunrise to catch some supernatural tones, we talk words into a little contrivance which will repeat our words and tones to the remotest generation of those who shall be curious to know whether we said those words in jest or earnest. All these mysteries made common and diffused certainly increase the feeling of the equality of opportunity in the world. And day by day such wonderful things are discovered and scattered abroad that we are warranted in believing that we are only on the threshold of turning to account the hidden forces of nature. There would be great danger of human presumption and conceit in this progress if the conceit were not so widely diffused, and where we are all conceited there is no one to whom it will appear unpleasant. If there was only one person who knew about the telephone he would be unbearable. Probably the Eiffel Tower would be stricken down as a monumental presumption, like that of Babel, if it had not been raised with the full knowledge and consent of all the world.

This new spirit, with its multiform manifestations, which came into the world nearly nineteen hundred years ago, is sometimes called the spirit of Christmas. And good reasons can be given for supposing that it is. At any rate, those nations that have the most of it are the most prosperous, and those people who have the most of it are the most agreeable to associate with. Know all men by these Presents, is an old legal form which has come to have a new meaning in this dispensation. It is by the spirit of brotherhood exhibited in giving presents that we know the Christmas proper, only we are apt to take it in too narrow a way. The real spirit of Christmas is the general diffusion of helpfulness and good-will. If somebody were to discover an elixir which would make every one truthful, he would not, in this age of the world, patent it. Indeed, the Patent Office would not let him make a corner on virtue as he does in wheat; and it is not respectable any more among the real children of Christmas to make a corner in wheat. The world, to be sure, tolerates still a great many things that it does not approve of, and, on the whole,

Christmas, as an ameliorating and good-fellowship institution, gains a little year by year. There is still one hitch about it, and a bad one just now, namely, that many people think they can buy its spirit by jerks of liberality, by costly gifts. Whereas the fact is that a great many of the costliest gifts in this season do not count at all. Crumbs from the rich man's table don't avail any more to open the pearly gates even of popular esteem in this world. Let us say, in fine, that a loving, sympathetic heart is better than a nickel-plated service in this world, which is surely growing young and sympathetic.

GIVING AS A LUXURY

THERE must be something very good in human nature, or people would not experience so much pleasure in giving ; there must be something very bad in human nature, or more people would try the experiment of giving. Those who do try it become enamored of it, and get their chief pleasure in life out of it; and so evident is this that there is some basis for the idea that it is ignorance rather than badness which keeps so many people from being generous. Of course it may become a sort of dissipation, or more than that, a devastation, as many men who have what are called "good wives" have reason to know, in the gradual disappearance of their wardrobe if they chance to lay aside any of it temporarily. The amount that a good woman can give away is only measured by her opportunity. Her mind becomes so trained in the mystery of this pleasure that she experiences no thrill of delight in giving away only the things her husband does not want. Her office in life is to teach him the joy of self-sacrifice. . . .

Let one consider seriously whether he ever gets as much satisfaction out of a gift received as out of one given. It pleases him for the moment, and if it is useful, for a long time; he turns it over, and admires it; he may value it as a token of affection, and it flatters his self-esteem that he is the object of it. But it is a transient feeling compared with that he has when he has made a gift. That substantially ministers to his self-esteem. He follows the gift; he dwells upon the delight of the receiver; his imagination plays about it; it will never wear out or become stale; having parted with it, it is for him a lasting possession. It is an investment as lasting as that in the debt of England. Like a good deed, it grows, and is continually satisfactory. It is something to think of when he first wakes in the morning — a time when most people are badly put to it for want of something pleasant to think of. This fact about giving is so incontestably true that it is a wonder that enlightened people do not more freely indulge in giving for their own comfort. It is, above all else, amazing that so many imagine they are going to get any satisfaction out of what they leave by will. They may be in a state where they will enjoy it, if the will is not fought over; but it is shocking how little gratitude there is accorded to a departed giver compared to a living giver. He couldn't take the property with him, it is said; he was obliged to leave it to somebody. By this thought his generosity is always reduced to a minimum. He may build a monument to himself in some institution, but we do not know enough of the world to which he has gone to know whether a tiny monument on this earth is any satisfaction to a person who is free of the universe. Whereas every giving or deed of real humanity done while he was living would have entered into his character, and would be of lasting service to him — that is, in any future which we can conceive.

Of course we are not confining our remarks to what are called Christmas gifts — commercially so called — nor would we undertake to estimate the pleasure there is in either receiving or giving these. The shrewd manufacturers of the world have taken notice of the periodic generosity of the race, and ingeniously produce articles to serve it, that is, to anticipate the taste and to thwart all individuality or spontaneity in it. There is, in short, what is called a "line of holiday goods," fitting, it may be supposed, the periodic line of charity. When a person receives some of these things in the blessed season of such, he is apt to be puzzled. He wants to know what they are for, what he is to do with them. . . . But

consider how full the world is of holiday goods —
costly goods too — that are of no earthly use, and
are not even artistic, and how short life is, and how
many people actually need books and other indispensable articles, and how starved are many fine
drawing-rooms, not for holiday goods, but for objects of beauty.

Christmas stands for much, and for more and more
in a world that is breaking down its barriers of race
and religious intolerance, and one of its chief offices
has been supposed to be the teaching of men the
pleasure there is in getting rid of some of their possessions for the benefit of others.   But this frittering
away a good instinct and tendency in conventional
giving of manufactures made to suit an artificial
condition is hardly in the line of developing the spirit
that shares the last crust or gives to the thirsty companion in the desert the first pull at the canteen.

Of course Christmas feeling is the life of trade
and all that, and we will be the last to discourage
any sort of giving, for one can scarcely disencumber
himself of anything in his passage through this world
and not be benefited; but the hint may not be thrown
away that one will personally get more satisfaction
out of his periodic or continual benevolence if he
gives during his life the things which he wants and
other people need, and reserves for a fine show in his
will a collected but not selected mass of holiday
goods.

HENRY TIMROD

1829–1867

TIMROD was both actually and typically a Southern poet. His birth in Charleston, South Carolina, and his life, misfortunes under the war cloud, and death in Columbia, identified him racially and locally with that part of our country; but, more than that, beneath his genuine poetic gift and the music of his verse, the delicate chivalry of his exaltation of woman and a certain strain of religious sincerity and reflectiveness were characteristic of the finer spirits of the South in his time, while the martial ring of his war lyrics during the great civil struggle was thoroughly expressive of his people. Both the Puritan poets, LONGFELLOW and WHITTIER, recognized and hailed him as of their high fraternity.

The best remaining piece of prose work from TIMROD's pen is the essay entitled "A Theory of Poetry," read by him for the benefit of a Soldiers' Hospital in Columbia in 1863. In it he takes issue with POE's position in his essay on "The Poetic Principle" [1] as to the basis of true poetry. Although POE, later, somewhat modified his exclusion of the didactic, granting that it might have some poetic justification, TIMROD's criticisms of his other omissions of poetic elements are very interesting and convincing. The essay was first printed, with comments by HENRY AUSTIN, in the New York *Independent* in 1901, thirty-four years after the author's death, and is well worth preservation.

[1] The same idea is similarly expressed in POE's "Philosophy of Composition," p. 97, herein.

A THEORY OF POETRY[1]

THERE have been few poetical eras without their peculiar theories of poetry. But no age was ever so rich in poetical creeds as the first half of the present century. The expositions of some of these creeds are not without some value; one or two, indeed, though incomplete, are profound and philosophical, but the majority are utterly worthless. Every little poet "spins, toiling out his own cocoon," and wrapping himself snugly in it, to the exclusion of others, hopes to go down thus warmly protected to posterity.

I shall pass most of these theories to consider only two; one of which I shall discuss at some length. The first is that definition of poetry which represents it simply as the expression in verse of thought, sentiment or passion, and which measures the difference between the poet and versifier only by the depth, power, and vivacity of their several productions. This definition was ably advocated not long ago in a well-known Southern periodical by one of the most acute of Southern writers. It would not be difficult to prove its total inadequacy, but I do not think it necessary to do so, except so far as the proof of that inadequacy may be involved in the establishment of a theory opposed to it.

The second theory which I desire to examine critically was propounded a number of years ago by the most exquisite poetical genius to which America has yet given birth.

Poe begins his disquisition with the dogma that a long poem does not exist; that the phrase "a long poem" is simply a flat contradiction in terms. He proceeds:

"A poem deserves its title only insomuch as it excites by elevating the soul. The value of a poem is in the ratio of this elevating excitement. But all excitements are, by a psychical necessity, transient. That degree of excitement which would entitle a poem to be called so at all cannot be sustained throughout a composition of great length. After the lapse of half an hour at the very utmost, it flags, fails — a revulsion ensues — and then the poem is in effect, and in fact, no longer such."

I am disposed to think that the young lady who pores over the metrical novels of Scott till midnight and wakes up the next morning with her bright eyes dimmed and a little swollen, or the young poet who follows for the first time the steps of Dante and his guide down the spiral abysses of his imaginary hell, could not easily be induced to assent to these assertions. The declaration made with such cool metaphysical dogmatism that "all excitements are, through a psychical necessity, transient," needs considerable qualification. All violent excitements are, indeed, transient; but that moderate and chastened excitement which accompanies the perusal of the noblest poetry, of such poetry as is characterized not by a spasmodic vehemency and the short-lived power imparted by excessive passion, but by a thoughtful sublimity and the matured and almost inexhaustible strength of a healthy intellect, may be sustained, and often is, during a much longer period than the space of thirty minutes. I am willing to grant, however, that this excitement has also its limit, and that this limit is too narrow to permit the perusal, with any pleasure, at one sitting, of more than a fraction of a poem the length of "Paradise Lost." I shall quote another paragraph and then proceed to show that such acknowledgment leads to no deduction that justifies the theory Poe has built upon it.

"There are, no doubt, many who find it difficult to reconcile the critical dictum, that the 'Paradise Lost' is to be devoutly admired throughout, with the absolute impossibility of maintaining for it, during perusal, the amount of enthusiasm which the critical dictum would demand. This great work, in fact, is to be regarded as poetical only when, losing sight of the vital requisite in all works of art, unity, we view it merely as a series of minor poems. If, to preserve its unity, we read it, as would be necessary, at a single sitting, the result is but a constant alternation of excitement and depression. After

314 BEST AMERICAN ESSAYS

a passage of platitude, which no critical prejudgment can force us to admire, there follows inevitably a passage of what we feel to be true poetry; but if, on completing the work, we read it again, omitting the first book — that is to say, commencing with the second — we shall be surprised at finding admirable that which we before condemned. It follows from all this that the ultimate or absolute effect of even the best epic under the sun is a nullity — and this is precisely the fact."

Let me call attention to the fact that, even if the argument I have just read prove all it assumes to prove, it amounts only to this: it shows, not that a long poem does not exist, or may not exist, but that, if there could be such a thing as a long poem, its effect, except as a series of short poems, would be null and void. This fact, however, if properly established, would be an almost sufficient justification of Poe's theory; and I only mention it by way of causing it to be remembered that the demonstration is not quite so direct and positive as appears at first sight, or as it might, if the author had analyzed the work of which he speaks and shown at what point the first poem ends and the second begins.

But I deny boldly and without reservation the truth of that assertion upon which the whole argument hinges; that, in order to preserve in effect the unity of a great poem, it should be read through at a single sitting. . . . It has been correctly remarked of the extracts which go by the name of

"The Beauties of Shakespeare" that those passages lose more by being torn from the context than the dramas themselves would lose by being deprived of those passages altogether. This is true also, though doubtless not to so great an extent, of "Paradise Lost," and it could not be true if each book or part of a book, when considered merely portions of a series of poems, could so strongly affect us as they do when regarded as the fractions of a harmonious whole.

For instance, the situation of the happy pair in Paradise is rendered a thousand times more pathetic than it would have been otherwise by our knowledge of the power of the tempter who is plotting their destruction without; and of that power we could have no adequate conception if we had not seen the mighty. Arch-demon, his form not yet deprived of all its original brightness, his face intrenched with the deep scars of thunder, treading in unconquerable fortitude the burning marl; or, if we had not beheld him in the mighty council assembled under the roof of Pandemonium, opening in haughty preëminence of courage and hatred the bold adventure of scouting with hostile purpose the universe of God Omnipotent; if we had not followed him in his dusky flight through hell and his encounter with the grim, though kingly Shadow; in his painful voyage through Chaos, and his meeting — in which the mean, but profound, subtlety of his genius is brought distinctly into action — with the Archangel Uriel; and so on down to the moment he alights upon the summit of Niphates and turns ·to reproach the Sun and blaspheme the Creator; in fine, if we had not from all these sources derived an indelible impression of the cunning, the ferocity, the indomitable pride and daring reckless-ness of his character.

Again, the fate of the guilty, but repentant, lovers touches us infinitely more deeply because we have been made familiar with the beauty of the home from which their sin had expelled them, that vast garden, which, with the eternal bloom of forests, abounds with fruits more precious than those of the Hesperides, amid undulations of hill and valley, with grottoes, fountains, and crispèd brooks, "rolling on Orient pearl and sands of gold," and feeding with nectar "Flowers of all hues and without thorn the rose"; a garden which with all this variety seemed almost as extensive as a kingdom, and is compact enough to occupy only the champaign-head of a steep and imperious wilderness that surrounds it as with a pro-tecting wall.   But, of course, that which affects us most profoundly, and that which the poet meant to affect us most profoundly, is not the loss of Eden, but the difference between the primal condition of inno-cence from which they fell (and which is described with a softness and purity no merely amatory poet has ever equaled), and the state of mind in which, after dismissal by the angel, they look back to behold the Eastern Gate, "With dreadful faces thronged and fiery arms," and then turning, with the world before them, but with slow and wandering steps,

"Through Eden take their solitary way."

I might go on and by minuter examination show still subtler connections between the several parts of the poem, but it is not necessary. I am satisfied to reaffirm my position that every portion of "Paradise Lost" is bound together by the closest relations, each helping to give force to all; and, just as the light about us is not produced solely by the rays of the sun, but is composed of millions of atmospherical and other reflections, so the ultimate and aggregate effect of this truly great creation is made up of innumerable lights and cross-lights that each book sheds upon the others. . . .

What, then, is poetry? In the last century, if one had asked the question, one would have been answered readily enough; and the answer would have been the definition which I dismissed a little while ago as unworthy of minute examination. But the deeper philosophical criticism of the present century will not remain satisfied with such a surface view of poetry. Its aim is to penetrate to the essence, to analyze and comprehend those impressions and operations of mind, acting upon and being acted upon by mental or physical phenomena, which when incarnated in language, all recognize as the utterance of poetry and which affect us like the music

of angels.   That this is the aim of present criticism
I need not attempt to show by quotation, since it
looks out from the pages of the most popular writers
of the day. . . .

I think that Poe in his eloquent description of the
poetical sentiment as the sense of the beautiful, and
in its loftiest action as a struggle to apprehend a
supernal loveliness, a wild effort to reach a beauty
above that which is about us, has certainly fixed with
some definiteness one phase of its merely subjective
manifestation.   It is, indeed, to the inspiration which
lies in the ethereal, the remote, and the unknown that
the world owes some of its sweetest poems; and the
poetry of the words has never so strange a fascination
as when it seems to suggest more than it utters;
to call up by implication rather than by expression
those thoughts which refuse to be embodied in language; to hint at something ineffable and mysterious
of which the mind can attain but partial glimpses.
But in making this feeling and this feeling only constitute the poetic sentiment, Poe simply verifies the
remark of one of the most luminous critics of this
country that we must look as little to men of peculiar
and original genius as to the multitude for broad
and comprehensive critical theories.   Such men
have usually one faculty developed at the expense
of the others; and the very clearness of their perception of one kind of excellence impairs their perception
of other kinds. . . .

In order to perceive the real narrowness of Poe's theory, it is but necessary to examine the list of those elements which he says induce in the poet the true poetical effect, and mark how carefully he selects only such appearances as are simply beautiful or simply mysterious, and how sedulously he excludes all of the sublime and terrible in the phenomena of nature.

"The poet," he says, "recognizes the ambrosia that nourishes his soul in the bright orbs of heaven, in the volutes of the flowers, in the low clustering of shrubberies, in the slanting of tall Eastern trees, in the blue distance of mountains, in the grouping of clouds, in the gleaming of silver rivers, in the repose of sequestered lakes. He perceives it in the song of birds, in the harp of Æolus, in the sighing of the night-wind, in the perfume of the violet and in the suggestive odors that come to him at eventide over dim oceans from far distant and undiscovered lands."

I have not enumerated all the influences to which he refers, but every one of them will be found upon examination to bear the same general character of quiet and gentle beauty. Let me ask in my turn whether there be no excitement of the poetical faculty in the clouded night as well as in the bright one; in the wrack of clouds by which the stars are driven in as well as in the purple islands and crimson archipelagoes of sunset; in the terror-stricken rain fleeing before the tempest as well as in the gentle and refreshing showers of April; in the craggy dangers

as well as in the blue distances of mountains; in
the rush of the tornado, which opens a road through
deep, untraveled, and illimitable forests, as well as in
the faint and fragrant sigh of the zephyr; in the
lightning that shatters "some great ammiral"
doomed never again to be heard of; in the ear-split-
ting crash of the thunder, the stricken pine, the
blasted heath; in the tiger-haunted jungles of the
Orient; in the vast Sahara, over which the sirocco
sweeps like a breath of hell; in the barren and lonely
cape strewn with wrecks and the precipitous prom-
ontory which refuses to preserve even a single
plank of the ships that have been crushed against
it; in the fearful tale suggested by the discovery of a
human skeleton upon a desert island; in the march
of the pestilence; in the bloody battles for freedom ;
and in the strange noises and wild risks of an Arctic
night, when the Great Pack has broken up and an
Arctic storm is grinding and hurling .the floes in
thunder against each other.

In the same manner, when the eloquent poet
comes to seek the mental or moral stimulants of
poetry, he finds them "in all unworldly motives, in
all holy impulses, in all chivalrous and self-sacrificing
deeds "; but he does not, like the profounder Wordsworth, find them in the tranquil comforts of home,
in the dignity of honest labor, in the charities of the
beggar, and in those everyday virtues over which
the human soul of Wordsworth's Muse broods in

pleased contemplation. He sees no appeal to the
faculties in the "common things that round us lie,"
in the fairy tales of science, in the magic of machinery, in the pen that writes and the types that im-
mortalize his argument, in truth as truth merely,
and in the lessons in which Nature is so bountiful
that they may be gathered from the very dust we
tread beneath our feet.

I think, when we recall the many and varied
sources of poetry, we must, perforce, confess that
it is wholly impossible to reduce them all to the
simple element of Beauty. Two other elements, at
least, must be added, and these are Power, when it
is developed in some noble shape, and Truth, whether
abstract or not, when it affects the common heart of
mankind. For the suggestion of those two additional principles, I suppose I ought to say that I
am indebted to Leigh Hunt; but I cannot help adding that I had fixed upon the same trinity of
elements long before I became acquainted with his
delightful book on Imagination and Fancy.

It is, then, in the feelings awakened by certain
moods of the mind, when we stand in the presence of
Truth, Beauty and Power, that I recognize what we
all agree to call poetry. To analyze the nature of
these feelings, inextricably tangled as they are with
the different faculties of the mind and especially
with that great faculty which is the prime minister
of poetry, Imagination, is not absolutely necessary

to the present purpose. Let us be satisfied with
having ascertained the elements which excite in us
the sentiment of poetry. . . .

The poet who first taught the few simple, but
grand and impressive, truths which have blossomed
into the poetic harvest of the nineteenth century
was Wordsworth. The poetic literature of the age
which preceded the appearance of Wordsworth was,
in general, wholly artificial and conventional. . . .
When he began to write, it was with the purpose of
embodying in all the poetic forms at his command
the two truths of which the poets and readers of his
time seemed to him completely incognizant. These
were, first, that the materials and stimulants of poetry
might be found in some of the commonest things
about us; and, second, that behind the sights,
sounds, and hues of external nature there is "something more than meets the senses, something
undefined and unutterable which must be felt and
perceived by the soul" in its moments of rapt contemplation. This latter feeling it is that constitutes
the chief originality of Wordsworth. It is not to be
found in Shakespeare or his contemporaries. It is
not to be found in Milton, and, of course, not in
Milton's successors; not in Dryden or Pope; not in
Thomson or Cowper. It appeared for the first time
in literature in the lines of Wordsworth written near
Tintern Abbey. Since then it has been caught up
and shadowed forth by every poet from Byron to the

present English Laureate [Tennyson]. I cannot understand how any one can read that profound poem
and then remain satisfied with the dictum of Poe
that the sole office of a poem should be the development of Beauty alone. . . .

Wordsworth could never have been brought to
agree with Poe that a true poem is written for the
poem's sake alone. The theory which Poe very
naturally evolved from his own genius Wordsworth
quite as naturally would have thought incompatible
with the high office of the poet as teacher, thinker, and
bard. On the other hand, the broader vision of
Tennyson has enabled him to detect the truth that
lies on the side of Poe and the truth that lies on the
side of Wordsworth. The proof that a poet may aim
at Beauty alone, without an ulterior purpose, he sees
in every daisy and buttercup of an English meadow.

> "Oh, to what uses shall we put
> The wildwood flower that simply blows?
> And is there any moral shut
> Within the bosom of the rose?"

Nevertheless does he recognize the right of the poet
to make his art the vehicle of great moral and philosophical lessons; nevertheless does he see his right
to grapple with the darkest problems of man's
destiny, to discuss the fears and perplexities of the
spirit and the faith that triumphs over them; and

even to drop now and then a silken line in the dim
sea of metaphysics. . . .

Oh! rest assured that there are no stereotyped
forms of poetry. It is a vital power, and may assume any guise and take any shape, at one time
towering like an Alp in the darkness and at another
sunning itself in the bell of a tulip or the cup of a
lily; and until one shall have learned to recognize
it in all its various developments he has no right to
echo back the benison of Wordsworth, —

> "Blessings be on them and eternal praise,
> The poets, who on earth have made us heirs
> Of Truth and pure delight in heavenly lays."

SIDNEY LANIER

1842–1881

PER aspera ad astra might have been the motto of this gallant spirit. Born in Macon, Georgia, LANIER, when hardly out of college, at the age of nineteen, enlisted in the Confederate army, and came out at the end of the struggle depleted of physique. Descended from a musical ancestry, he was born a musician. His earliest passion was music. Of the six instruments he played, his favorite was the flute, and he managed to keep one with him through war and captivity, for the solace of himself and others. A great reader, especially in the English classics, his second passion was poetry, which he held as a variety of music.

Life went hard with LANIER after the war, through varied experience in several callings, — teaching, law-practice, and, after removing to Baltimore (1873), signalizing his devotion to music by playing the flute in the Peabody Symphony Orchestra. In that city, however, a volume of his poems and some literary lectures made his fine qualities more publicly known, and he became, in 1879, lecturer on English literature in Johns Hopkins University. Cheered by a noble wife and loving children, he battled bravely with the mortal disease that was upon him, and besides his professional duties edited for boys several of the elder classics — Froissart, King Arthur, and the Mabinogion. These were widely approved, and his exquisite poetical gift won its way with the discriminating. Since his decease in 1881 his lectures and essays, which had appeared in various periodicals, have been gathered and published in the more permanent book form: "The English Novel and its Development" (1883), "The Science of English Verse" (1885), "Music and Poetry" (1898), from which last is here reprinted the essay on music, "From Bacon to Beethoven" (omitting some of the detailed illustrations of his argument). In 1884 also was issued a volume of his collected "Poems," with a finely appreciative memoir by Dr. WILLIAM HAYES WARD.

FROM BACON TO BEETHOVEN[1]

THEMISTOCLES being "desired at a feast to touch a lute, said 'he could not fiddle, but yet he could make a small town a great city.' If a true survey be taken of councilors and statesmen, there may be found (though rarely) those that can make a small state great and yet cannot fiddle; as, on the other side, there will be found a great many that can fiddle very cunningly but yet . . . their gift lieth the other way, to bring a great and flourishing estate to ruin and decay. And certainly those degenerate arts and shifts whereby many councilors and governors gain both favor with their masters and estimation with the vulgar deserve no better name than fiddling, being rather pleasing for the time, and graceful to themselves only, than tending to the weal and advancement of the state which they serve."

My Lord Bacon has here used the term "fiddling" — with a propriety wholly unsuspected by himself — to denote the whole *corpus* of musical art. He clearly believes that in discussing the value of musical as opposed to political affairs he has expressed the pithiest possible contempt for the former by the mere

[1] From "Music and Poetry," by SIDNEY LANIER; copyright, 1898, by MARY D. LANIER.

327

nickname he has given them in translating the *mot* of Themistocles.

It was just about the time when the wise fool Francis was writing his essay *Of Kingdoms and Estates* that the world was beginning to think earnestly upon the real significance of tones; for it was in this period that music — what we moderns call music — was born. The prodigious changes which the advent of this art has wrought in some of our largest conceptions could not have been foreseen even by the author of the *Instauratio Magna*. . . .

The amiable Tyndall relates that when he was once about to perform a new experiment for Mr. Faraday in his laboratory, the latter stopped him, saying, "First tell me what I am to look for." Following this wise precaution, let the reader look for, and carry mainly with him, in the following discussion, these principal ideas: —

That music is the characteristic art-form of the modern time, as sculpture is of the antique and painting is of the medieval time;

That this is necessarily so, in consequence of certain curious relations between unconventional musical tones and the human spirit, — particularly the human spirit at its present stage of growth;

That this growth indicates a time when the control of masses of men will be more and more relegated to each unit thereof, when the law will be given from within the bosom of each individual, — not from

without, — and will rely for its sanctions upon
desire instead of repugnance;

That in intimate connection with this change in
man's spirit there proceeds a change in man's relations to the Unknown, whereby (among other things)
that relation becomes one of love rather than of
terror;

That music appears to offer conditions most favorable to both these changes, and that it will therefore be the reigning art until they are accomplished,
or at least greatly forwarded.

Perhaps the most effectual step a man can take in
ridding himself of the clouds which darken most
speculations upon these matters is to abandon immediately the idea that music is a species of language,
— which is not true, — and to substitute for that the
converse idea that language is a species of music.
A language is a set of tones segregated from the great
mass of musical sounds, and endowed, by agreement,
with fixed meanings. The Anglo-Saxons have, for
example, practically agreed that if the sound *man* is
uttered, the intellects of all Anglo-Saxon hearers will
act in a certain direction, and always in that direction
for that sound. But in the case of music no such
convention has been made. The only method of
affixing a definite meaning to a musical composition
is to associate with the component tones of it either
conventional words, intelligible gestures, or familiar

events and places. When a succession of tones is played, the intellect of the hearer may move; but the movements are always determined by influences wholly extraneous to the purely musical tones, — such as associations with words, with events, or with any matters which place definite intellectual forms (that is, ideas) before the mind.

It is to this idiosyncrasy of music that it owes the honor of having been selected by the modern Age as a characteristic art-form. For music, freed from the stern exactions of the intellect, is also freed from the terrible responsibilities of realism.

It will be instructive to array some details of the working of this principle.

Let the general reader recall to himself three great classifications of human activity. The universe consists (say) of man, and of what is not man. These two being coexistent, it is in the nature of things that certain relations shall straightway spring up between them. Of such relations there are three possible kinds, regarding them from the standpoint of man. These kinds are the intellectual, the emotional, and the physical. Whenever a man knows a thing, the intellectual relation is set up. When he loves or desires a thing, the emotional relation is set up. When he touches or sees a thing, the physical relation is set up.

Now, whatever may be the class of relations with which music deals, it is *not* the first class above

named, — the intellectual. This has sometimes
been doubted. But the doubt is due mainly to a
certain confusion of thought which has arisen from
the circumstance that the most common and familiar
musical instrument happens to be at the same time
what may be called an intellectual instrument, —
i.e. the organ of speech. With the great majority
of the human race the musical tones which are most
frequently heard are those of the human voice.
But these tones — which are as wholly devoid of
intellectual signification in themselves as if they
were enounced from a violin or flute — are usually
produced along with certain vowel and consonantal
combinations which go to make up words, and which
consequently have conventional meanings. In this
way significations belonging exclusively to the *words*
of a song are often transferred by the hearer to the
tones of the melody. In reality they are absolutely
distinct.

In other words, the intellectual relations are not
affected by pure tones, — not by the tones of the
human voice any more than the tones of a violin.
Whenever intellectual relations are determined by
tones, it is not in virtue of their character as tones,
but because of certain conventional agreements
whereby it has been arranged that upon the hearing
of these tones, as upon the hearing of so many signals,
the intellects of the auditors will all move in certain
directions. It may strengthen the conception of this

principle to recall here that other signals than tones might have been agreed upon for this purpose. Gestures, indeed, are used with quite as much effect as tone-language in many dramatic situations, and constitute the entire speech of many persons. The selection of tones, rather than of other sorts of signals, to convey ideas has not been made because the tones had intrinsic significations, but upon purely *a posteriori* and economic considerations, the main one being that there is no means of producing so great a variety of signals with so little expenditure of muscular force comparable to that of the human voice. . . .

Once for all, — for it is a principle of such fundamental importance as to warrant its repetition in many forms, — musical tones have in themselves no meaning appreciable by the human intellect. . . .

A painting is an imitation, upon a flat surface, of things which are not flat; it is an imitation, upon a surface lying wholly in one plane, of things whose planes lie at all manner of angles with each other; it is an imitation of three dimensions by two, and of horizontal distance upon vertical distance. These imitations . . . can be accomplished because human vision is not unerringly keen.

It is through the limitations of the eye that painting is possible. Perhaps this could not have been properly understood before Bishop Berkeley unfolded the true nature of vision and the dependence of the reports brought in by the sense of sight upon many other matters which are the result of judgments founded on experience. It may fairly be said to have been established by that acute speculator that we do not *see* either distance or magnitude, — that is, that these two particulars are not immediate deliverances of the sense of sight, but are the results of a comparison which the mind draws between present and certain remembered appearances gathered by touch, hearing, and other senses. This comparison is made rapidly, and the judgments founded on it are practically instantaneous; but the fact remains that distance and magnitude are mainly not given by the eye, but deduced by reason as inferences from several particulars which have been communicated by other senses in addition to sight.

It is, then, this defective organ which is practiced upon (of course not in the bad sense) by the art of painting. Every one, therefore, upon approaching a painting, goes through a preliminary series of allowances and of (in a certain sense) forgivenesses. These allowances are made so habitually that they frequently become unnoticed, and many will be surprised at remembering that they are made at all. But something like this typic discussion always occurs in practice when one is before a painting for the first time. "Here," says the eye, "is an imitation of a mountain."

"Absurd," replies the judgment, which has often

before tested the reports of the eye by reports of the touch, the ear, and other senses, and has learned to correct them accordingly; "the mountain is a mile high, while the canvas is not three feet. But let it pass." . . .

Now, it is easy to conceive a stage of growth of the human spirit when the necessity of making these realistic comparisons would be no hindrance at all, but a refreshment and an advantage. In the medieval time, for example, when the subtle disquisitions of the schoolmen abandoned the real entirely and busied themselves with pure figments of human fancy, — when bigotry was piled upon bigotry and fanaticism upon fanaticism, until all trace of the actual earth and of actual human nature was obscured, — in such a time, men's minds would experience a sense of relief and of security in contemplating works of art composed of firm and definite forms whose accuracy could be brought to satisfactory tests of actual measurement. Accordingly, we find the artist of the medieval time to be a painter, seeking refuge from the instabilities and vaguenesses of the prevalent thought of the time in the sharply outlined figures which he could fix upon his canvas.

These considerations apply with still greater force to the antique time, with its peculiar art of sculpture. In an age when men knew so little of the actual physical world that the main materials and subjects of thought were mere fancies and juggles of ingenious speculators, it must have been a real rest for the mind to fix itself upon the solid and enduring images of undeceptive stone which the artists furnished forth from their wonderful brains and chisels. The need of such rest, though not, of course, consciously recognized by the sculptors, was really the reason of their being. In such matters Nature takes care of her own. She knows the peculiar hunger of an age, and fashions the appropriate satisfactions to it.

Here, now, we are arrived at the crisis of the argument. What has been said of the relations of sculpture and painting to the times in which they flourished is but the special application of a general underlying principle which may be thus stated: The Art of any age will be complementary to the Thought of that age.

In the light of this principle, let us examine the attitude of music towards the present time. *A priori*, one will expect to find that in an age of physical science, when the intellect of man imperiously demands the exact truth of all actual things and is possessed with a holy mania for reality, the characteristic Art will be one affording an outlet from the rigorous fixedness of the actual and of the known into the freer regions of the possible and of the unknown. This reasoning becomes verified as soon as we collate the facts. With sufficient accuracy in view of the size of the terms, it may be said that the rise of modern music has been simultaneous with

that of modern physical science. And what more
natural ? I have endeavored to show that music
is of all arts that which has least to do with realism,
that which departs most widely from the rigid defi-
nitions and firm outlines which the intellect (I use
this term always in its strict sense as referring to the
cognitive or thinking activity of man, in contra-
distinction to the emotional or conative activity)
demands. In music there is no preliminary allowance to be made by the ear, as was alleged to be
made by the eye in painting; there is no forgiveness,
in consideration of the impossible; there is no question of *vraisemblance*, no chill of discussion, at the
outset. Even in the case of programme-music, where
a suggestion is made to the intellect by imitation of
familiar sounds, the imitation is, as already shown
[as in the *nightingale* passage in Beethoven's Pastoral
Symphony], really no imitation, does not pretend
to be or set up for a *vraisemblant* representation, but
is a mere hint, with purposes wholly ulterior to and
beyond the small puerility which imitation would be
if sought as an end in itself. Moreover, in all cases
of programme-music, even if the attempt at carrying along the intellect fails, the music as an emotional
satisfaction remains. If bad as a programme, it is
still good as music.

Music, then, being free from the weight and burden
of realism, — its whole *modus* being different from
that of imitative and plastic art, — its peculiar

activity being in the same direction with that of those emotions by which man relates himself (as I hope to show further on) to the infinite, — what more natural than that the spirit of man should call upon it for relief from the pressure and grind of Fact, should cry to it, with earnest pathos, "Come, lead me away out of this labyrinth of the real, the definite, the known, into, or at least towards, the region of the ideal, the infinite, the unknown: knowledge is good, I will continue to thirst and to toil for it, but, alas! I am blind even with the blaze of the sun; take me where there is starlight and darkness, where my eyes shall rest from the duties of verification and my soul shall repose from the labor of knowing"?

But this is only a rudimentary statement of the agency of music in modern civilization, intended to bring prominently forward its attitude towards science. The musician is the complement of the scientist. The latter will superintend our knowing; the former will superintend our loving.

I use this last term advisedly, intending by it to advance a step in the investigation of the nature of music. For the mission of music is not merely to be a quietus and lullaby to the soul of a time that is restless with science. This it does, but does as an incident of far higher work.

On an earlier page, the reader's attention was recalled to three classes of activities by which a man relates himself to that part of the universe which is not himself, — namely, the cognitive (or "intellectual," as I have used the term here, not to be too technical for the general reader), the emotional, and the physical.   Now, man strives always to place himself in relation not only with those definite forms which go to make up the finite world about him, but also with that indefinite Something up to which every process of reasoning, every outgo of emotion, every physical activity, inevitably leads him, — God, the Infinite, the Unknown.   The desire of man is that he may relate himself with the Infinite both in the cognitive and in the emotional way.   Sir William Hamilton showed clearly how impossible was any full relation of the former sort, in showing that cognition itself was a conditioning (*i.e.* a defining, a placing of boundaries appreciable by the intellect), and that therefore the knowing of the Infinite was the conditioning of the Unconditioned, — in short, impossible.   This seemed to preclude the possibility of any relation from man to God of the cognitive sort; but Mr. Herbert Spencer has relived the blankness of this situation by asserting the possibility of a partial relation still.   We cannot think God, it is true; but we can think *towards* Him.   This in point of fact is what men continually do.   The definition in the catechism, " God is a spirit, infinite, eternal, and unchangeable in His being, wisdom," etc., is an effort of man to relate himself to God in the cognitive, or intellectual, way: it is a thinking towards God.

Now, there is a constant endeavor of man, but one to which less attention has been paid by philosophers, to relate himself with the Infinite not only in the cognitive way just described, but also in the emotional way. Just as persistently as our thought seeks the Infinite, does our emotion seek the Infinite. We not only wish to think it, we wish to love it; and as our love is not subject to the disabilities of our thought, the latter of these two wishes would seem to be capable of a more complete fulfillment than the former. It has been shown that we can only think *towards* the Infinite; it may be that our love can reach nearer its Object.

As a philosophic truth, music does carry our emotion towards the Infinite. No man will doubt this who reflects for a moment on the rise of music in the Church. The progress of this remarkable phenomenon will have probably come, in some way, under the notice of the youngest person who will read this paper. . . .

Everywhere one finds increasing the number of fervent souls who fare easily by this road to the Lord. From the negro swaying to and fro with the weird rhythms of "Swing Low, Sweet Chariot," from the Georgia Cracker yelling the "Old Ship of Zion" to the heavens through the logs of the piney-woods church, to the intense devotee rapt away into the Infinite upon a Mass of Palestrina, there comes but one testimony to the substantial efficacy of music in this matter of helping the emotion of man across the immensity of the known into the boundaries of the Unknown. Nay, there are those who go further than this: there are those who declare that music is to be the Church of the future, wherein all creeds will unite like the tones in a chord.

Now, it cannot be that music has taken this place in the deepest and holiest matters of man's life through mere fortuitous arrangement. It must be that there exists some sort of relation between pure tones and the spirit of man by virtue of which the latter is stimulated and forced onward towards the great End of all love and aspiration. What may be the nature of this relation, — why it is that certain vibrations sent forward by the tympanum along the bones and fluids of the inner ear should at length arrive at the spirit of man endowed with such a prodigious and heavenly energy, — at what point of the course they acquire this capacity of angels, being, up to that point, mere particles trembling hither and thither, — these are, in the present state of our knowledge, mysteries which no man can unravel.

It is through this relation of music to man that it becomes, as I said in the principles affirmed at the outset, a moral agent. . . .

One hears all about the world nowadays that art is wholly un-moral, that art is for art's sake, that art has nothing to do with good or bad in behavior. These are the cries of clever men whose cleverness can imitate genius so aptly as to persuade many that they have genius, and whose smartness can preach so incisively about art that many believe them to be artists. But such catch-words will never deceive the genius, the true artist. The true artist will never remain a bad man; he will always wonder at a wicked artist. The simplicity of this wonder renders it wholly impregnable. The argument of it is merely this: the artist loves beauty supremely; because the good is beautiful, he will clamber continuously towards it, through all possible sloughs, over all possible obstacles, in spite of all possible falls.

This is the artist's creed. Now, just as music increases in hearty acceptance among men, so will this true artistic sense of the loveliness of morality spread, so will the attractiveness of all that is pure and lovely grow in power, and so will the race progress towards that time described in the beginning of this essay as one in which the law would cease to rely upon terror for its sanction, but depend wholly upon love and desire. . . .

Never was any art so completely a household art as is the music of to-day; and the piano has made this possible.

As the American is, with all his shortcomings of other sorts, at any rate most completely the man of to-day, so it is directly in the line of this argument to say that one finds more "talent for music" among the Americans, especially among American women,

than among any other people. The musical sense
is very widely diffused among us, and the capacity
for musical execution is strikingly frequent.

When Americans shall have learned the supreme
value and glory of the orchestra, — when we shall
have advanced beyond the piano, which is, as matters
now exist, a quite necessary stage in musical growth,
— when our musical young women shall have found
that, if their hands are too small for the piano, or
if they have no voices, they can study the flute, the
violin, the oboe, the bassoon, the viola, the violon-
cello, the horn, the corno Inglese, — in short, every
orchestral instrument, — and that they are quite
as capable as men — in some cases much better fitted
by nature than any man — to play all these, then
I look to see America the home of the orchestra,
and to hear everywhere the profound messages of
Beethoven and Bach to men. . . .

As for Beethoven, it is only of late that his happy
students have begun to conceive the true height and
magnitude of his nature. The educational value of
his works upon the understanding soul which has
yielded itself to the rapture of their teaching is un-
speakable, and is of a sort which almost compels
a man to shed tears of gratitude at every mention
of this master's name. For in these works are many
qualities which one could not expect to find coher-
ing in any one human spirit. Taking Beethoven's
sonatas (which, by the way, no one will ever properly

appreciate until he regards them really as symphonies, and mentally distributes the parts among flutes, reeds, horns, and strings as he goes through them), his songs, his symphonies, together, I know not where one will go to find in any human products such largeness, such simplicity, such robust manliness, such womanly tenderness, such variety of invention, such parsimony of means with such splendor of effects, such royal grandeur without pretense, such pomp with such modesty, such unfailing moderation and exquisite right feeling in art, such prodigious transformations and re-transformations of the same melody, — as if the blue sky should alternately shrink into a blue violet and then expand into a sky again, — such love-making to the infinite and the finite, such range of susceptibility, such many-sidedness in offering some gift to every nature and every need, such comprehension of the whole of human life.

There is but one name to which one can refer in speaking of Beethoven: it is Shakespeare.

For as Shakespeare is, so far, our king of conventional tones, so is Beethoven our king of unconventional tones. And as music takes up the thread which language drops, so it is where Shakespeare ends that Beethoven begins.